HINDUTVA
A Challange to Multi-cultural Democracy

HINDUTVA
A Challenge to Multi-cultural Democracy

C.P. Bhambhri

SHIPRA

(2017, First Published in 2003)

Rs. 995, US$ 33

ISBN: 978-81-7541-137-1

2024 Impression, PoD

Hindutva: A Challenge to Multi-Cultural Democracy

Published by:
SHIPRA PUBLICATIONS
LG 18-19, Pankaj Central Market,
I.P. Ext., Patparganj, Delhi 110092, India
+91 11 22235152/6152; 9650028065
info@shiprapublication.com
www.shiprapublication.com

Preface

The Bharatiya Janata Party, whether in government or in opposition, cannot be discussed, understood and analysed without keeping in mind the Hindutva ideology of the Sangh Parivar. The BJP is just a political face of the Rashtriya Swaymsevak Sangh and other sister organisations established by the RSS for the promotion of the ideology of Hindutva. The real meaning of state power for the BJP and the Sangh Parivar can be understood only if attention is sharply focused on the project of Hindutva. The Vajpayee-led coalition government at the Centre and the BJP governments in Gujarat or Himachal Pradesh or Uttar Pradesh are acting as a government of the Hindus, for the Hindus and by the Hindus.

This study of Hindutva : A Challenge to Multicultural Democracy is an attempt to prove that BJP-in government along with the Hindu Joint Family has used its governmental power to divide Indian citizens on the basis of their religious identity. A fundamental principle of multi-cultural democracy is that the universal right of citizenship has to be reconciled with special rights of multiple cultural groups. Every multicultural democracy has been involved in a struggle to find a proper equilibrium between equality of citizens and special rights for diverse cultural groups. The plurality of cultural groups has to be recognised, respected and protected in a democracy and the ideology of Hindutva is fundamentally opposed to the idea of special group rights for minorities. It is not without reason that the Vajpayee government appointed a National Constitutional Review Commission to rewrite the secular and democratic Constitution of India. The Republican Constitution of India has harmonised the universal right of every individual citizen with special rights for cultural minority groups. How can such a Constitution be acceptable to the believers of Hindu Rashtra?

The Vajpayee government's record of the three years of governance has been examined in this study around its domestic and foreign policies. Foreign and defence policy of the Vajpayee government is based on a projection of military and nuclear power of the Indian state with a view to put China and Pakistan on notice. Not only this, the Vajpayee-led government during its two *Avatars* (two Births) of 1998-99, 1999-2002 has made every effort to win over the support of American state and in a manner of speaking the Vajpayee government's foreign policy has been very simple: Pro-America and anti-Pakistan. The Sangh Parivar views Muslims as opponents of Hindutva and Pakistan being a Muslim country is considered as a natural enemy by the Vajpayee government. The study brings out clearly that the targeting of minorities has been the main plank of the Sangh Parivar which has operated under the protective umbrella of the BJP-led Central Government and if any evidence were needed to prove that the Sangh Parivar felt encouraged to launch its anti-Muslim and anti-Christian tirade the state of Gujarat has amply proved it. The Narendra Modi government in Gujarat has achieved kind of a record of persecution of unprotected Muslim minority.

The study of Hindutva: A Challenge to Multi-cultural Democracy is a description and analysis of the record of governance of the party of the Hindus and also the activities of the Sangh Parivar with special reference to its linkages with other political formations like the opposition parties. The BJP style of governance, and its various acts of ommission and commission have been highlighted with a view that it is not a party "with a difference" as claimed by its leadership. It is party with a "difference" as shown in its study because the practice of its ideology has created Hindu-Muslim divide.

Contents

1
Introduction

Hindutva: A Challenge to Democracy

Western Democratic theory and praxis "is a historical product" (Sartori) and its evolutionary character can be understood by referring to John Locke's "*Two Treatises of Government*" (1689/80), John Stuart Mill's "*On Liberty*" (1859), "*Considerations on Representative Government*" (1861) and finally a seminal contribution by John Rawls' "*A Theory of Justice*" (1971). These classics by Locke, Mill and Rawls have conveyed a message that democracies have evolved from the earlier system of "social exclusivism" of large segments of society from political participation to the present system of "all inclusive" participation by all citizens of regimes which are practicising liberal competitive democracy. Democracies have gradually extended the meaning of representation and participation and after establishing the principle of universal adult franchise, democracies are now moving towards the goal of establishing 'gender neutral', 'race neutral' and 'religion neutral' political and social order. Further, Marxist social and political theory's claims launched a frontal attack against John Locke or John Stuart Mill or John Rawls' liberal theory of free and independent citizen enjoying universal privileges by raising the issue of social equality which was a logical consequence of 'the unequal distribution of resources in society.' J.S. Mill's *On Liberty* has been criticised because it completely ignores that the social membership and social participation of individuals in politics is determined and decided by social relations of individuals and groups in the overall productive system of society. It has led Bryan S. Turner to observe that "...definition of citizenship places the concept squarely in the debate about inequality, power differences and social class, because citizenship is inevitably and necessarily bound up with the problem of the unequal distribution of resources in society".[1] While recognizing that equality and its reconciliation with liberal principles of political democracy is problematic,

Sartori observes that "The principle of social equality, instead, remains a characteristically democratic preoccupation. Liberalism does not reject it out of hand, but is not very sensitive about this problem".[2] Sartori continues to struggle with 'liberalism', 'democracy' and 'social equality' and maintains that "....., liberalism is the theory and practice of individual liberty, juridical defense and the constitutional state"[3], and 'democracy' is a political system which strives for the creation and establishment of equality. Many Western scholars have argued that in democracies the underclass or the nineteenth century characterisation of the underclass as lumpen proletariat are protected by welfare state which has facilitated the creation of social conditions for full participation of citizens in public life. With the emergence of New Right in the West, any quest for social equality in participatory democracy has been completely pushed back by the ideologues of "free market economy" and non-regulatory democratic state. Many western writers, who are not Marxists, are also concerned with "neo-liberal classical" market-led societies and the emergence of "new underclass" in these societies under the impact of Reagan-Thatcher-Chirac led New Right regimes. Bart Van Steenbergen comments: "Tolerating the existence of such an underclass, however, betrays the basic values of citizenship. Therefore, its mere existence poses a challenge to the moral foundations of our society".[4] While believers of liberal democracy dismiss the problems of socially exploited underprivileged strata of society as their "moral dilemmas", Marxist Social Theory takes the bull by its horns by attacking the foundational principles of capitalist democracy because liberal democratic theory and praxis, with all its variations and modifications, is not able to answer a basic question : How can a citizen freely participate in governance in a society which is absolutely unequal and unjust? The high priest of democratic theory, Robert A. Dahl concludes his work on *Democracy And Its Critics*: that democratic journey from 'city–state' to 'nation–state' in "Tomorrow's World" has taken us to global and transnational institutions for governance. While Dahl expresses his satisfaction that, "equal rights of citizenship have been extended to virtually all adults", the closing decades of twentieth century have created a new situation because of the emergence of 'global decision makers' and Dahl characterises it as 'the third-transformation' of democracy from city-state to national state to internationalisation of rule making and decision making. How do democracies cope with the challenges of the twenty first century? Dahl concludes that "This emerging possibility means that in order to maintain the vitality of the democratic process, democratic institutions within countries would need to be improved. For one thing, stronger democratic institutions would provide whatever democratic control may be possible over the authority delegated to transnational decision makers. Democratic controls will help to prevent delegation from becoming alienation".[5] Samuel J. Huntington is talking of "fourth democratic transformation" by suggesting that democracy equated with good governance is a global phenomena and every country is wanting to establish western type of liberal competitive democratic institutions; and the collapse of erstwhile Russian and East European Communist regimes in the decade of 1990s is a testimony, according to Huntington, that "every country is wanting western type of democratic institutions for governance". It is a triumph of western democracies over every other model of governance. For Huntington this is the meaning of the beginning of 21st century.

While modern democratic political systems in western capitalist countries suffer from many infirmities and deficiencies, a few important rights have been secured by the citizens in democratic countries. When Thomas Jefferson observed in 1776 that "all men are created equal", blacks and women did not have any rights and the American Twentieth Century has ended with the "inclusion" of all previously "excluded" social groups and democratic rights have been won by the erstwhile deprived, disenfranchised and disempowered groups on the basis of their own struggles against social discriminations. Even until the Twenties or Thirties social theories of "scientific racism" were in circulation in the west and fascism and Nazism practiced such a "racist science". It does not mean that universal democratic rights of the citizens have become real in the west. Liberal democracy in the west has established "necessary conditions" for citizens to participate in social struggles for converting "formal democratic rights" into "substantive human freedoms." What has been achieved in western democracies is the result of human struggles and such struggles are still continuing to expand the areas of freedom in western societies?

While democracies are nowhere safe and constant vigilance has to be exercised by citizens for the defence of their rights, democracy in India is in danger because the Sangh Parivar (Hindu Joint Family) does not accept, even in principle, the idea of equal democratic citizenship for all Indians irrespective of their religion, caste, creed, sex or language. What is the definition of India given by the believers and practitioners of what is popularly known as *Hindutva*? If the foundational principle of democratic political system is rule of law and equality of every citizen, the fundamental belief of the ideologues of *Hindutva* is that India is a Hindu country and Hindus have a right to demand "loyalty from other minority groups like Muslims and Christians". If democratic government accords full recognition to all plural and diverse social and cultural groups, *Hindutva* is committed to the establishment of "One Country, One Culture and One nation" in India. If democratic institutions for governance in every plural society are organised on the basis of juridically guaranteed opportunities for equal and active participation of all citizens in governance, the Sangh Parivar is extremely hostile to the idea of guaranteed rights for all groups in society. Equality of citizens is not acceptable to the forces of *Hindutva*. The Sangh Parivar is engaged in the establishment of *Hindu Rashtra* (Hindu Nation) and *Hindu Raj* (Hindu State) by rejecting and liquidating plural cultural traditions of the country. The Constitution of republican, democratic and secular India is not acceptable to the practitioners of *Hindutva* because they reject the principle of equal citizenship and believe in the doctrine of equal status to Muslims and Christians whose Holy places are outside India. India belongs to Hindus and other minority cultural groups are expected to win over the goodwill of the majority community and also willingly accept their 'minority status". *Hindutva* and democracy are involved in an antagonistic contradiction and there is no meeting point between the two. Pralay Kanungo, while describing the mission of RSS observes : "Its ideologues explain that Keshav Baliram Hedgewar (18880-1940) founded the organisation with the objective to unify and revitalise the Hindu community and to establish India as a Hindu Rashtra. M.S. Golwalkar, the second Chief of the RSS (committed himself) to achieve 'the all-round glory and greatness of our Hindu Rashtra".[6]

The goal of *Hindu Rashtra* cannot be achieved without capturing state power and the whole energy of RSS 'family' is devoted for spreading its anti-pluralist, anti-democratic and anti-secular message with a view to mobilise "awakened Hindus" for bringing a party of the Hindus, for the Hindus and by the Hindus into the corridors of power. In their multi volume study on *Fundamentalisms* Martin E. Marty and R. Scott Appleby (eds) have brought into sharp focus that "all religious mobilizations are inevitably political"[7]. Every member of the Sangh Parivar has been actively promoting exclusivist Hindu identity and the state power under BJP governments is exercised for consolidating exclusivist and specially privileged Hindu community. It deserves to be clearly mentioned that the "quest of Sangh Parivar" to establish "Pure Hindu Nation-State" is based on a well-developed concept of the "Other" and "enemies" and logically it is socially divisive and based on violence in society. Lahouari Addi writes :

> "A political community that is held together solely by nationalist ideology will never enjoy lasting peace. There will always be ...a purer than thou dynamic that claims a monopoly over pure nationalism".[8]

A pure Hindu state shall mean total destruction of culturally pluralist and diverse society of India and the forces of *Hindutva* will not be able to achieve their goal of establishing a Hindu nation-state without violent civil war in the country. Many a time, the growth of the Sangh Parivar in the decade of 1990s has been explained by observing the Right-wing shifts in society, polity and economy of the country and it has been suggested that the shift in India is closely linked with the emergence of Sangh Parivar which is full fledged Hindu Rightist organisation and ideology. In a limited sense, it can be maintained that the rise of Sangh Parivar is reflective of the emergence of Hindu Right-wing forces in society because any right wing force practices inequalitarianism and the believers of *Hindu Rashtra* do not believe in the equality of Indian citizens. The Sangh Parivar is much more than the traditional Rightists in politics like Donald Reagon of America or Margaret Thatcher of England or Jacques Chirac of France. What were the electoral promises of President Chirac's Centre-Right platform during the June 2002 elections in France? President Chirac's centrist and rightist allies promised to crack down on crime, reform the lumbering administration and placate business leaders by lowering income tax rates. Traditional Right in Europe is business friendly, and American or British or French governments under the Right wing parties also protect and promote interests of the business classes in their countries when Right is in power. Jonathan Freedland commenting on "George Bush Jr.'s 100 days in power" commented under the caption "Presidency of dunces" that "It is an appalling record, assembled in less than 14 weeks. What it amounts to is the wish list of the wealthy wing of the Republican party granted in full Big business does not just have influence over this administration—it is the administration."[9]

Similarly Ambani and other leaders of Big Business in India can walk into the corridors of power and the obliging BJP, as a party of propertied classes, is ready to willingly exercise state power for the benefits of the property owning classes. In this respect, BJP is a 'Right-wing' party like the American Republican or British Conservative parties. But the BJP is much more than the traditional Right-wing platform in politics. A section of French voters were led by La Pen who contested the French elections of March 2002 on racist anti-immigration platform. Similarly, the British National Party won three seats in the election of June 2001 on the basis of racist anti-immigration ideology. France's National Front or the British National Party or the Danish People's Party or the Austrian Freedom Party or the Italian National Alliance and the Northern League are all like BJP and the commonality is that these parties are racist right wingers and the BJP is Hindu majority Right-wing party. While the extreme rightists of Europe indulge in hate campaign against "foreigners" the BJP targets Muslims and Christians in India.

Hindutva integrates Hindu religion-based culture with political power to create a polarised society based on the concept of the "Other" and "social exclusivism". Hence *Hindutva* is a total negation of democracy and Indian Constitution.[10] German philosopher Hebermas alerted everyone about the dangers of the "project of cultural identity" by suggesting that human brings are being taken for a ride in the name of glorious cultural past. People should critically accept or reject traditions. It deserves to be clearly stated that the Sangh Parivar (Hindu Joint family) is a well-knit ideological front to promote Hindu cultural/religious values and BJP is just a political branch of the RSS controlled Parivar. Jana Krishnamurthy, the erstwhile BJP President, enlightened us about the inner-relationship among the various sub-organisations established by the *Rashtriya Swayamsevak Sangh*. He stated that: "There can be honest difference of opinion within Parivar, the BJP is the only organisation in the political field. All the other organisations have their own specialised field. So one can understand if their approach is different because they view things from outside the political field." He continued further: "There is no tension. There may be occasional friction. It is expected in any family. But then family is a family, and family ties do not get broken by friction"[11]. *Rashtriya Swayamsevak Sangh* (the RSS) is the hyphen that joins and the buckle that binds all branches of the Parivar. The RSS is the creator of every outfit of the Parivar. The present RSS *Pramukh Sarsangh Chalak*, K.S. Sudarshan, acted as the 'watchdog' of the BJP government and he appointed Madan Das Devi, the Joint General Secretary of the RSS, as a coordinator between the RSS and the BJP-in-Government. L.K. Advani, while deposing before the Liberhan Commission of inquiry observed: "BJP and RSS shared historic ties and the ban imposed by the Janata Party on Jan Sangh members not to associate themselves with RSS saw the birth of BJP."[12] He further continued: "We were part of the Janata party till 1980. In that year a resolution was passed by the party that none of its members could have any affiliation with RSS. This is what made us launch BJP. This is the historic nexus that BJP has with RSS."[12] Since RSS is the creator and controller of the BJP ideology, the belief system of every member of the BJP whether 'in government or in party' is conditioned by *Brahamanical*, *Vedic*, Sanskrit definition of Hinduism. K.B. Hedgewar, M.S. Golwalkar and V.D. Savarkar as official translators of Brahamanical Hindu social philosophy have conditioned the thinking and praxis of every BJP functionary. Murli Manohar Joshi, the Minister of Education, is promoting the project of fictionalised interpretation of history with a view to substantiate, a historically false claim, that Aryan Hindus are the indigenous and original inhabitants of India, *i.e. Bharat Varsh*. The purpose of making a claim that Aryan Hindus are the real Indians is to project Muslim and Christian communities as non-Indian outsiders. The prosecution of Hindus as "insiders" by Muslims and Christians, who are "outsiders", is a cornerstone of the ideology of *Hindutva* and political project of this ideology is to "cleanse" Hindu India from the influences of "outsider" Muslims and Christians. M.S. Golwalkar rejects the idea of territorial plural nationalism and he states that "there was a full-fledged ancient nation of the Hindus, and the various other communities, the Jews and Parsis, the Muslims and Christians which were living in the country were here either as guests or invaders[13]."

The task of BJP-in-government is to faithfully implement the ideology of Hindu cultural nationalism as propounded by the *Sarsangchaalk* whom the RSS *Swayamsevaks* including Atal Bihari Vajpayee, L.K. Advani, Murli Manohar Joshi and other *Swayamsevaks* of the BJP government pay their obeisance. The tragic happenings in the Gujarat state under the BJP government can be explained by linking Hindu anti-minority agenda pursued by Chief Minister Narendra Modi. To sum it up, the Sangh Parivar is fully engaged in exercising state power for the purposes of establishing *Hindu Rashtra*. It is not without reason that the BJP government appointed a so-called National Commission for the Review of Constitution because the Republican Secular constitution of India is not in conformity with the ideology of the practitioners of *Hindu Raj* (Hindu State).

What is the explanation for the growth of the forces of *Hindutva* in the country? How has the ideology of *Hindutva* based on 'social exclusivism' of the majority Hindus from minority communities captured the minds of different social strata of the Hindu community? The practitioners of *Hindutva* believe that Hindus are 'first class citizens' and Muslim and Christian minorities are 'second class citizens' in Hindu India. How has this completely 'undemocratic' belief system come to influence the so-called Hindus in a Hindu majority country?

A social system (whole) is much more than the sum total of its various parts. Aristotle alerted us that various parts of a social system can not be equated with the total system because 'system' has great power of integrating all its components into a very powerful social whole. Apart from warning about the complexity of social system, Aristotle defined the task of political science in a very modest manner. Aristotle noted that the "actions which political science investigates, admit of such variety and fluctuation....we must be content, then in speaking of such subjects....to indicate the truth roughly and in outline ....for it is the mark of an educated man to look for precision in each class of things just so far as the nature of the subject admits."[14] If social system is much more than the sum-total of its parts and, following Aristotle, if political science explanations are intended "to indicate the truth roughly and in outline....", an attempt may be made to offer a few interconnected explanations for the growth of political Hinduism in the decade of 1990s.

A few salient facts may be mentioned to properly contextualise the phenomena of the growth of Hindu majoirtarian fanatics during the 1990s. First, the decade of 1990s witnessed a break with the past forty years of post-independence India not only because 'one party domination of the Congress' over country's politics came to an end, and the whole philosophy of economic planning for growth with distribution was given a goodbye in the 1990s. Second, if on the one hand, unstable and unprincipled coalition governments have been formed at the central government level during the 1990s, on the other, whole society of India has been fed on the rhetoric of globalisation, liberalisation and privatisation. The Indian state has retreated or rolled back not only from the management of Indian economy, the leaders of the Indian state have not been able to project any large social and cultural goals for the whole society. Third, in the absence of any alternative large social goals, the upwardly mobile middle class has successfully projected the social goals of consumerism, individualism, economic competition and freedoms for the market oriented economic transactions and activities. Not only this. The upwardly middle classes have publicly identified themselves with *Brahamanical* ritualised Hindu religion and the Hindu masses have begun to exhibit their active and enthusiastic public participation in ritualised Hindu festivals. A public display of Hindu religious rituals and festivals like *yatras* has become an order of the day. In this atmosphere of heightened Hindu religious assertion the RSS, the VHP, Bajrang Dal *et al* have succeeded in linking activised Hindu religious believers with political ideology of Hindu Sangh Parivar. The Indian mass media, print and visual, have contributed to the growth of public exhibition of Hindu ritualised religious festivals.

It is suggested here that assertion of aggressive Hindu identity during the 1990s is a consequence of the absence of any other alternative powerful social goal which could have captured the imagination of Indian citizens. Human beings need a picture of the future. Human beings wish to construct their society on the basis of large social ideals, goals and dreams. India of the 1990s has witnessed that only the manipulators of *Hindutva* have succeeded in mobilising different strata of society including the underclass or lumpen proletariat for the public demonstration of an exclusivist Hindu identity in public life. A goal-oriented and powerful social alternative to the practitioners of ownership of India for the Hindu only has been found completely absent during the 1990s. Hindu fanatics are marching forward because not only their 'ideological appeal' achieved a level of legitimacy among the Hindus, the success of Hindu demagogues is also explainable because of the absence of any powerful alternative social goal in the life of ordinary Indians. Hindu ideologues have succeeded in filling up a social vacuum by spreading the message of 'Hindus for the Hindus' and 'India belongs to Hindus only'. It seems appropriate to refer to Nehru's phase of politics when Hindu sectarian forces were completely marginalised, even vanquished. Nehru provided a philosophical framework for a newly independent country and he linked goals of national reconstruction by emphasising the overall "objective" of achieving and establishing a just and an equitable social and democratic order. It deserves to be emphasised that the Nehruvian project of modern democratic nation-state made different sections of society extremely enthusiastic for the promised future. India of the 1990s does not offer any promises or hopes for the future to the deprived strata of society and in this stage of social hopelessness, the poor have also become the carriers of the ideology of Hindu upper caste and exploiting classes. The poor and marginalised sections, including the lower middle classes, in the present stage of social pessimism, have been successfully indoctrinated by the promoters of aggressive *Hindutva*, and the Sangh Parivar has succeeded in making Hindu *Rashtrawadis* aggressively take on their "Enemies", *i.e.*, Muslims and Christians.

How have the believers and practitioners of aggressive and militant Hinduism succeeded in selling the idea of a need for defence of Hindus from "Enemies"?

The decade of 'globalisation, liberalisation and privatisation" has injected a powerful dose of economic individualism among the propertied classes, and they are also searching for Hindu cultural identity by bringing a meaning to their 'economistic' daily life. The acceptability and respectability of Hindu priestly class has increased among the Hindu propertied castes and classes. Hindu mythological movies, television serials along with aggressive patriotic symbols have come to occupy an important place in the day-to-day life of successful Hindu traders, businessmen, professionals and opinion makers. It is not an accident that retired judges, army, police and other functionaries of the Indian state are actively involved in promoting the ideology of the Sangh Parivar. The Vishwa Hindu Parishad-led *Ram Janmabhoomi* movement has been guided by highly educated and very successful Hindu professional classes. Kar Sevaks of the VHP or Bajrang Dal may belong to poor and deprived social classes but the real leaders of the ideology of aggressive and militant anti-minority *Hindutva* are Hindu propertied classes who have become extremely prosperous during the last fifty years of post-independence India.

Rural and urban unemployment situation has become quite "grave" in the decade of 1990s and irrespective of statistical sophistry of the government agencies, G.K. Chadha and P.P. Sahu have given a timely warning that the post-reforms (1991-2002) phase of rural economic development has shown "Setbacks in Rural employment.[15] C.P. Chandra Sehkhar and Jayati Ghosh in their evaluation of the "decade of economic reforms" confirm that "rural dynamism" is a myth because of "great slowdowns in the rate of job generation."[16] The Annual Economic Survey (2001-2002) of the government of India admits to the slowdown of economy because of "demand constraints"[17]. If unemployment is increasing and if ordinary wage earners are just struggling to sustain themselves, the demand for goods required for mass consumption will go down. The Indian capitalist market has a narrow social base because more than 500 to 600 million deprived, poor and marginalised population of the country is just not economically capable to sustain a rapid economic growth. Further, public sector employment is on the decline because of new anti-public sector economic policies of the government, and employment in the agricultural sector is also witnessing a decline or extremely slow growth as testified by the Government of India Economic

Survey for 2001-2002. The impact of this crisis-ridden economic situation is felt by the labouring classes. The prevailing 'social pessimism' is a direct result of the deep economic crisis of India, and in such a situation of deep social crisis, either socially revolutionary or socially conservative and 'backward looking' social ideologies are successful in capturing the mind of the struggling masses. This is the meaning of dialectical process in society. The 'backward looking' social forces of *Hindutva* have succeeded by mobilising the large majority of socially depressed strata by creating an imaginary picture of 'monstrous' minority Muslim and Christian communities.

It is not only in India that the ideology of 'targeting specific minority social groups' as social enemies has succeeded in times of 'deep social crisis', European history tells us that racist, anti-Jew and anti-foreigner sentiments have always emerged during the periods of European crisis. Hitler and Mussolini succeeded in establishing the most brutalised regimes during inter-war periods in Germany and Italy because both these societies were in deep crisis and Hitler's goal of the "Germanising" of conquered Europe carried a great emotive appeal with the German society. The goal of Hinduisation of India, the "Germanising" of conquered Europe, and other militarist hate oriented ideologies carry great emotive appeal to the frustrated and depressed large strata of crisis ridden societies. In May 2001, race riots took place in England. Riots of Oldham of May 2001 have been explained on the basis of growing economic crisis in that area. Oldham is North East of Manchester where cotton mills are closing and unemployment situation has assumed serious proportions. The idea of "enemy" whether racial or religious or foreigner attracts special attention because deep social divide becomes a reality during serious social crisis. *Hindutva* is selling the idea that "...this land is – and always has been, mine". Hitler had also sold the same idea to the Germans and all racist theories are built around "us" against "them". It is not without reason that racist anti-foreigner British National Party won three seats in the general elections of June 2001 and out of these three, two seats were won in the crisis ridden Oldham and the third in Burnely.[18]

The politics of *Rathyatras* in the decade of 1990s should attract special attention for analysis because the ideology of hatred is carried on the shoulders of large majority of disempowered masses. The BJP ruled state of Gujarat witnessed real communal holocaust because the state apparatus was controlled by fanatic Hindus. A party of the Hindus, for the Hindus, and by the Hindus has succeeded in teaching a lesson to the 'hapless' and 'helpless' Muslim minority in Gujarat. The state apparatus was used by the Hindu government (BJP) to either physically liquidate or completely terrorise and marginalise the minority communities. Dr. Parveen Bhai Togadia, VHP International General-Secretary, observed that Godhra carnage reflected the "*Jihadi* mentality of the Muslims, the subsequent events of Gujarat were proof of the Hindu awakening."[19] National Human Right Commission commented on Gujarat that "Despite the measures reportedly taken by the state government, which are recounted in its report of 12 April that report testifies to the increasing numbers who died or were injured or deprived of their liberty and compelled to seek shelter in relief camps. The Commission has, therefore, reached the definite conclusion that there was a comprehensive failure of the state to protect the constitutional rights of the people of Gujarat."[20] Sunder Singh Bhandari, an RSS activist, as a Governor of Gujarat state met the Prime Minister Atal Bihari Vajpayee and Home Minister L. K. Advani with a suggestion to hold elections for the Gujarat State Assembly. When Gujarat state was burning, the Sangh Parivar wanted elections to be held during such a disturbed situation. The Sangh Parivar wanted the 'newly awakened Hindus' of Gujarat to vote for the Hindu party which will keep on teaching lessons to the minorities. The two day meeting of the VHP Kendriya Margdarshak Mandal warned Muslims that "if they continue to take the country towards partition", they would have to stay in refugee camps like Gujarat."[21] Mr. Singhal claimed "that the recent communal violence in Gujarat symbolised the first "positive response of Hindus to Muslim fundamentalism in 1,000 years."[22]

John Stuart Mill must have anticipated the capacity of Hindu majoritarianism to subvert democracy when he observed in his classic *On Liberty* (1859):

> "When society itself is the tyrant-society collectively over the separate individuals who compose it-..it practices a social tyranny more formidable than any kinds of political oppression, since.....it leaves fewer means of escape, penetrating much more deeply into the details of life, and enslaving the soul itself. Protection, therefore, against the tyranny of the magistrate is not enough : there needs protection also against the tyranny of prevailing opinion and feeling, against the tendency of society to impose…its own ideas and practices as rules of conduct on those who dissent from them ..and to compel all characters to fashion themselves on the model of its own."[23]

The above very perceptive observation of J. S. Mill against Hindu majoritarians helps us in summing up the above discussion that Sangh Parivar is anti-democracy because it is imposing "qualifications" for participation in representative elected Parliament and State assemblies. A certificate or testimonial of loyalty or patriotism is essential for minorities if they wish to live like "citizens" in Hindu India.

How has the Sangh Parivar won over the loyalties of entrepreneurial, professional and other social groups in support of the project of Hindu India? Hindu petit–bourgeoisie as a "monied" class is exhibiting its new economic and social status by appropriating Hindu religious symbols, rituals and socially conservative belief system. The role of priest in the daily life of the rising Hindu petit-bourgeoisie has assumed great significance and it has become a 'status symbol' with the *nou-veau* rich class to exhibit their identification with all kind of important Hindu gods and godmen. Hindu identity is a status symbol with the upwardly mobile middle and upper middle classes. May 11-13, 1998 was celebrated by Hindu propertied classes as a moment of arrival of nuclear Hindu India. The Sangh Parivar claimed that 'nuclear weapon state status' achieved on May 11-13, 1998 has compelled the powerful countries to take India seriously in world affairs. The Sangh Parivar has played on the fictitious emotions of the socially successful Hindus that Hindu identity is their real benchmark. The new awakening among Hindus about their identity as claimed by the Sangh Parivar is getting support of socially successful Hindus. Aijaz Ahmad narrates the story of BJP-led central government from 1998-2002 and concludes :

> "We are faced with the classic situation of a pre-fascist upheavals. What used to be the political centre has collapsed, with the Congress reduced to a parliamentary minority and all the rest so splintered as to be assimilated into support for the fascist project as small, ineffectual groupings : The BJP rules on the strength of its own inner cohesion and the obedience of those splinters..., the machinery of terror in the hands of fraternal organisations such as the VHP and the Bajrang Dal,...., a sufficiently large proportion of the state personnel and the privileged professional strata allied with it,...., rapid changes in the social and cultural environment which favour its ideological position, ..., and negatively, isolation and relative weakness of the Left and the labour movement,...."[24]

All this put together has worked in favour of *Hindutva.* Indian democracy is under siege because the ideology of *Hindutva* is total negation of every foundational principle of constitutional democracy established by the post-independence nationalist leadership. The Sangh Parivar is an enemy of Indian democracy because it does not accept the principle of equality of citizenship. This is the essence of anti-democratic Sangh Parivar. A telling example of Sangh Parivar's total absence of faith in secular democratic Republican Constitution of India is provided by the role of Hindu Shankracharya in resolving the Temple-Mosque dispute. In democracy, it is the task of an elected government to deal with public disputes and it is not at all the concern of Hindu priests to intervene in public dispute.

Conclusion: Is BJP Different ?

The Bharatiya Janta Party got a great success by projecting itself as a "party with a difference" because Indian voters were completely disenchanted with corrupt and cynical Congress party which had ruled/misruled over the country for forty years of post-independence India. Rajiv Gandhi revived the confidence of the Indian voter in the Congress by projecting himself as "Mr. Clean" and by publicly denouncing "power brokers" in his party during the centenary celebrations of the Indian National Congress in 1985. An important section of intelligentsia and the leaders of mass media had raised great public hopes by projecting Rajiv Gandhi as a leader who was not brought up in the Congress culture of "corruption". The camels' back was broken when the controversy on the purchase of "Bofors Gun" from the Swedish company burst in public because it was concluded that Congress could not have "Mr. Clean" and the Congress political culture of corruption and bribes was deeply institutionalised and even Rajiv Gandhi could not rise above the "logic of corruption". Not only this. Indira Gandhi's Emergency Regime of 1975-77 had completely disillusioned democratic public opinion and the Indian voters began to look for "alternative" parties because Indira Gandhi's authoritarian and centralist regime was considered as a great threat to the survival of Indian democracy.

The BJP leadership succeeded in winning over a sizable section of Indian voters including intellectuals by promising an alternative of good governance in the place of Congress party's misgovernance. Can such a claim of the BJP as a "*party and government with a difference*" be sustained and maintained on the basis of some available facts? A few well known facts may be mentioned to refute the party's claim to be "*different*" from the much maligned Congress party. First , the Congress party was always involved in internal factionalism and factional leaders were quite busy in continuous "struggle for power" for the displacement and replacement of congress Chief Ministers or ministers. The BJP has been completely infected by this disease of the Congress. Kalraj Mishra resigned from the Uttar Pradesh BJP Presidentship on June 5, 2002 by publicly stating that the party was involved in "infighting" among top leaders and "indiscipline" prevails in the party. Jana Krishnamurthy, the erstwhile BJP President, observed that he would have to discuss with party's national leadership about "internal dissensions among party leaders in Uttar Pradesh." Ms. Mayawati, as Chief Minister of Uttar Pradesh, has exploited "factionalism" of UPBJP, and thrown away the policy of "quota within quota" for the most backward castes. Lalji Tandon and Om Prakash Singh, as BJP ministers in the Ms. Mayawati coalition government, supported the "reversal" of reservation policy by Mayawati inspite of the fact that this policy of "quota within quota" was proclaimed by their own party Chief Minister Raj Nath Singh. The BJP, as an alliance partner of the BSP in Uttar Pradesh, has been a party to an utter nonsensical policy of the Chief Minister who has fixed caste-based percentages for the posting of heads of police stations. Is it BJP's model of "*governance with a difference*"? The BJP along with Mayawati is pursuing a policy of complete *casteisation* of state machinery in U.P. Second, unlike corrupt Congress party governments, the BJP proclaimed its commitment to "corruption free" public life.

While the Tehelka exposure of Bangaru Laxman of the BJP is an old story, Arun Shourie and Parmod Mahajan, two BJP central government ministers, have fought pubic battles on the role of Tatas in the affairs of Videsh Sanchar Nigam Limited. L.K. Advani had to intervene to settle the dispute between his two BJP colleagues in the government. Further, the BJP has not cleared the confusion on VSNL because Arun Shourie has alleged that "disinvestment" decisions by the government are attracting "corporate rivalries" and different business houses are exercising their influence on government decision-making. Arun Shourie had warned Parliament also about Air India disinvestment controversy because "Corporate rivalry was casting a shadow on the disinvestment process and scaring away bidders." How can corporate houses fight their battles without support of the BJP bigwags? Like congress party, the BJP has also developed a so-called "High Command" to deal with factional rivalries of BJP-led state governments. In Gujarat, the BJP changed three

Chief Ministers from Shankar Singh Vaghela to Keshu Bhai Patel to Narendra Modi and in Uttar Pradesh the same story was repeated where Kalayan Singh was replaced by an ailing Ram Prakash Gupta but later he was also given marching orders by the "High Command" and Rajnath Singh became the Chief Minister. Even now Kalraj Mishra is alleging that BJP in Uttar Pradesh is a divided house.

While the upshot of above narration is that the BJP-in-government has been in no way different from the Congress party, the claim of the BJP leadership of being "different" than other democratic parties deserves to be validated by shifting the focus from "routine BJP governance" to its "*real agenda for governance.*" Since the BJP is not like any other party or political group in India, evaluative yardsticks to understand its "inner dynamics" will have to be clearly spelt out. The real issue is : what does state power mean for the BJP and other affiliates of the Sangh Parivar? Every political party or group has a "definition of state power" and it deserves to be examined while evaluating the reality of BJP. Michel Foucault, French philosopher, alerted us by saying that "power comes from below; that is, there is no binary and all-encompassing opposition between the rulers and the ruled at the root of power relations, and serving as a general matrix-no such duality extending from top down and reacting on more and more limited groups to the very depths of the social body". The real focus of Foucault is that 'power is dispersed through a network of relationships which make up society and is based on discourse." Foucault's insights on power make us analyse BJP's capacities to reach the multitude of Hindu social groups on the basis of a monolith "discourse" for the construction of *Hindu Rashtra* and Hindu identity in a Hindu majority country. It is not accidental that television and radio are considered very powerful visual media for the spread of message of Hindu discourse by the BJP. The Ministry of Information and Broadcasting is always given to a BJP activist in "coalition governments" led by the BJP. Similarly, Ministry of Education is also managed by the BJP for the purpose of spreading the message of *Hindutva* through educational institutions. The BJP always attacks Muslim community's *madarsas*, (Islamic schools) but the Sangh Parivar itself is involved in a very large school education programme for the promotion of *Hindutva* consciousness among the children. While the Sangh Parivar activists target the Muslims visiting Holy Mecca for Haj with the support of public funds, huge public money is spent on Hindu ritualistic festivals. The Sangh Parivar has brought into active public life Sants and Sadhus to spread the message of *Hindutva*. The Vishwa Hindu Parishad and other leaders of the Sangh Parivar have always maintained that every activity regarding the movement for *Ramjanmbhoomi* is decided by Dharam Sansad or Sant Sammalans. During the decade of 1990s, the Sangh Parivar, with the full support and patronage of the BJP governments, has activised all religious and mythologically associated Saints and Sadhus to take the message of *Hindutva* to the masses of India. Shankracharyas have been brought into politics and with the support of the BJP governments distinction between religious/spiritual leadership of Hindu Shankracharyas has been consigned to the dustbin of history and religious leaders have become political messengers. The "discourse" of *Hindutva* and the instruments for the spread of the message of the Parivar's ideology of *Hindutva* has been actively supported by the BJP governments. If the BJP leadership resurrects V.D. Savarkar as a great Hindu nationalist or L.K. Advani uses the opportunity of the so-called historic Sindhu river in Leh to spread the message of great Hindu tradition, the Indian masses are fed everyday on the Hindu symbols of martyrdom and chivalry in struggles against foreign invaders of India. *We the Hindus* of India are true custodians of *Hindu Rashtra* and the state power, in the hands of the BJP, is meant to promote this ideology of strong, militant *Hindutva*. BJP is a different party than the other parties because it believes in the purity of its ideology and belief systems and it has gained an opportunity to spread its ideological message with the help of state power. It is true to maintain that state power is an "instrument" in the hands of every party and political group but the BJP holding the state power has different meanings because it is used as an "instrument" for the promotion of the ideology of One Nation, One Culture and One Country. The tragedy of Gujarat under the leadership of the Narendra Modi Government has proved the argument that the BJP is different than other political parties. The Muslim minority in Gujarat is convinced that atrocities against the community have been committed with full support of the BJP state government. Dr. Parveen Bhai Togadia, VHP's international general-secretary, maintained at *Purna Ahuti Mahayagna* held at Ayodhya on June 2, 2002 that while Godhra reflected the "Jihadi mentality of the Muslims, the subsequent events in Gujarat were proof of Hindu awakening." Hindu awakening is the agenda of the Sangh Parivar and it can be achieved by polarising India into "*We the Hindus*" and "*the other*", the Muslims and Christians. BJP is a party with a difference because no other party is practitioner of the ideology of polarization of Hindus and Muslims. If Congress is a weak democratic secular party, the other parties are just casteist and regionalist. The BJP is the only alternative party with an alternative ideology to the wishy washy programme of casteist or regionalist parties which are just opportunistic political actors.

In summation, it may be mentioned that BJP has two different faces and there is no meeting ground between the corrupt or faction ridden BJP-in-government and BJP using state power as an instrument for the spread of its ideology of *Hindutva*. BJP-in-government seems to be making opportunistic compromises with its coalition partners, but BJP-in-government has shown no vacillation or ambivalence for using state power for the construction of the imagined reality of *Hindu Rashtra*.

The greatest success of BJP lies in making every secular party to play safe with the so-called Hindu sentiment. The BJP has succeeded in making the myth of hurt Hindu sentiment as a real political issue and in this respect it is a party with a difference.

BJP-in-Government is pursuing its own agenda of constructing Aryan Hindu history by making myths like "River Saraswati" or Rama of Ramayana look "real" to prove great Hindu ancestry of the real inhabitants of Hindu India. In this project of construction of a non-existing golden age of Hindus of ancient India, the Sangh Parivar has mobilised all kind of Shankracharyas and priests for influencing the gullible Hindus that they had a great past which was destroyed by Muslim invaders, who are the real enemies of great Hindu civilisation.

BJP-in Government is implementing its agenda of *teaching a lesson* to Muslims and Christians by patronising Hindu fanatics who are indulging in destroying Mosques and Churches V.D. Savarkar's definition of *Hindutva* is actually practiced by the BJP-in-Government, whether at the Centre or in the States. The Narendra Modi government presided over the physical liquidation of Muslims for three months. The state of Gujarat simply burnt from March to May 2002 because the state government controlled by the Hindus was not expected to protect the lives and property of the helpless Muslim minority. In 1923 V.D. Savarkar in *Hindutva : Who is a Hindu?* emphasised that "Hindutva is not identical with what is vaguely indicated by the term Hinduism". There is "a clear line of demarcation between the two... Hindutva is not identical with Hindu *Dharma*; nor is Hindu *Dharma* identical with Hinduism". And S.S. Savarkar, the publisher, wrote in the preface : "Veer Savarkar had to coin some new words such as '*Hindutva*'..." Is it not expected of L. K. Advani as Home minister of the BJP-led central government to sing praises of Savakrar and declare the jail complex in Port Blair as a national memorial in honour of the hero of the forces of *Hindutva*? If on the one hand Tapan

Raychaudhuri in his essay on *Swami Vivekananda's construction of Hinduism* writes that "he was among the earliest nationalist thinkers to claim the Indo-Islamic past as part of the Indian heritage", on the other, he castigates the forces of *Hindutva* by saying how "the VHP has the audacity to claim him as their own." *Hindutva* as constructed by Sangh Parivar and promoted by BJP-in-government has specific goal of pursuing an anti-Minority project of its own brand. Robert A. Dahl in his book *Democracy And Its Critics (1989)* mentions that democracy had adversarial critics" and "sympathetic critics' and devotes his attention to examine the "adversaries" and "sympathetic critics" of democracy. He concludes the book by commenting on '*Democracy in Tomorrow's World*' and '*Sketches for an Advanced Democratic Country*'. Dahl concludes : "Yet the vision of people governing themselves as political equals, and possessing all the resources and institutions necessary to do so, will, I believe, remain a compelling if always demanding guide in the search for a society in which people may live together in peace, respect each other's intrinsic equality, and jointly seek the best possible life".[25]

What is the future vision of the Sangh Parivar? Where does 'democracy based on the principle of equality of all citizens' fit into the project of Hindutva? Is democratic political system safe in the hands of committed anti-minority Sangh Parivar? The answer to this question is a Big No. Democratic political system of India is not at all safe from the attack and assaults of committed anti-minority *Hindutva*. BJP-in-Government has an "adversial" relationship with secular, democratic pluralist political system of India. *Hindutva* and Indian democracy can not co-exist because *Hindutva* is ideologically committed to establish Hindu majority state which is a negation of the very idea of democratic rights of every citizen irrespective of caste, creed, religion, sex and colour.

REFERENCES

1. Bryan S., Turner: "*Contemporary Problem In the Theory of Citizenship* in Bryan S., Turner (Ed.) *Citizenship and Social Theory*: New Delhi: Sage Publication 1993, p. 3
2. Giovanni Sartori: *Democratic Theory*: New Delhi: Oxford University Press: 1965, p. 335
3. *ibid*, p. 364
4. Bart Van Steenbergen: *The Condition of Citizenship*: New Delhi Sage Publication 1994: p. 4
5. Robert, A. Dahl: *Democracy And Its Critics*: New Haven: Yale University Press 1989, pp. 320-21.

6. Pralay, Kanungo: *RSS Tryst with Politics: From Hedgewar to Sudarshan*: Delhi: Manohar, 2002
7. See Martin E. Marry and R. Scott Appleby (Eds) *Fundamentalisms observed*, vol. I (Chicago: Chicago University Press, 1991 also see other volumes 1992 1993, 1994, 1995)
8. Lahouari, Addi : "*The Failure of Third World Nationalism*" : quoted by Peter Juviler and Sherrill Stroschein : *Political Science Quarterly*, volume 114, Number 3, 1999, pp. 450-51.
9. The *Guardian*: Europe: April 25, 2001, p. 7.
10. Also see Jorge Larrain: *Ideology and Cultural Identity: Modernity and the Third World*: Polity Press, 1994.
11. Interview of Jana Krishnamurthy, *The Indian Express*: New Delhi: May 29, 2001.
12. L.K. Advani: *Statement before Liberahan Commission*: *The Indian Express*: New Delhi: June 13, 2001.
13. M.S. Golwalkar, *Bunch of Thoughts* p. 182, quoted by Kanungo (2002) p. 116.
14. Aristotle quoted by Richard Mecheon: (ed) *The Basic Works of* Aristotle: New York : Random House, 1941, p. 936.
15. G.K. Chadha, P.P. Sahu: "*Post-reform setback in rural employment: Issues that need further serutiny*." Bombay, *Economic Political Weekly*, May 25-31, 2002, vol. XXXVII, no. 21, pp. 1998-2026.
16. C.P. Chandrasekhar and Jayati Ghosh: *The Market that Failed: A Decade of Neoliberal Economic Reforms in India* : New Delhi Leftword Books, 2002.
17. *Economic Survey*: 2001-2002: New Delhi: Government of India: March 2002.
18. Gary Younge: "*After Burnley and Oldham, there is no such thing as a black British experience: There are several*". *The Guardian*: London, June 28, 2001, p. 7.
19. *Asian Age* : New Delhi June 7, 2002, p. 1
20. *The Statesman*: New Delhi: June 8, 2002, p. 4.
21. Ashok Singhal, VHP leader: *The Hindu*, New Delhi, June 23, 2002, p. 1.
22. *The Hindu*: New Delhi June 23, 2002, p. 1.
23. J.S. Mill quoted by Sartori, *op. cit.* p. 99.
24. Aijaz Ahmad, "*Cry the Beloved Country*" : *Frontline*, Chennai. Vol. 19, no. 13, June 22-July 5, 2002, p. 116.
25. Robert A. Dahl: *Democracy And its Critics* New Haven, Yale University Press, 1989, p. 341.

2

Governance for Hindutva

Priestly Takeover of Secular Governance

The Sangh Parivar has once again succeeded in reviving the movement for the construction of Ram Temple at the so called *Ramjanmbhoomi* site in Ayodhya. An obliging Prime Minister who himself maintained on December 6, 2002 that the Ram Temple reflected "national sentiments", started negotiations with the Vishwa Hindu Parishad, a "frontal organisation" of the Sangh Parivar, for the modalities of performing *puja* on the undisputed/disputed site for the construction of the Ram Temple.

The VHP leadership pretended to reject the stand taken by the Prime Minister on the issue of *puja* and it was claimed that he had asked the RSS to intervene between the VHP and the Vajpayee-led coalition Government, as if the RSS and VHP were working at cross purposes. On March 4, 2002, the Ramjanmbhoomi Nyas (RJN) Chief Ramchandradas Paramhans proclaimed that he had told the Prime Minister that "he would not meet him again on the issue". On March 5, we were informed by the same Paramhans that "RSS is no different from us. It is my eyes, hands, my entire being". This statement of Paramhans completely exposed the well-known linkages between every member of the Parivar, including Atal Bihari Vajpayee. The VHP leadership raised the antenna when Acharya Giriraj Kishore publicly maintained that "we will not change the programme under any circumstances as the decision has been taken by the sants". The VHP has also led a "*Sant Chetavani Yatra*" from January 21 to 27, 2002 to warn the Government not to create any obstacles in the way of the construction of the temple at Ayodhya. The BJP-led Government was in a fix when on February 27, 2002, Acharya Giriraj Kishore of the VHP shut the doors of negotiations with the Prime Minister by observing that "we do not have the authority to postpone the temple construction date. The decision was taken by the Dharmacharyas (Hindu religious heads) and only they can change it". Since the Saints and Sadhus had been elevated to the position of real decision makers by the Sangh Parivar, Shankracharya Swami Jayendra Sarswati of Kanchipuram landed in Delhi on March 4, 2002 to mediate and negotiate with the Vajpayee Government and the luminaries of the Sangh Parivar on the terms and conditions for performing the Puja on March 15. The Shankracharya got actively involved in negotiations and many leaders like R. Venkataraman, a former President, Ranganath Mishra, a former Chief Justice, and legal luminaries were consulted by him in order to facilitate the Hindu organisations to perform *puja* at Ayodhya on March 15. What are the consequences of involving "priestly" class in resolving inter-community or inter-group public disputes or conflicts? Is India not moving towards the establishment of a Hindu theocratic state when the "priestly class" has succeeded in supplanting the state in performing its legitimate constitutional obligations of dealing with public issues, including inter-community religious disputes?

A few facts may be mentioned to alert democratic public opinion in India that the active involvement of the 'priests' in public decision making processes will make India a full-fledged Hindu theocracy. The Sangh Parivar and its various frontal organisations have always maintained that any court verdict on the temple-mosque dispute is irrelevant because the birthplace of Ram is a "matter of faith among the Hindus" and "matters of faith" are not sub-judice. The story does not end there. Ramchandradas Paramhans of RJN claims that the date of the *puja* decided by the Dharmacharyas is irrevocable because priests are superior to the Government of India and once the priests have decided, the Government cannot be permitted to override their decision. Not only this. The real goal of the Sangh Parivar is to create a complete Hindu-Muslim divide and in the pursuit of this objective they have tried to project the temple-mosque dispute as a conflict between two religious communities. If it is a Hindu-Muslim dispute, it falls in the domain of Hindu and Muslim priestly classes, and the Sangh Parivar would like Shankracharyas to play an active pubic role on behalf of the Hindus. Since the logic of the Sangh Parivar is acceptable to the Muslim communalists, they have also activated their Mullahs and Maulanas of the All-India Muslim Personal Law Board and the Babri Masjid Action Committee to intervene on behalf of the Muslim community and defend the Muslim cause at Ayodhya. The Hindu and Muslim communalist parties, organisations and leaders have been struggling to create a monolithic Hindu and Muslim community so that communal organisations can claim to be "authentic" spokespersons of their respective communities. Priests emerge as the real reference point of public disputes if they are represented in religious idiom as is the case regarding the current dispute and this is projected by communalists as an alternative to the democratic secular state. The Indian state is the final arbiter in every public dispute and inter-community questions cannot be handed over to the priests by the political class.

The Constitution has created a sovereign, democratic, republican state which is the legitimate guarantor of the rule of law and rights of citizens, irrespective of their religion, faith or creed. The basic structure of the Constitution is threatened if priests and not an elected Parliament become the real representatives of the "general will" of the people of India. Elections provide legitimacy to democratic governance with the mandate that public affairs will be managed by its institutional mechanisms. In an elective democracy priests have no authority in public affairs. India is witnessing a complete subversion of constitutional democracy by the emergence of anti-constitutional centres of power represented by the priestly class. Instead of priests being ejected from pubic disputes, the Indian state itself has abdicated its legal authority, thereby deliberately and consciously providing "space" to the priests, and therefore authority that is completely denied to them by the Constitution. It is one thing for individual political leaders to visit individual Shankracharyas and receive their blessings for success in politics; it is quite another for the Prime Minister of India to negotiate with the priestly class by according it a respectability which is not given to them by the constitutional law of India. It is worth reminding the motley crowd of leaders like V.P. Singh, P.V. Narasimha Rao and others that they should publicly own their acts of omission and commission by involving Shankarayas or Shahi Imams in public disputes because only then the gang of four ex-Prime Ministers can alert the country that the Vajpayee Government is leading India towards a great disaster. Are the allies of this unnatural National Democratic alliance aware of their past commitments to socialism and secularism? Will they stand up or allow the Sangh Parivar to transform India into a Hindu theocracy where the authority of Shankracharyas will be supreme?

The issue is not the success or failure of the Shankracharya as a negotiator or mediator. The central issue is: How does a secular democratic state keep the "priests" out of public domain? Jawaharlal

Nehru believed in this approach and he warned the first President of India, Dr. Rajendra Prasad not to publicly associate with the ceremonies of the purification of the Somnath temple because the state should not be seen associating itself with the priests. The upshot of the above discussion is that the Sangh Parivar is deliberately and consciously involving Hindu priests in the affairs of the state because a secular constitution is not acceptable to the forces of *Hindutva*. It is for the opponents of the philosophy of the *Hindutva* to demand that the state does not stray from the secular path. It is not priests but the Prime Minister who should be in the driver's seat in democratic India. (*March 21, 2002, The Pioneer*)

Promotion of Religiosity by a Secular State

The BJP-led Government of Uttar Pradesh has created a great public controversy by introducing a Bill on the Places of Worship. This legislation has been reserved by the State Governor for the approval by the President. This action of the BJP Government of Uttar Pradesh has once again brought into sharp public focus the issue of the role of the secular state while dealing with places of religious worship.

The defenders of the Bill introduced by the Uttar Pradesh Government to regulate the places of worship argue that similar laws have been passed by the Madhya Pradesh and Rajasthan State Governments. Secondly, after the demolition of the Babri Masjid on December 6, 1992. Parliament passed a law for the protection of places of religious worship. The argument is if Parliament can legislate for the protection of religious places, then the State legislatures can also pass laws for the regulation of places of worship. Thirdly, it has been suggested that colonial India had a tradition of the state legislating for the maintenance and management of places of worship; an important example is the Sikh Gurudwara Prabandak Committee Act which was passed on the demand of the Akali Dal, a platform of the Sikh community. Fourthly, all-important temples of India from Tirupati to Vaishno Devi have management boards with government functionaries working in cooperation with the temple priests. The upshot of the argument in defence of the regulatory powers of the Indian state, irrespective of its secular character, is that every public institution or organisation has to be regulated by the state and public places of worship cannot be an exception.

Further, the Indian state not only regulates the places of worship, it also very actively patronises some places of worship. As Governor of

Jammu & Kashmir, Mr. Jagmohan worked overtime to make *darshans* to the temple at Vaishno Devi very comfortable for devotees. As Union Minister of Urban Development, he is actively involved in the "development of a residential pilgrim centre near the Laxmi Narayan temple, popularly known as Birla Mandir of Delhi". Ministers and chief ministers openly identify themselves with places of worship by becoming chairpersons or presidents of the management boards of these institutions. Punjab Chief Minister Parkash Singh Badal, is not the only one who is involved in the politics of religious affairs. Mr. Om Prakash Chautala, the Chief Minister of Haryana is chairman of the Shree Sheetala Mata Devi Shrine Board. State governments have frequently exercised their powers to take over the management of places of worship and to reconstitute or dismiss their management boards. Central and State governments are involved in litigations regarding the problems of management of religious places.

Should leaders of the Indian state openly identify themselves with places of worship and purely religious festivals and rituals? This question had been raised just after Independence when the then President Rajendra Prasad wanted to attend the consecration ceremony of the Som Nath Temple and Nehru publicly advised him not to associate himself with the activities of the temple. Not only this, in the 1950s, the Kumbh Mela was held at Allahabad and President Prasad joined in the holy bath. Since the State administration was busy in making arrangements for the President's holy bath, lakhs of devotees who had gathered at Allahabad could not be regulated. In the stampede that followed hundreds of people died. The media took the President to task on the wisdom of visiting the Kumbh Mela.

In a multi-religious country, functionaries of the secular state end up patronising every religion, seer or place of worship on the basis of a spacious and facile argument of equal respect for all religions. *Eid milans*, *Iftar* parties, *Ram lilas*, Krishna temples in Mathura and Varanasi, Tirupati temple and places of worship or rituals of an important religious sect receive great, though formally equal attention of the leaders of the secular state. While playing this game of "equal respect for all religions" leaders of the Indian state have come to be identified with majority Hindu religious places of worship.

A distinction has to be maintained between the regulatory powers of the Indian state, and active promotion and patronage of places of worship by state functionaries. Religious beliefs are a private affair of citizens and under the Constitution every citizen has freedom to practice his religion.

But the association of state functionaries with places of worship makes religion a public affair. The secular state of India has legitimised and solidified religiosity, alongwith religious superstitions, because state functionaries are proud of their association with places of worship and religious rituals. Public association of public functionaries with public places of worship has seriously compromised the legitimacy of secularism as practiced by the Indian state. The functionaries of the secular state have to keep themselves at a respectable distance from religious functionaries in religious places because their public identification with places of worship or religious ceremonies has done harm to the actual functioning of the secular state of India which has come to be suspected to be a Hindu state.

Moreover, in a country where cultural practices and performances are intertwined with specific religions, public functionaries cannot maintain that their association with a cultural festival is a secular activity. How can association with ritualistic cultural festivals in a multireligious country be accepted as a practice of neutrality by functionaries of the state?

Similarly, the Indian state has been accused of religious biases while performing their regulatory functions in relation to places of worship. Why should elected political leaders and permanent civil servants be associated with the actual management of temples or gurdwaras? Places of religious worship should be managed by the community of believers. In the age of the roll back state and amid the downsizing of the bloated bureaucracy, the Indian state should abandon its powers of regulation and management of the places of worship. The community should manage its own religious affairs subject to the ordinary laws of the land.

The Constitution of India clearly states that "The state shall not discriminate against any citizen on grounds only of religion..." We have to go a long way even to achieve this goal of non-discriminatory secular state. Religious distancing has increased in Indian society and many a time functionaries of the Indian state have been accused of practising religious preferences while performing public duties. In such a situation, the state regulation of places of worship should be kept to the minimum. The Supreme Court of India has in many important judgements made a distinction between the "essentials" and "non-essentials" of different religions.

A religious believer has a right to build a place of worship and manage it. The Indian state while performing its regulatory functions in relation to the places of worship should confine itself only to its essential role of maintaining law and order during religious festivals and implementing its normal ordinary laws while dealing with places of worship.

A secular state, whose credentials are already suspect, should withdraw itself from promotion of religiosity in public and the management of places of worship. Only Nehru had seen the folly of state functionaries identifying themselves with religiosity. His successors have complicated the issues which now deserves rectification. (*May 12, 2000, The Pioneer*)

Poll in the BJP's Court

Lok Sabha and State Assembly elections in India have become as frequent as Hindu religious festivals. Indira Gandhi delinked Assembly and Lok Sabha elections in 1971 and 1972. Her spurious argument: National issues should be focused during Lok Sabha polls and local issues raised during Assembly elections. The catalogue for Assembly elections in 2003 and 2004 is quite formidable. Himachal Pradesh and Gujarat (unless the latter has elections in October) will go to the polls early 2003; Madhya Pradesh, Rajasthan, Delhi and Chhatisgarh later that year 2003 which will witness polls in six States. Early-2004: Orissa, Karnataka and Bihar will see electoral battles. The Lok Sabha polls are to be held in October 2004.

These electoral battles are crucial for the BJP. In the 2002 Assembly elections, the party suffered decisive defeats in UP, Uttaranchal, Punjab and Manipur, and secured a small success in Goa. If the 2002 story repeats itself in 2003 and 2004, the BJP will be marginalised. To checkmate its electoral decline, the Sangh Parivar has activated its organisational units, and the BJP leadership is setting the party house in order.

The BJP has at its service well-knit, ideologically-committed and cadre-based organisations—the RSS, the Bajrang Dal, the VHP, the ABVP. *Hindutva* ideology and solid organisational backup is its strength. Its all-India competitor, the Congress, falls far behind in terms of "ideological purity" and organisational strength. The Sangh Parivar spreads the *Hindutva* message, and elections are the Hindu Parivar's collective activity. Not without reason, Mr. Atal Bihari Vajpayee reshuffled his Council of Ministers on July 1, and Mr. K. Jana Krishnamurthy was replaced as party President by Mr. Venkaiah Naidu, with Mr. Arun Jaitley becoming party spokesman. Mr. Vinay Katiyar was shifted from the Bajrang Dal to the post of UP BJP chief. The Cabinet reshuffle and the appointment of Mr. L.K. Advani as Deputy Prime Minister are one aspect of the exercise. The other part of BJP's surgical operation is the appointment of new party functionaries.

French scholar M. Duverger, in his seminal work on modern political parties, maintains that "modern political parties" are different from their late-18th or 19th century counterparts in that they are extremely organised. Robert K. Merton, an American sociologist, alerted us by pointing out that the "party organisational machine" controls a party, and it is the "organisational machine men" who are a party's real leaders.

This applies to the BJP, which has not only strengthened its party "machine" but also stated that the Ram temple is on the party agenda. The commitment to Ram temple was reiterated by Mr. Vajpayee in Lucknow on June 28. At Kurukshetra, RSS ideologue M.S. Vaidhya said "courts cannot do anything" because "it is a matter of faith". Not to be left behind, the BJP chief in UP, Mr. Katiyar, asserted that a grand temple would be built at Ayodhya.

However, ideology and party organisation are a necessary but not sufficient condition for electoral victory in a highly competitive pluralistic democracy. The Congress rules 14 States despite its "wishy-washy" ideology. The BJP could not receive a mandate of more than 20 per cent of voters during the 1999 Lok Sabha polls. This, despite the fact the party raised the highly emotive issue of Kargil. The elections in Uttaranchal were contested by the BJP on the plea that its political opponent, the Congress, was opposed to the creation of the State. Yet, Uttaranchal's voters defeated the party.

Hence, the strength of the BJP and the Sangh Parivar is also a serious political limitation. *Hindutva* does not appeal to a large number of voters who view socio-economic realities without the blinkers of faith. They look beyond *Hindutva* during elections—consider the 1993 polls in UP, Madhya Pradesh, Himachal Pradesh and Rajasthan. The BJP projected itself as "martyr" to the cause of Lord Ram, appealing to the emotions of Hindu voters after the Babri Masjid demolition. The events in Ayodhya on December 6, 1992, did not strike a chord with so-called Hindu voters. The BJP was defeated in UP, the land of Ayodhya, and in Madhya Pradesh and Himachal Pradesh.

The BJP's anti-Pakistan and anti-ISI campaign during the 1999 Lok Sabha elections did not enthuse the Hindu voter. It was supported by the same percentage of one-fifth of the voters as in the 1998 Lok Sabha polls. V.D. Savarkar's idea of "Hinduising politics and militarising Hindudom" has not paid off, despite the BJP's rhetoric about India achieving 'nuclear status' in 1998. BJP leaders do not draw correct conclusions from electoral victories or defeats. Why did the Congress under Rajiv Gandhi obtain three-fourths majority in the 1984 Lok Sabha elections but only 220 seats in 1989? An emotive appeal can succeed only once. Indira Gandhi's assassination in 1984 brought dividends but Rajiv Gandhi's assassination in 1989 made a marginal difference to the Congress's electoral fortunes. Similarly, in the 1970 Lok Sabha elections, Indira Gandhi could project Congress stalwarts as reactionary with her "*Garibi Hatao*" slogan.

The BJP has reached its electoral peak. It cannot mobilise its Hindu constituency on any "emotive" issue. Its attempt to polarise society has serious limitations. Within the Hindu community, caste plays a spoilsport. Mr. Katiyar is a Bajrang Dal fanatic, but his nomination as UP BJP chief was owing to his Kurmi caste. The 'backward caste' platform has many claimants—Mr. Mulayam Singh Yadav, Mayawati and Kalyan Singh. Social polarisation on the basis of religion leads to social violence, as in Gujarat from February to May 2002. It cannot lead to electoral victories. Mr. Rajnath Singh, former BJP Chief Minister of UP, announced a policy of "quota within quota" for the "most backward castes". His hopes of political reward from these sections in the Assembly elections of 2002 were belied.

The BJP may have brought in new faces to counter the Congress's high-profile Chief Ministers like Mr. Ashok Gehlot of Rajasthan, Mr. Amarinder Singh of Punjab and Mr. Digvijay Singh of Madhya Pradesh, to name a few. It is a well-known strategy of parties to learn from opponents. Ms. Sonia Gandhi has successfully projected the performance-oriented leaders of Congress-ruled states, with whom the BJP's 'new faces'—Mr. Katiyar, Mr. Venkaiah Naidu (the third BJP President in 18 months), Mr. Arun Jaitley and others—will have to compete.

The question is: What is the place of governance and performance in the BJP scheme of things? The Cabinet reshuffle and new party appointees offer nothing to voters. How can film actors improve the country's governance? How can the economy be revived by shifting Mr. Jaswant Singh to Finance? How can the West's coercive diplomacy in the India-Pakistan stand-off be countered by Mr. Yashwant Sinha? If he failed as Finance Minister, he cannot be expected to succeed as Foreign Minister. Musical chairs are not a surrogate for performance.

Setting its house in order, the BJP offers nothing to voters save the bankrupt ideology of *Hindutva*. A monolithic Hindu community does not exist and cannot be created by raising slogans—be it the Ram temple,

Hindu India or the Pakistani threat. The politics of protecting Hindus from "enemies, domestic and external" has lost its electoral appeal and the BJP has reached a dead-end. It does not have a nation-building or developmental programme that can inspire the electorate. The Congress has not succeeded at the State level because of new leaders. Its Chief Ministers have made a definite impact by focussing on development. By contrast, BJP Chief Ministers in UP in the recent past or presently in Gujarat or Himachal Pradesh have not provided good governance. This is the BJP's real challenge. (*July 20, 2002, The Pioneer*)

Autonomy Fever and the BJP

Many tall claims were made by the BJP leadership and its allies while releasing the election manifesto of the National Democratic Alliance for the 1999 Lok Sabha elections. It was proclaimed that Atal Bihari Vajpayee was quintessentially a believer and practitioner of accommodative political culture of coalitional politics. It was further maintained that regional aspirations of the allies of the BJP would be well looked after and that 24 political parties were enthusiastic to accept the leadership of the BJP.

The BJP had claimed that the presence of regional parties in the central government would ensure that specific regional problems would get resolved in the council of ministers. But important regional parties and groups like Akali Dal, Asom Gana Parishad, DMK, PMK, MDMK and National Conference represented in the council of ministers have been airing serious grievances against the excessive centralisation of Indian federalism under the BJP-led government.

The National Conference, a partner of the NDA government, has formally approached the central government for a discussion on 'autonomy' for J&K. Prakash Singh Badal of Akali Dal and Prafulla Kumar Mahanta of Asom Gana Parishad have come out openly in favour of more 'autonomy' for the states. The claim of the BJP that a coalition government under its leadership at the Centre would be the best arrangement for resolving Centre-state problems has thus been belied.

The demand for 'autonomy' by the state governments and regional political parties is based on their quest for regional-cultural identity which is perceived as threatened by an all-India national party like the BJP and earlier the Congress. There is, however, a basic difference between the approach of the Congress and BJP on autonomy. Congress believes that India is multi-cultural and its cultural diversities have to be promoted and protected, whereas BJP believes that India is "one country, one culture and one nation."

While the Congress was reluctant to grant autonomy to the states, it had never refused to negotiate with regional groups on the issue of more powers for the state governments. It is worth mentioning that when the issue of state autonomy was getting hot in the mid-1980s, the Indira Gandhi government appointed Justice R.S. Sarkaria to undertake a full review of Centre-state relations in India.

Justice R.S. Sarkaria, in response to demands for more autonomy to the states on July 9/10, 2000 observed that without amending the Constitution of India, the central government could transfer many powers to the states from the Concurrent List of the Indian Constitution. But how can BJP resolve any issue raised by the regional and sub-regional groups by providing them more powers under the existing Constitution since the Sangh Parivar does not accept the basic pluralist philosophy underlying the Indian constitution?

The Sangh Parivar has always believed and practised the politics of strong and centralised *Hindu Rashtra* because the Parivar firmly believes that Hindus have always suffered because of the central government's ineffectiveness in dealing with centrifugal tendencies. The BJP government is facing a fundamental contradiction between its ideology of exclusivist *Hindu Rashtra* and demands of cultural pluralists represented by chief ministers and regional parties.

The BJP-led central government also does not have any answer to the growing regional imbalances within India under the impact of globalisation and privatisation. The decade of 90s has changed the face of India. Southern states of Tamil Nadu, Andhra Pradesh and Karnataka are attracting high investments for Information Technology, and Maharashtra and Gujarat are also favourite destinations of foreign investors. What about the backward states of Uttar Pradesh, Bihar, Madhya Pradesh and Rajasthan?

The Indian federal system has entered a stage where serious conflicts shall emerge between developed regions and backward states. Backward states will demand more financial support from the Centre and the developed states will oppose this demand on the ground that backwardness of these states is depriving them from their own legitimate share in national fiscal resources. An acute competition has already developed among various regions because the beneficiaries of new economic policy regime consider the backward states as a great drain on national fiscal resources. New demands for autonomy are likely to emerge from forward and developed states as they will not like to share their benefits of development with poor cousins like UP, Bihar, MP and Rajasthan.

The above discussion reveals that demands for autonomy by the states are not going to end simply because the central government is reluctant to concede such demands. Autonomy for the states is an important agenda of Indian politics in the 21st century, and it has to be tackled with great sensitivity on the part of the Central Government. Federalism is always a balancing system between the powers of the Centre and status of the state governments and a new dimension has been added to this issue because of globalisation of our economic policies. The demands for autonomy cannot be rejected without proper negotiations with a spirit of give and take by the central and state governments.

The autonomy fever will continue to plague the body politic of India because the emerging scenario of developed regions versus underdeveloped and backward regions will intensify inter-regional conflicts. The central government will always be under pressure from competing and contending regional forces for more autonomy to the states in the name of development or assertions of cultural identities. (*July 21, 2000, The Observer*)

Bloated from Gorging on Power

Mr. Atal Bihari Vajpayee, in his address to the captains of industry on December 16, said that "the mindset of the Indian bureaucracy is a great roadblock" to the speedy implementation of economic reforms. He added that every prime minister in the Nineties faced an obstructionist bureaucracy, and promised to streamline the administrative machinery by "downsizing" the bloated bureaucracy by 2004.

The Indian bureaucracy is fully integrated with the political class and politicians, bureaucrats, industry and powerful agricultural sections are a close-knit ruling class. The bureaucracy is a power centre because of its linkages with other power centres. Each of these groups is mutually supportive. A sea change has taken place in the power of the bureaucracy since the Nehru era and the licence-permit raj to the Nineties, which has been characterised as the phase of the "retreat of the state" and the de-bureaucratisation of the Indian society and economy. The much-maligned Nehru phase did not have "jumbo-sized" ministries, which are a common feature of the weak factionalised coalitions of the 1990s. This is not confined to the Centre: the state governments have many more ministers than in the 1950s and '60s. Instead of shutting down ministries and departments created to respond to the needs of state-led economic development phase of Nehru, the Nineties have seen the creation of new departments, ministries and specialised "regulatory" agencies to manage economic liberalisation.

Nehru's Council of Ministers consisted of cabinet ministers, ministers of state, a few deputy ministers and parliamentary secretaries. The cabinets of the Nineties consist only of cabinet ministers and ministers of state. Nehru worked with limited secretarial staff, the prime ministers of the Nineties have a large and powerful prime minister's office. A large cabinet requires a huge bureaucracy to serve it. In these changing times, the bureaucracy at the Centre, like their political masters, have added new designations and status symbols which has made governance not only expensive but also cumbersome. The staffing pattern of Home Minister L.K. Advani is: one Home Secretary, three Special Secretaries, one or two Additional Secretaries, 14 Joint Secretaries, and numerous Deputy and Under Secretaries.

Every minister has facilitated large bureaucracies and special categories for officials depending not on job needs but to satisfy personal ego. Bureaucrats believe that if there can only be one Home Secretary, there is no limit on the number of Special Secretaries, a designation which in Nehru's time was rare. The prime minister's office and the prime minister's personal secretary is a very powerful watchdog of the interests of the fraternity of bureaucrats.

If the bureaucracy is to be streamlined, it is essential to diagnose the reasons which make bureaucrats powerful. The way in which the Fifth Pay Commission recommendations were accepted and implemented by a great liberaliser like P. Chidambaram shows that bureaucratic power and strength can only be cut down if the existing centralisation of power in the central and state governments is tackled by evolving transparent decision-making based on checks and balances. Centralisation is the real villain of the piece.

Politicians centralise power to take care of their special constituencies. Powerful social groups appreciate centralisation because they feel comfortable dealing with ministers and the higher bureaucracy and the business classes get quick decisions by lobbying with them. Politicians have the alibi that without practising the politics of patronage they cannot win an election.

How does the bureaucracy fit into this system of centralisation of power? It is the hyphen that joins the buckle that binds the political class with powerful economic and social strata. It is a permanent factor in decision-making while politicians are transitory in the unstable and fractured coalitions of the Nineties. Political and business leaders who want a particular decision cannot succeed without the consent of the bureaucracy.

Mrs. Indira Gandhi really laid down the foundations of a centralised system of decision-making, for she found that an unwilling bureaucracy could queer the pitch for her. If on the one hand she talked of a "committed bureaucracy", on the other she established her own prime minister's office under a trusted Principal Secretary like P.N. Haksar and P.N. Dhar. The same practice continues with the Vajpayee government with Messrs Haksar and Dhar having been replaced by Mr. Brajesh Mishra, who is the real hand of the prime minister. Ms. Jayanti Natarajan, was not wide of the mark when she said that "no politician in his life can be as corrupt as a bureaucrat". Our focus is not on corruption, but on the system of centralisation of power whose mainstay is the Indian bureaucracy. A political controversy on the Bofors deal can seal the fate of a Rajiv Gandhi and the bureaucrats involved in the affair can retire.

Mr. Vajpayee has wrongly focused attention on the bloated bureaucracy. The real reason for the bureaucracy's malfunctioning is the centralisation of power to which politicians, the business class and the bureaucrats have contributed because of self-interest. The alternative system of decentralised, participatory and transparent decision-making is the only method to tackle bureaucrats' arrogance of power. A large number of ministers in the field of social welfare and human resource development are not at all required at the centre. The reason for their continuance in the age of liberalisation is that bureaucrats want to be at the headquarters of decision-making in Delhi or the state capitals.

Active governmental and bureaucratic decision-making is the only method to deal with the bureaucracy's centralising tendency. The government of West Bengal successfully practised a people-led exposure of the bureaucracy because Operation Barga succeeded when local people came forward to identify the benami owners in the villages. The suggestion is not for a toothless Panchayati Raj but for a real restructuring of bureaucratic functioning which has created a mystique about itself. (*December 28, 2000, Financial Express*)

Ideology and Opportunism

The pre-poll drama in Tamil Nadu, Pondicherry, Assam, West Bengal and Kerala by the national/regional parties is a repeat of the one performed in the decade of the 1990s, which was characterised by the interplay of politics of ideology with opportunism. The politics of alliance formation for the forthcoming five Assembly elections is a kind of replay of the events preceding the Lok Sabha elections of 1989, 1991, 1996, 1998 and 1999. A few salient features of the politics of the decade of the 1990s may be mentioned to substantiate the argument that Indian politics has decisively arrived at a stage where the so-called ideological parties are continuously engaged in the politics of opportunism, and this kind of opportunistic politics of alliances has decisively benefited the BJP.

First, all anti-Congress political formations of the Left, Right, Centre and Regionalists have succeeded in displacing the Congress from the centre-stage of Indian politics. In this process, the Congress has been pushed out and the space vacated by it has been gradually occupied by the BJP. Every kind of opportunistic alliance was made by anti-Congress formations and every non-Congress government at the Centre in the 1990s existed and survived on the basis of courtesy and whims of the BJP. Mr. V.P. Singh became the Prime Minister in 1989 with the so-called outside support of the BJP. Then, Messrs H.D. Deve Gowda and I.K. Gujral in 1996 and 1998 as prime ministers of shaky and unnatural alliances legitimised the BJP in the eyes of the voters, who started accepting the BJP propaganda as "party with a difference".

Not only this. Many of the alliance partners of the Singh/Gowda/Gujral governments did not hesitate to form partnership with the BJP-led coalition governments of 1998 and 1999. Mamatas, Jayalalithas, Karunanidhis, Naidus, Badals or Abdullahs faced no crisis of conscience in walking out of the so-called "secular alliances" of Messrs Singh or Deve Gowda or Gujral to join hands with the so-called communalists. It is surprising that "People's Front" of the Left parties (with Mr. Mulayam Singh Yadav and Mr. Laloo Prasad Yadav) has been floated again to counter the Congress and the BJP, without realising that the opportunistic politics of the 1990s has legitimised the communal politics of the BJP, and that this Party has ceased to be a political untouchable because so many leaders, groups and parties have shared power with the "outcaste" representative of *Hindutva*.

Second, politics of opportunism and compromises is not confined only to the Central Government because the same political drama is being replayed in the states. Again the beneficiary of such unprincipled politics is the BJP. M. Karunanidhi, the secular partner of many anti-Congress formations, has successfully accommodated the BJP for the forthcoming State Assembly elections in Tamil Nadu. Then, Ms. J. Jayalalitha cannot attack Mr. Karunanidhi on this issue because her AIADMK shared power with the BJP at the Centre in 1998.

The Assembly elections in Assam provide yet another example of how the BJP is "marching on" with the support of regional formations. The AGP Government of Prafulla Kumar Mahanta is a committed anti-Congress regionalist, and in this game the BJP is a beneficiary because during the elections, the party will play its only Hindu card very effectively by targetting the Muslims of Assam and by raising the bogey of "Assam under siege by the Bangladeshi Muslims". Mr. L.K. Advani, the Union Home Minister, has repeatedly made a distinction between Hindu Bangladeshis migrating to India and Muslim Bangladeshis. The AGP-AASU will have to compete against the Sangh parivar on the sole issue of Assamese identity because the AGP is not able to distinguish between its secular definition of Assamese identity and its opposition to Bangladeshi migrants. While the AGP is confused about identifying and targetting the so-called foreigners in Assam, the BJP offers a clear alternative before the voters by making a distinction between an unwanted Bengali Muslim foreigner and legitimate Hindu Bengali migrant from Bangladesh to Assam. The AGP has created a climate where the dividends will be enjoyed by the BJP.

The secular Mamata Banerjee of Trinamool Congress too is politically legitimising *Hindutva* in West Bengal, not only by sharing power at the Centre with the BJP-led NDA, but also by accommodating the BJP in the forthcoming Assembly elections. Ms. Mamata Banerjee is following the same path in West Bengal as that of the Left parties. The Left Front made all sorts of political arrangements to defeat the Congress and now it is left to Ms. Banerjee — by following in the footsteps of the Left parties — to make every kind of alliance with the sole purpose of defeating the Left Front in West Bengal. Anti-Congressism of the Left has been replaced by anti-Left Frontism of the Trinamool leadership. It is advantage BJP. What is the explanation for the surrender of ideology by the so-called believers of ideological politics? How can M. Karunanidhi of the anti-Brahman, anti-God DMK help in the growth and expansion of a party of the Hindus, by the Hindus and for the Hindus? How can anti-Brahman political and secular formation in Tamil Nadu accept practitioners of Brahamanical Hinduism? The first explanation for the emergence of ideological opportunism lies in the "logic of power". Political power *per se* has become the goal of a large number of political leaders, groups and formations. The winning of an election is an essential passport to power, patronage and personal aggrandisement. This is the reason why parties and groups are multiplying and every caste or sub-caste leader is engaged in opening a political shop for the purpose of winning an Assembly or Lok Sabha election.

The pre-election drama of walking-in and walking-out of individual leaders from their political shops has been clearly witnessed in Tamil Nadu. Mr. P Chidambaram of the TMC walked over to Mr. Karunanidhi of the DMK who has an alliance with the BJP. Tamil Nadu has many claimants of Dravidian heritage, which is co-terminus with their caste, sub-caste and backward caste and really backward castes. These appropriators of Dravidian culture do not feel inconvenient while walking towards Mr. Karunanidhi or Ms. Jayalalitha. Victory in election has become the only aim of fragments of political class and after winning a seat, these patriotic leaders see "riches and luxuries". Politics has been a lucrative activity because it is a profitable business.

If one side of the story of Indian politics is underscored by opportunism, the other side of the picture is that in this opportunistic game, the party of *Hindutva* is making every effort to emerge as a formidable pole at the all-India level. Moreover, in achieving the goal of an all-India party of the Hindus, the BJP's real target is the declining pan-Indian Congress party. Hence, the BJP is practicing politics of ideology and giving the impression of being an opportunist coalition-maker. The BJP has used every opportunity to extend its influence and even unreliable allies like Ms. Mamata Banerjee, Ms. Jayalalitha or Ms. Mayawati are important because under their umbrella, the BJP can displace the Congress and create a political space for itself from J&K to the North-East.

Politics of opportunistic alliances has not only legitimised the BJP in Indian democracy, it has helped the party in decimating its sole enemy, the Congress party. The Congress, with all its weaknesses, remains an all-India secular political formation and *Hindutva* cannot become an all-India political force without annihilating the practitioner of "weak secularism". A weak secularist, however, is much better than a full-fledged communalist. In sum, it may be maintained that the mask of opportunism worn by the BJP-led NDA is only one side of the picture. The other side is revealed by the successes of the BJP in promoting its agenda of *Hindutva*. (*April 6, 2001, The Pioneer*)

Governance Sans Ideology?

An extremely astounding statement of L.K. Advani that the 'people of India want governance that is largely ideologically neutral' deserves to be analysed in the light of fifty three years' experience of democratic governance of post-independent India. The claim made by Advani that 'de-ideologised' governance of India can deliver the goods and take the country forward in the context of new challenges of the Twentyfirst century may be examined in the light of the larger issue of the role of ideologies in the making or unmaking of human societies. Incidentally, Mr. L.K. Advani, himself is a product of a very rigid and puritanical school of ideology represented by the RSS. Mr. Advani, Mr. Vajpayee or others like them are in the centre stage of politics because they are champions of the ideology of *Hindutva*, and if they abandon the essence of *Hindutva*, they will disappear. This fact is testified by Advani; and UP and Gujarat BJP Chief Ministers keep identifying themselves in public with the RSS.

Every social-philosophical ideological framework is based on a value structure and a world view on whose foundational principles human beings define their social existential goals and values of life. Ideological value framework plays an important role, along with concrete experiences of social existence in determining the level of social consciousness, and since social experiences of human beings differ from one another, they construct different world views and ideologies and this leads to ideological contests among different social groups. Hence, we as humans are following different ideological paths to shape our society, and multiple social groups are involved in the struggle to capture state power for the promotion of their cherished ideological goals for building of the social life. The BJP-led coalition government at the centre cannot be an exception to the rule that the Sangh Parivar has been involved in a serious struggle to capture power for implementation of the ideological goals cherished by the forces of Hindutva.

Not only this. The Sangh Parivar and its political outfit, the BJP, have contested against many prevailing ideologies and world views and in this contest, they have not only offered a social critique of the ideologies pursued by other social groups, they have propounded their own specific ideology of *Hindu Rashtra* and *Bhartiyata*. If this is not the case, then Mr. Vajpayee and Mr. Advani and others would not repeatedly claim that their "own" agenda of the abolition of Article 370 of the Constitution, or the formulation of the Uniform Civil Code or the construction of the *Ramjanmbhoomi* at Ayodhya can not be implemented at present because the BJP has not secured a clear political mandate from the voters. A clear implication is that some issues can wait till the party gets a clear political mandate. If Mr. Advani believes that de-ideologised government is the real preference of the Indian voter, the BJP-led state governments of Gujarat, UP and Himachal Pradesh will have to be evaluated on this yardstick. Since these three state governments came to power on the basis of the electoral support extended by a large section of Hindus, the minorities in these states feel insecure because the state governments are the custodians of the interests of the Hindus. The governments led by the BJP have given enough evidence that they are promoting the ideology of *Hindutva* on the basis of governmental power.

The economic policies pursued by the NDA government during its one year in office expose its claim to ideologically neutral governance. The decade of 1990s has witness very serious ideological competition and contest on the issues of caste versus class based politics, religion versus religion based politics, and self-reliance versus internationally dictated neo-classical economic policies of globalisation, privatisation and dismemberment of the public sector. The BJP-led government is pursuing an ideologically oriented economic policy by accepting that the market-led and not the state-led path of economic development is suitable for resolving the problems of poverty and massive unemployment. It is an ideologically loaded fetish that "market" and not "state" can bring economic development for a country and that the large majority of the poor will be the beneficiaries of the market generated economic forces. The American economist Friedmann's prescriptions, or Reaganonomics of the US or Thatcherism of England or IMF-World Bank prescriptions for economic growth are based on the ideology of market. The BJP-led coalition government is encouraging private global and domestic capital play an active role in the economic growth of India. Is this economic policy of the Vajpayee government ideologically neutral? A powerful social constituency is supporting the BJP because it is pursuing the ideology of market-led economic growth.

The foreign policy pursued by the NDA government has shown clear pro-US tilt and a bias in favour of Western capitalist countries. This is because it is operating on the basis of an ideology of capitalist development of India in close alliance with developed capitalist countries of the West. The Vajpayee government has activised powerful associations of Indian capitalist classes like the FICCI, the ASSOCHAM, IIC and captains of industry to actively participate in the policy making and economic decision-making processes of the government within the country, and also to establish institutional linkages with global capitalism. The Vajpayee government has not shown any ambiguity or doubts on the path of market-led capitalist development of India on the basis of close collaboration and association with global capitalism. The Vajpayee government is a facilitator and catalyser for the growth of market forces in the country, and its result is that the upwardly-seeking rent-seeking middle class, the surplus generating peasantry and every strata of the capitalist classes including the predatory capitalist groups are thriving under the ideological umbrella of the government.

The Vajpayee government has assisted in the creation of an ideological nexus among the political and bureaucratic classes along with the other strata of society who are beneficiaries of economic policies and the whole governmental effort is focussed on the social needs and social welfare of 250 million Indians only. The poor of India have been socially ejected by the market-friendly policies of the Vajpayee government. The most important example of the ideological coherence of the Vajpayee government is provided by the social and ideological integration of the well-off Indians with Western capitalist countries which is a logical result of government policies based on pro-domestic capitalism and their partner allies in the capitalist West. This integration is the result of the market-friendly ideology pursued by the Vajpayee government.

An important ideological plank of the Vajpayee government has been based on the concept of "one country, one culture". Such ideological pursuits have brought into sharp focus the question of: what is India? What is the definition of India? Is it *Brahamanical* Hindu India? The BJP leadership pays lip service to the concept of "unity in diversity" of India. The Sangh Parivar demands that the Muslims should "*Indianise*" themselves. It has targeted the Christian community and is playing with fire in the North-East. It and the BJP have characterised the policy of the Congress as pseudo-secular. This is the essential ideological mindset of the Sangh Parivar. The BJP government is pursuing a clear-cut cultural-ideological agenda of *Hindutva* and this has alienated the minority communities in the country.

Mr. Advani's formulation of ideologically neutral government is flawed because he and the BJP are involved in deep ideological struggles and the goal of every ideological group in a democracy is to capture state power for the implementation of its ideology. During one year of the Vajpayee-led government, India has witnessed ideologically committed government in every field of public life and every public discourse has been ideologically formulated whether in Parliament or outside the corridors of power. (*October 31, 2000, The Pioneer*)

Communalisation of the State Apparatus

A Believer in the impartiality of the custodians of rule of law receives a shock when he finds that they are guided by religious-communal considerations while dealing with situations of inter-religious community conflicts. The issue of discriminatory behaviour by the "men in uniform" has been raised once again by some Muslim leaders from Kanpur. A section of the minority community in Kanpur feels that the Provincial Armed Constabulary of Uttar Pradesh did not behave in an even handed manner while dealing with Hindu-Muslim riots. It has alleged that the Uttar Pradesh police have a bias in favour of the majority community.

It is not the first time that the police and the civil bureaucracy involved in maintaining law and order have been perceived as anti-minority while dealing with situations of social conflict. The Srikrishna Report on the Mumbai riots clearly identified important police officials who acted very aggressively as partisan Hindus while performing their public duties. Ms. Nirmala Deshpande in her deposition before Justice Liberahan Commission of Inquiry on the events of December 6, 1992, at Ayodhya stated on February 8, 2001, that "...it looked as if the police and the administration were commanded by the 'organisers'. ...the local police told the workers of (her organisation) the Akhil Bharat Rachnatmak Samaj, 'You also pick up a hammer and give it (the dome) a blow'." Ms. Deshpande clearly stated before the Commission that many district officials were working in favour of the forces of *Hindutva* and that "those who did not subscribe to their ideology were under pressure".

The above-mentioned facts and observations bring into sharp focus the important issue of the ongoing process of communalisation of the apparatuses and functionaries of the Indian state. How can 'secularism', a foundational principle of our Constitution, be safe in the hands of state functionaries who are practitioners of religion-based communalism? Such a question has also attracted the attention of the believers in the rule of law in Western democracies in relation to racial biases of the state functionaries and many serious efforts have been made to deal with open or clandestine racial prejudices of the guardians of the rule of law. It deserves to be mentioned that the Western democracies have brought the issue of '*race*' into public discourse but Indians feel shy about discussing the ongoing communalisation of society, polity and bureaucracy.

A systematic penetration of communal ideology among the state functionaries began with the post-election scenario of 1967 when the

Congress was defeated in all the major States and the voter had not given a clear verdict in favour of any alternative. The post-1967 phase of politics witnessed the emergence of unstable and opportunistic alliances of parties and, for the first time in post-independent India, the Jana Sangh shared power with the faceless and shapeless Samyukta Vidhyayak Dal. The Jana Sangh treated Uttar Pradesh as a social laboratory for the extension of its ideological base among the state functionaries by joining the State Government of a crowd of parties.

Hence, it should not come as a surprise to liberal democrats in India when the police are found instigating the so-called *kar sevaks* to destroy the Babri Masjid or when the functionaries of the state are found to be Hindu partisans while dealing with Muslim or Christian minorities during and after riots. Mr. Justice Srikrishna came face to face with the practitioners of aggressive *Hindutva* during the post-Babri Masjid demolition riots in Mumbai because Shiv Sainiks and RSS workers were comfortably sitting in public offices under the protective umbrella of Mr. Bal Thackeray and the Sangh Parivar in Maharashtra.

The 1990s witnessed the growth of *Hindutva* and also public demonstration of communal bias by the state apparatus which has failed to protect Muslims and Christian minority groups especially in Gujarat under the Keshubhai Patel Government. Mr. Keshubhai Patel and the Sangh Parivar emerged on the public scene in Gujarat when the Nava Nirman Samiti launched a movement in 1974 against corruption in the Chimanbhai Patel-led Congress(I) State Government. The Sangh Parivar has not looked back since and is now firmly entrenched in Gujarat. It is not without reason that Mr. Keshubhai Patel as Chief Minister of Gujarat enthusiastically welcomed state functionaries with an RSS background. Like Uttar Pradesh from 1967, Gujarat from 1974 has witnessed the penetration of the RSS in Government agencies.

Hindu communal organisations are successfully spreading their ideological message among the state functionaries under the umbrella provided by the Atal Bihari Vajpayee Government at the Centre. How can destroyers of churches or Christian missionary schools be punished when the *Hindutvawadis* allege that Christians are involved in large-scale conversion of Hindus? How can minorities feel secure with the practitioners of the politics of hate and also in the absence of neutrality of the state apparatus?

The experiment of minority representation in agencies of the state is of doubtful utility because any communal representation in the Government cannot ensure secular functioning of the state functionaries.

If the problem of *Hinduisation* of the state apparatus is not tackled, the induction of minority groups in Government will not help cleanse the system because the real issue is to get rid of the believers and practitioners of communal ideology and make the state apparatus an instrument of secularism. Western democracies have created autonomous inter-race committees which citizens can approach with complaints and grievances about race-based discrimination.

In Western democracies every institution, Government or autonomous, has provisions and clearly laid down procedures for tackling race-related grievances of employees or citizens. Indians have to tackle the problems of communalisation of state functionaries not only at the levels of Central or State Governments, but also in towns and cities because every city is inhabited by multiple religious, linguistic and other minority groups.

The visits of the National Minority Commission members to Gujarat to investigate the complaints of Christians against state employees had a very limited impact. If Mr. Justice Srikrishna's specific report on the misconduct of the Mumbai police remains unattended for eight years, the significant interventions of the National Human Rights Commission or the Minority Commission are going to be very time consuming.

Government employees in India work under 'rules and conditions of service' and their violations are institutionally punished. A quick punishment of a properly identified biased and prejudiced Government functionary is required to clean the corridors of power of communal elements. This goal can be achieved if every city or town of India has quasi-judicial commissions for dealing with the complaints of minority communities against the local administration. The larger issue of secularism versus communalism in India can be resolved only in the mega political society but the day-to-day issue of communal bias of the state functionaries should be tackled immediately to restore the confidence of the minorities in the majesty of the rule of law. An alienated and insecure minority always adopts the path of violence and becomes anti-democracy. (*April 11, 2001, The Hindu*)

The Politics of Resignations

George Fernandes while joining the Vajpayee government on October 14, 2001, said he had come back "on the specific request of Prime Minister" and further added there was no "moral question" involved in his being in the Cabinet and Defence Ministry. For the first time in the history of India, a Prime Minister took a public stand that a person can resign on "moral question" — because *Tehelka* caught a party president accepting "bribe relating to purchase of defence material" in the official residence of the Defence Minister — and the same Prime Minister and his very tall colleague now make a statement that there was no "moral" question involved in the *Tehelka* episode and such a "suspect" can continue to perform his old responsibilities. Corruption in public life is a "moral" act in India.

And who takes such a position? The Prime Minister of a country who was compelled to appoint the Justice Venkataswami Commission to inquire into serious issues raised by the *Tehelka* expose and apportion appropriate blame on the guilty who used Defence Minister's official residence to make money in a completely illegal manner.

A few facts need to be mentioned to substantiate the argument that the Vajpayee government is the chief legitimiser of corruption in public life. March 16, 2001, was a great day for Indian democracy because Vajpayee announced the setting up of an inquiry, under the Commission of Inquiry Act, 1952, to "probe the allegations in the *Tehelka* expose." On October 14, 2001, the Prime Minister, without waiting for the inquiry commission report, reinducted Fernandes and handed him the same defence portfolio.

This after the Venkataswami Commission said the tapes were genuine. The Prime Minister by his action showed contempt for the judicial correctness and publicly admitted that Fernandes and his associates have not misused and abused the official status of the Defence Minister. Mamata Banerjee of the Trinamool Congress, who left the NDA on the continuation of Fernandes after Tehelka expose, now became the first vocal and active supporters of his reinduction. Thus, every partner of the NDA government is a party to the acts of corruption in public life and the "chief umpire" of the NDA government is a head of legitimiser of corruption in national life.

It is not at all suggested that Nehru, Indira Gandhi and Rajiv Gandhi's phases of leadership did not witness great scandals involving acts of corruption by high dignitaries in the government and the party organisation. Nehru appointed the Justice Chagla Inquiry Commission, and on the basis of its findings removed T.T. Krishnamachari, who was the Finance Minister. Nehru did not stop there. He appointed the Justice Das Inquiry Commission and the government accepted the findings of inquiry commission and asked Pratap Singh Kairon, the Chief Minister of Punjab, to resign from his job. The real argument which deserves to be made here is that all anti-Congress political formations, groups and tall leaders beginning with the Jayaprakash movement of 1974-75 had always targeted the Congress for creating a "political culture of corruption in public life." Every ruling group, or leader has politically benefited by painting the Congress as the fountain source of corruption in public life. The present beneficiaries of the anti-corruption JP movement like Atal Bihari Vajpayee, L.K. Advani, George Fernandes, Laloo Prasad Yadav *et al* have all become practitioners of politics of corruption against which they pretended to struggle for 40 years. V.P. Singh, Chandra Shekhar, H.D. Deve Gowda, I.K. Gujral and A.B. Vajpayee are considered the five Pandavas of Indian politics who have benefited by fighting against the Kauravas who practiced the evil of lowering standards in public life. These five Pandavas targeted Rajiv Gandhi for his alleged involvement in Bofors scam. Nothing has been proved till today while the country has waited for 13 years to find out the guilty persons involved in Bofors' gun deal. Vajpayee could not wait for a few months for the inquiry commission report. Even before the report is submitted, everyone is back to power with the open approval of the Prime Minister. The BJP leadership had always claimed that they believed in maintaining very high standards in public life. BJP claimed that it was a "party with a difference." Truly, it is a party "with a difference", because it had a party president Bangaru Laxman who was caught accepting bribe in public. It is a party with a difference because it is happy to share power with suspected and tainted leaders whether corrupt or criminals.

Fernandes was a "rebel" of Indian politics and he projected himself as a great "anti-establishment" fighter. The rebel George has been tamed by the same "corrupt establishment" against which he pretended to fight. The new George says that PM's invitation to occupy a lucrative chair cannot be refused because moral questions do not arise when the Prime Minister offers you a job. The worst part of the story is that the so-called NDA "celebrated" the judicial indictment of Chief Minister J. Jayalalitha because as a convict she could not occupy public office under the Constitution but supporters of the NDA can enjoy the fruits of power because the inquiry commission can be appointed and dismissed by their own fraternity in the market of politics.

To sum up, the Vajpayees, the Georges, the Mamatas and others have openly and publicly agreed that corruption in public life will be rewarded and 'morality' in public affairs will be 'exchanged' with contempt for all institutions of governance. (*October 21, 2001, Deccan Chronicle*)

Is BJP Really Going the Congress Way?

A very important public meeting was held at Jaipur on October 14, 2001 to celebrate 75 years of the RSS, and chief K.S. Sudarshan addressed the Rashtriya Shakti Sangam's 60,000 strong cadre and urged them to "take the message of Hindu pride before the masses". The BJP celebrated its own "two years" of power at the Centre and every fora was used to "project its achievements" from October 1999 to October 2001. At Agra, the Jan Sangh's Avatar BJP celebrated its "twenty years" on October 13, 14, 2001. Then, at a gathering of RSS and BJP leaders on October 17, 2001, Vajpayee stressed that "the Sangh ideology had gained wide acceptance in the country". He further said that "The very fact that Advaniji and myself are where we are today shows that we have been accepted by the people and there is no discrimination against us". Vajpayee asserted that the Sangh Parivar is in the mainstream with its own "distinct ideology". L.K. Advani remarked, at the National Executive meeting of the BJP on October 20, 2001, on the "congressification of the BJP". He said that the people did not want "the BJP to resemble the Congress even if it could become a "better Congress". He did not stop here and observed on October 21, 2001, that the "People are already saying that we are resembling Congress...they expect us to be the real BJP". A very significant issue has been raised by Advani who wants a "real BJP" which is not a "counterfeit of the Congress". It deserves to be asserted that the BJP can never be like the Congress, and the Congress, irrespective of its past policy blunders and opportunistic ideological compromises, would never become a BJP. BJP and Congress are two fundamentally "opposites" of Indian politics and it is not without reason that the BJP leadership has always maintained that politics has to be polarised between them. BJP is involved in a basic struggle to become a real all-India alternative to the "pseudo-secular Congress" which is alleged to have always "pampered the minorities". The so-called "minorityism" of the Congress has been the focus of attention for the BJP. BJP and Congress are real political opponents and it is not without reason that in spite of many flaws, Congress has never participated or supported "from inside or outside" a BJP-associated government. Every other Messiah of secularism of Indian politics, except the Congress, has legitimised the BJP in Indian politics.

The history, the ideology, and the foundational principles of the Congress and BJP are a study in contrast. Congress was a "social platform" for all sections of society who were mobilised for the struggle against colonial rule. While Congress provided a comprehensive social and political umbrella to every community of India Dr. K.B. Hedgewar founded the RSS in 1925 at Nagpur for the "defence of Hindus"; and he accepted the ideology of the Hindu Mahasabha as propounded by Veer Savarkar which is described by the present BJP leadership as "cultural nationalism" or "One Nation, One People, One Culture". Second, all children of RSS like the BJP, Bajrang Dal, Vishwa Hindu Parishad, ABVP, EMS, etc are involved in promoting the Hindu cause which the Sangh Parivar equates with "national culture". Every organisation and every movement of the Sangh Parivar including the BJP has mobilised Hindus to safeguard *Hindu Rashtra*, and everyone in the Sangh Fraternity is very committed to take revenge against the so-called "hurt and humiliated Hindu sentiment". Congress has never launched any "culturally and socially exclusive" political movement. While the VHP leadership was involved in the October 17, 2001 entry into the prohibited area of *Ram Janmabhoomi* at Ayodhya, Sonia Gandhi, on the same day, was addressing a Congress party *Parivartan Rally* at Lucknow where she asserted "Congress does not belong to any one section of the Indian people".

Advani stated on October 21, 2001 before the BJP National Council that "If we had not taken up the *Ram Janmabhoomi* issue as a symbol of cultural nationalism, we would not have progressed so much". He further stated that "It convinced people of certain and sharp distinction between positive secularism and pseudo- secularism". In contrast Sonia Gandhi while addressing a political rally, in Meerut on October 20, 2001 exhorted, "party men not to rest until they had succeeded in extricating the state (UP) from multiple problems of communalism, casteism and slow pace of development".

Why has Congress been abandoned by some of its own important social constituencies? Muslims are angry with the Congress because it compromised with its own ideology, history and traditions while dealing with the challenges posed by the Sangh Parivar. Sonia Gandhi admitted this at Meerut party rally that "we failed to gain faith of the people and party has learnt a lesson from its experience. But this has given a major setback to the (UP) state". It was expected that the Congress would take up the challenge of the Sangh Parivar; instead, the Congress party and government collapsed like a house of cards because it wanted to play petty "tricks" in politics when its very own existence and survival had been challenged by its own main political opponent.

Ultimately, L.K. Advani's real BJP" can never be like even a defeated Congress. It is not only that Congress and BJP are ideologically poles apart, Congress does not have organisational equipment and resource like the Sangh Parivar. Every child of the RSS is a believer, promoter and protector of the 'purity' of the ideology of *Hindutva*. Congress party cadre is 'middle-of-the-road' practitioner of liberal secularism; the cadre of the Sangh Parivar is fanatically committed to the ideology of *Hindu Rashtra*. A telling example of fundamental difference between the BJP and the Congress can be seen when they are in government. Congress party is an open book and factionalism is its essential feature. If Narasimha Rao is Prime Minister, Arjun Singh of the Congress must 'plant' news in the newspapers, and Sita Ram Kesari must play the same factional role while dealing with Narasimha Rao. BJP-in-Government has implemented its agenda of so-called *cultural nationalism* and its top leadership has never forgotten the essential commonality of goals. That the BJP government should remain in power is the primary goal of the BJP leadership because only then can it implement its own agenda of National Reconstruction and National Rejuvenation. Congress is a platform and Congress leaders can walk out or walk into the party at their own convenience. But Vaghela or Kalyan Singh or Madhok can not walk in or walk out of the Parivar at their individual sweet will. A Congressman or woman of yesterday does not feel uncomfortable in going out or coming in the party but the doors of the BJP are always closed for the 'indisciplined' and 'deviant' leader. BJP is a party with its own ideological purity, recognised leadership and a method of functioning where dissidence is punished and never rewarded. Congress is just its opposite. How can the two ever meet? The Congress and BJP are products of different interpretations of what is India. The BJP is growing because it has never abandoned that India is Hindu, and Congress can face the BJP and Sangh Parivar only if it firmly upholds that India as an idea is pluralist and culturally extremely diverse. (*November 10, 2001, The Pioneer*)

Tell It As It Is? In defence of media

Mr. L.K. Advani as I&B Minister of the Janata Party Government in 1977-79, castigated the Indian media, observing that during the infamous Emergency regime of 1975-77, the media was "asked to bend, and instead they crawled" before the Government. And now the Sangh parivar is alleging that the media has sensationalised the events of Gujarat from February 27 to March 5, 2002. The Sangh Parivar is upset with the

Indian media because governments, both at the Centre and the State of Gujarat, have been completely exposed for their serious acts of omission and commission during the genocide of Gujarati citizens.

During the days when Gujarat experienced large scale killings, burning of property and human beings, Parliament was shut because of the Annual Budget and due to the death of Lok Sabha Speaker G.M.C. Balayogi. In these circumstances, the only watchdog was the media and they provided yeoman service during the carnage in Gujarat. If the media had not shown the photographs of criminal mobs who were involved in swiftly eliminating the Muslim minority in Ahmedabad and Baroda in newspapers of March 1, and if multiple TV channels had not shown the visuals of the ghastly activities indulged in by sword-wielding mobs on the streets of Gujarat, the Central Government would not have cared to deploy the army to deal with the situation where the State Government had simply failed to perform its job of maintaining law and order.

Defence Minister George Fernandes was shown struggling with the mobs in Ahmedabad and the whole country was shaken by the sight of Mr. Fernandes guiding the law-enforcing agencies to perform their duties towards the beleaguered and innocent men, women and children who had no defenders against the merchants of death. If the media, print and TV had not informed the Indian public that Mr. Narendra Modi, the BJP Government's Chief Minister, had explained away the pogroms in Gujarat as a "reaction" to the burning of Kar Sevaks at Godhra on February 27, 2002, there would have been no pressure on the Government or the Sangh Parivar to either govern or get out. It was the media that informed the nation that Gujarat was burning and because of the total callousness of the Narendra Modi Government the media exposed the communal side of the Gujarat State machinery. An Indian police service officer, a High Court judge and a former Congress party MP, were defenceless. If the media had not informed the whole country about the helplessness of the Muslim elite during the carnage in Gujarat, the concern for the lives and property of those threatened would not have become a national agenda.

While Gujarat was burning Prime Minister Vajpayee said that the "events in Gujarat have brought about a national shame". The media, unlike the Prime Minister, was not talking of sentimental things like national shame. It was showing us the naked face of death looming over the minorities in Gujarat. The people of India were completely shaken when they saw the photograph of a young Muslim with folded hands and tears in his eyes, asking for the security of life, and a 4-year old child with

90 per cent burns. The country of Gandhi wept bitterly on the man-made tragedy of Gujarat.

All hell broke out in Gujarat because the media correctly informed us that the bandh call (in reality revenge call) has been given by the party in Government. A free press is the pillar of civil society and this freedom, with great sense of responsibility, conviction and courage was exercised to educate and inform the people of India on the "pogrom in Gujarat". Discussions on TV and analyses in newspapers further helped the people outside Gujarat learn about the complicity of the communalised state apparatus in dealing with problems of the security of the helpless victims.

Interviews with the victims of the tragedy of Gujarat further educated the citizens outside the state that a partisan government has miserably failed even to provide proper relief to the refugees of riots. It is absurd to maintain that the media should not tell the real story during riots because it inflames others and it becomes difficult for the Government to manage the situation. Should the media show happy marriage processions when the reality is the ugly face of mob fury. The demand from the media is either speak lies or remain light-lipped and let the rioters under the benign protective umbrella of the powers-that-be to perform their task of religious cleansing. Instead of criticising the media, the Indian people should be grateful to the only autonomous watchdog of the society; parliamentary debates end up in partisan one-upmanship, and it is a game between the defenders and the critics. Further, the presence of different newspapers and TV channels is good in a democracy because no one can act as a hegemonist. This is precisely the reason that governments fear media organisations that are beyond its control.

The riots were stopped by a reluctant Government on the basis of public opinion created by the media against the machinations of the Sangh Parivar. The media ought to keep it up. (*March 10, 2002, The Sunday Pioneer*)

A Socio-Cultural Study of Gujarat: Is there a way to change people's mindset?

Gujarati society seems to be completely brutalised because the killings of innocent men, women and children for nearly two months have not brought millions of "people with conscience" on the roads to launch a strong satyagraha to stop this unparalleled tragedy in recent times. Has Gandhi left any positive impact on Gujarati society? A few well-known facts may be mentioned to substantiate the argument that the happenings of Gujarat are not comparable even to the post-Partition tragic events of 1947-48.

First, Gujarat has a fully constituted and organised state apparatus, which is expected to deal firmly with any law and order problem, including inter-community conflicts and disputes. On the eve of Partition, neither Pakistan nor India had the time and opportunity to put their house in order. But the Gujarat of 2002 is not India or Pakistan of 1947-48. Second, the 'presence' of the Army in Gujarat did not make any difference to the killers, who seemed to have had a free hand for more than two months.

A Ministry of Home Affairs report released by Mr. L.K. Advani mentions that "in order to cope with the situation and maintain law and order", the Government of Gujarat "immediately deployed 66 companies of the reserve police, 18 columns of the Army and 28 companies of paramilitary forces". And in spite of this, the Home Ministry itself tells us that 824 people died, 2,082 were injured, and 10,200 houses, 12,200 shops and 3,002 vehicles were destroyed.

Third, the visit of the Prime Minister made no difference to the state government and its law and order machinery in dealing with the riots. Mr. Atal Bihari Vajpayee was projected as a leader in the Nehruvian mould, but now one feels that such a comparison was the greatest humiliation for Nehru. The first Prime Minister's conduct during the post-Partition riots stands in sharp contrast to Mr. Vajpayee's rationalisation of the Gujarat tragedy at the Panaji (Goa) session of the BJP on April 12. Nehru did not play tricks or petty games when the country was burning in 1947-48. As against this, Mr. Vajpayee attempted to dilute the tragedy of Gujarat.

Fourth, the National Human Rights Commission, the National Minorities Commission and the National Women's Commission have unanimously blamed the Narendra Modi government for serious acts of omission and deliberate commission while dealing with Hindus and Muslims in a discriminatory manner.

Fifth, the print and the audio-visual media completely exposed the biases and prejudices of the Modi government in the discharge of its constitutional obligations during the riots. It is for the first time in the history of independent India that a state government has been accused of indulging in "genocide" of its own citizens.

While the above narration is limited to the events from March to April, 2002, the discussion needs to be expanded to understand the reality of Gujarati society which has lived from violence to violence and riot to riot during the past 55 years. An enquiry into the social dynamics of the state is essential to find an answer to the question: why has Gujarat experienced violence with regular intervals? Why has Mr. Modi been lionised as "Chhote Sardar", *i.e.*, after great Sardar Patel? Why did Sabarmati Ashram established by Gandhi attract derisive and abusive epitaph from communalists? Why is the memory of the destruction of the Somnath Temple by a Muslim invader is still kept alive? Why is it that the communalists of Gujarat are not able to forget the "destruction of the Somnath Temple" after destroying hundreds of mosques and dargahs during these two months of rioting and killings?

It deserves to be mentioned here that aggressive, militant and violent struggles have been the order of the day in Gujarat. The major Hindu-Muslim riot of 1969 had completely shaken the late Frontier Gandhi, Khan Abdul Ghaffar Khan, who was then on a visit to India. After witnessing the gory events he simply "wept". Similarly, Morarji Desai launched an aggressive anti-Congress government campaign in 1974. The Navnirman Samiti spearheading the movement for the dismissal of the then corrupt Congress government in the state had indulged in law-breaking activities. Incidentally, the Samiti in 1974 had ample representation of RSS workers. During the 1990s these RSS workers emerged as leaders of the BJP in Gujarat.

Similarly, a very powerful anti-reservation movement launched by high-caste middle class Hindus in 1984 ended up in communal violence. It was not without reason that Mr. L.K. Advani started his Ram Janmabhoomi Rathyatra from Somnath. It led to communal violence, now a regular feature of Gujarat.

What is the explanation for the continuing communal divide in Gujarat? First, Gujarati society is torn between the memory of Mehmood Ghaznavi and that of Mahatma Gandhi. The Gujarati middle class still talks of Prithviraj Chauhan's defeat at the hands of Mehmood. The Gujarati Hindu is highly religious and ritualistic, and in this cultural setting, the manipulation of the historical reality at the hands of Muslims becomes a readymade fodder for the aggressive forces of *Hindutva*.

Second, the first major controversy in public life after Independence was the reconstruction of the Somnath Temple under the close supervision of Sardar Patel himself. The Nehru-Rajendra Prasad controversy over the President's participation in the religious ceremonies regarding the Somanth Temple is well known, but it is not brought to public notice that the Gujarat Congress had extended an enthusiastic support for the renovation of the destroyed temple. Further, it is also not known that Nehru's influence on the thinking of the Congressmen in Gujarat was minimal, nearly non-existent, because Sardar Patel had controlled the organisation with an "iron hand" from 1926 to 1947.

Indulal Yajnik, a mild socialist, became the Gujarat Congress President for one year only, and Patel saw to it that such a thing was never repeated. Thus, politically, Gujarat is polarised between full-blooded *Hindutva* and a soft-pedalling "Hindu" Congress. Indira Gandhi tried to change the social caste-class composition of the Congress, and Madhavsinh Solanki, as a symbol of her new social engineering, was ousted by the powerful Patels of Gujarat.

Third, during the national movement, Bombay witnessed powerful communist and socialist trade union struggles in the 1930s. The Gandhi-controlled trade unions in Gujarat were always made to compromise with the Gujarati capitalists like Jamnalal Bajaj. Not only this, Gujarat did not witness any militant peasant movement on the pattern of that in West Bengal or in Telengana in the erstwhile Hyderabad State.

Militancy for social and secular causes was conspicuous by its absence in Gujarat. An important impact owing to the absence of militant trade union and peasant struggles in Gujarat was felt on the social order because the strong control of the high castes over Gujarati society was never completely shaken. Every social, cultural and political mobilisation in Gujarat—whether the anti-Congress struggle of 1974, the anti-reservation movement of 1984 or the Ram Janmabhoomi Rathyatra of 1990 and the subsequent events—has had one common factor, *i.e.*, the domination of high caste middle class Hindus.

The Hindu ethos of Gujarati society remains unquestioned because no movement either of peasants or workers or students has stepped out of the existing normative structure of that society. Even the Gujarati diaspora remains linked with the inherited Hindu ethos of its place of birth. It is not incidental that the Gujaratis abroad were highly active in supporting the victims of the earthquake, and just a year later they have nothing to offer to the victims of the worst riots. While sitting in foreign countries, they have Hindu-versus-Muslim feelings. It is not without reason that the Vishwa Hindu Parishad is a recipient of great financial generosity of Hindu Gujaratis and Maharashtraians settled in foreign countries.

This, however, does not mean that secular Indians have to give up Gujarat and hand it over to the fanatic manipulators. The moral of the above description is that weak or soft secularism in the garb of Hinduism will not serve the purpose of confronting communalism in Gujarat. It is necessary to target those responsible for creating communal cleavages, but this alone is not enough to deal with the religious hatred prevailing there. It is the responsibility of the country as a whole to protect the life and property of every citizen without any distinction of caste, colour, creed or religion.

The real message from Gujarat is that the socio-cultural roots of Hindu communalism have not been either identified or targeted even by the secular parties and autonomous secular institutions of civil society. Gujarat has paid a very heavy price because secularists have always made tactical compromises. The Congress party in Gujarat has to accept the responsibility for its failure to confront openly and aggressively communal social and political tendencies in the state. The conscience-keepers of Gujarati society owe an explanation to the larger Indian society for passively tolerating the growth of communalism. Riots are a consequence of the deep-seated social and historical causes, and Gujarat has once again proved it. However, the state can be pulled out of its fanatic mindset by the intellectual class, which can project an alternative secular worldview to the people there.

India Under Siege

It may look plausible to suggest that every state in India has its own 'distinctive historical memories' and thus the tragedy of Gujarat as witnessed during March and April of 2002 should be explained in the context of specificities of politico-cultural and historical settings of that state. This line of argument makes the proponents of Gujarati 'uniqueness' argue that Gujarat has many a time witnessed violent outbreaks in post-independence India.

This logic of situating the tragedy of March and April in the local historical settings of the Gujarati society is much too simplistic because the current happenings are closely linked and integrated with the growth of aggressive *Hindutva* at the all-India level. The Narendra Modi government could not have carried out its agenda of militant and violent *Hindutva* without the protective umbrella of the Vajpayee-led Central Government and without the social sanction and support of the believers of *Hindutva* in other parts of India.

The entire country is under siege because the growth of Hindu communalism has impacted not only Gujarat but also large sections of society across the states of India. If it is accepted that the forces of *Hindutva* are involved in dividing Hindus and Muslims throughout the country and Gujarat is just one flashpoint, the explanation for the understanding of the fast ongoing process of Hindu-Muslim divide will have to be found in the *shifts* which have taken place in Indian politics during the 20th century.

Indians have witnessed secular versus communal ideological contests throughout the 20th century. The Partition of Bengal of 1905-11 by Lord Curzon on the basis of Hindu versus Muslim, the establishment of the sectarian Hindu Mahasabha and Muslim League in 1906 and 1907 and the politics of separate community-based electorates were all attempts to institutionalise a Hindu-Muslim divide by the colonial rulers which in turn was supported by Hindu Mahasabha leaders like V.D. Savarkar and Mohammad Ali Jinnah of the Muslim League. The politics of separatism was contested and opposed by the Gandhi-Nehru Congress, socialists, communists, trade unions and kisan sabhas.

With the end of World War II in 1945, the agenda of Indian independence became central to negotiations between the colonial rulers, Congress leaders and Muslim League. The Gandhi-Nehru Congress opposed and contested the religion-based definition of India by the Hindu Mahasabha, Muslim League and the British colonisers. The events moved fast from 1945 to 15 August, 1947, and a partitioned India emerged as independent, democratic and secular state. The Constitution of Republican India firmly laid down the foundations of a state which was prohibited from showing any special preference or indulging in any discrimination against any citizen on the basis of religion, sect, belief or creed.

While the Partition of India led to the rejection of the Muslim League's separatist religious politics, a section of Hindu communalists did not accept secularism as a foundational principle of the Indian Republic despite the fact that the Indian judiciary has many a time declared 'secularism as a basic structure of the Constitution.' An independent India launched its democratic journey on the basis of a rejection of the demands of Hindu and Muslim communalists and 17 years of Nehru's government witnessed the complete marginalisation of the Hindu communalists.

An important question that arises: How has a marginalised and ostracised *Hindutva* emerged as a mainstream phenomenon enjoying great social sanction at the end of the 20th and beginning of the 21st century? What happened to the secular project of post-independence India which was at its commanding heights during the Nehru and to an extent, Indira Gandhi governments? Hence, Bhikhu Parekh is completely off the mark when he proclaims in his contribution to *Seminar* (513, May 2002) that, 'This great political project... (cannot be revived) by simple minded secular opponents whose thinking has advanced little since Nehru's death. 'Nehru's ideal of secularism as enshrined in the Constitution of India is adequate to politically confront and oppose the rising tide of Hindu communalism.

Incidentally, Professor Parekh should know that Gujarati society remained quite insulated from the influence of Nehru. On the contrary, conservative Hindu leaders of the Congress party influenced Gujarati society (C.P. Bhambhri, 'A Socio-cultural Study of Gujarat', *Tribune*, 6 May 2002). The so-called culturalists like Bhikhu Parekh or Ashis Nandy deserve to be reminded that Karl Marx had alerted us (*On the Jewish Question*) that once a state is politically formed, secularism becomes a political and not a religio-cultural or theological issue. Nehru understood this clearly and he fought political battles against conservative Hindus in his own party and the forces of *Hindutva* within the country.

Hindu communal forces have extended their influence in India's public sphere because of the grand failures of secular parties, groups, leaders and intellectuals. A few facts may be mentioned to substantiate the argument that political compromises of the opportunist secular formations have facilitated the consolidation of *Hindutva*. First, blind anti-Congressism brought Hindu communalists to share power with self-appointed secularists. Second, the Jayaprakash Narayan movement of 1974-75 further legitimised the Sangh Parivar because in Gujarat and Bihar, the JP movement was actively supported by the RSS alongwith socialists and others. We have the testimony of George Fernandes about JP's admiration for Narendra Modi: 'JP used to mention his fascination for this youthful leader of Gujarat at least 10 times a day. He looked to him as *roshni* (beacon of light)' (*The Statesman*, Delhi, 4 May 2002).

Third, former prime ministers like V.P. Singh (1989-90), and the present prime minister, Atal Bihari Vajpayee (1999), have one thing in common, *i.e.* either a central government is formed with outside support of the BJP or a BJP-led government is formed with the support of 'regional-secular allies'. During the decade of the 1990s, *Hindutva* defined the agenda of Indian politics and Congress prime ministers like Rajiv Gandhi (1984-1989) and P.V. Narasimha Rao (1991-1996) were made to react and respond to the programmes decided by *Hindutva*. The so-called secular prime ministers like Rajiv Gandhi, V.P. Singh or P.V. Narasimha Rao became passive spectators and showed little initiative while dealing with the *Ram Janmabhoomi* movement. *Hindutva* marched forward in the 1990s because the secular political parties and leaders did not challenge it.

The decade of the 1990s witnessed the emergence of militant and ferocious anti-minority *Hindutva* along with the so-called 'soft *Hindutva*' of the secular governments, parties and leaders. Finally, *Hindutva* is not considered a dirty word and state power has been handed over to the Sangh Parivar by Naidu of Andhra Pradesh, the Dravidian leaders of Tamil Nadu, the Chautalas and Ajit Singhs of Jat castes and socialists like George Fernandes, Sharad Yadav and Ram Vilas Paswan. The Dalit leader Mayawati has no difficulty in legitimising the real '*Manuwadi* party' of the Hindus.

It is well known that an idea or ideology or movement succeeds because it is responsive to the felt needs of the people. Ideologies do not hang in the air and least of all *Hindutva* because the socio-cultural base of India can become fertile for the manipulation of Hindus by Hindu demagogues. It is also a fact that an idea or ideology or a movement, including *Hindutva*, can be opposed, contained and marginalised by a powerful opposite idea or ideology or movement. Nehru effectively contested *Hindutva* in the 1950s and till the mid-1960s; it is now becoming unstoppable because the so-called secularists have either joined the bandwagon of *Hindutva* or are not ready to confront the ideology of 'religion-based politics'.

Further, it is not a simple question of communalism versus weak and compromising secularism because the central issue is: who should wield state power in India? M.S. Golwalkar, the RSS Sarsanghchalak had said in 1940 (*What is Hinduism?*) that, 'The non-Hindus of India must learn to respect and hold in reverence Hindu religion, must entertain no idea but glorification of the Hindu race and culture and may stay in the country wholly subordinated to the Hindu nation.' Should Indian state power be handed over to Golwalkar's *swayamsevak's* like Atal Bihari Vajpayee, Narendra Modi and others to practice the teachings of their Master?

In summation, it may be mentioned that *Hindutva* has to be confronted politically by politicians who attach value to principle over pragmatism, to convictions over opportunism and to composite culture over culture of political opportunism. If the politicians do not recover secular space, all of India will shortly witness events like Gujarat. Nehru had linked secularism with socialism because demagogues of every variety can manipulate unemployed and deprived individuals and groups. Globalisation, privatisation and liberalisation have created a 'goalless society' because consumerism cannot inspire the masses. A politics of social goals is the need of the times and only this can contain Hindutva. *(June 2, 2002,)*

Is Hindu Goodwill It? Constitution Says No

The Hindu versus Muslim construction is based on the total ideological architecture of the 'One Nation, One Country, One State' belief of the Sangh Parivar but such an authoritative construction of a monolith Hindu community is based on complete ignorance of the ideologues and intellectuals of the Parivar because the existence of an authentic Hindu majority (community) is a complete myth. There is nothing like a Hindu religion. At best, we have plural Hindu religions, and internally, highly differentiated Hindu believers who have their own symbols, rituals, reference points and historical memories.

If for the Sangh Parivar, the Vedas are sacred Hindu texts, Sanskrit is an authentic Hindu language and Brahmins are official interpreters and custodians of Hindu religious scriptures and rituals, Phule of Maharashtra, Ramaswami Naicher of Tamil Nadu, B.R. Ambedkar of the Republican Party of India and intellectuals and leaders of the Bahujan Samaj do not accept the Brahamanical Sanskrit, and the Vedic brand of Hinduism. On the contrary, the Bahujan Samaj of Dalits claim a majority as opposed to the believers and practitioners of Brahamanical Hinduism—Hindus as defined by the Sangh Parivar are not a majority in India, and if this minority comprising Hindu high castes want to live safely, it must win the "goodwill of the Dalit majority".

The crux of the issue is: What is the definition of India? The British Colonial rulers partitioned Bengal in 1905 on the basis of separateness of Bengali Hindus from Bengali Muslims and in this context Hindu Mahasabha and Muslim League were born in 1906 and 1907; and Hindu-Muslim separatism was practised by Hindu and Muslim leaders under the patronage and protective umbrella of the colonial rulers who believed in the policy of "divide and rule".

This definition of Hindu-Muslim separatism was rejected by a large number of social, cultural and political movements of 20th Century India. India cannot be defined either in terms of Hindu majority of the V.D. Savarkar type or Muslim minority of Jinnah. And these were not the only "two" main contestants defining the meaning of India. In opposition to the Hindu-Muslim monolithic identity was placed a very powerful definition of plural, diverse, culturally robust and multi-lingual, multi-religious, multi-regional, multi-national India.

The beauty of India lies in its diversity of cultures, festivals, dresses, literatures, beliefs and plural historical memories. A very powerful anti-colonial movement was built by mobilising all social groups, and in the process of the historic struggle against colonialism, India was constructed around the idea of "Unity in diversity".

Indians defined their plural and diverse Indianness during the struggle for freedom and in it the Hindu and Muslim construction of "two Indias" was rejected. The Constitution of India, which is a product of the struggle for Independence, concretised "plural definition of Indianness" by guaranteeing "equal rights" for all citizens irrespective of religion or creed. This is the reason why the Sangh Parivar does not accept the Republican Constitution of India.

While the Sangh Parivar believes that minority religious communities are "second class citizens" who need the "goodwill of the Hindu majority" for their "survival", the Constitution mandates a State that protects every citizen equally. In the schema of the Sangh Parivar, minorities have to earn their rights, if any, by winning over Hindu sympathy. The Constitution does not provide any right to any community to act as a "guarantor" of the rights of other individuals or groups.

A democratically elected Parliament and other secular institutions of governance are the only "custodians" of the equal rights of citizens. Hence the Sangh Parivar and the Constitution are involved in an antagonistic contradiction because if, on the one hand, for Atal Bihari Vajpayee, building a Ram Temple reflects "national sentiment" because Nation is equated with Brahamanical Hinduism, on the other, for the Indian state, "judiciary" is the only arbiter of group disputes.

Supreme Court-ordered *status quo ante* on March 15, 2002 hurt, according to the Sangh Parivar, "the sentiment of millions of Hindus". The Court rejected the argument of a myth known as Hindu sentiment for a Ram temple at Ayodhya and protected the rule of law in the country. If for the Sangh Parivar Ram Temple is a "core issue", for Indians the central issue is: How to defend a secular and democratic state from a Parivar that completely negates democracy?

Indianness is not co-terminus with the *Brahamanical Hindutva* of the Sangh Parivar. And if the definition of the Sangh Parivar is accepted, genocide against minorities will become the order of the day in the whole of India. Fascism equates nationhood with racial or blood purity and superiority of one group, and democracy defines the principle of equal citizenship for everyone without any concept of superiority of the majority.

Thus the Sangh parivar's philosophy is fascist in practice and completely undemocratic in spirit. We must either defend the secular, democratic, republican Constitution or end up like Pakistan and Bangladesh. (*March 24, 2002, The Sunday Pioneer*)

Battle Royale and the Idea of India

The Prime Minister and the Leader of the Opposition have a clearly defined constitutional and political role in a parliamentary democracy. While the Prime Minister is the Head of the Government, the Leader of the Opposition is expected to keep the former constantly on his toes; otherwise governance can become arbitrary.

Of late, Mr. Atal Bihari Vajpayee and Mrs. Sonia Gandhi have been seen in a confrontational mood, both within and outside the Parliament. Both have expressed serious differences on public issues, and many a time these clashes have degenerated into a personal slinging match. Apropos the ongoing violence in Gujarat, Mrs. Gandhi has accused the Sangh Parivar of indulging in communal violence under the protective umbrella of the Central and the State governments. Mr. Vajpayee has accused the Congress leader of fomenting trouble, whereas she is expected to provide a healing touch. Without trivialising the issues raised by Vajpayee and Sonia as personal likes and dislikes, the speeches during the CII annual meeting on April 25 and 26, 2002, contain fundamental differences between the two vis-à-vis their "definition of India". Both have taken a public position where there is no meeting point.

In the context of the violence in Gujarat, Mrs. Gandhi, while attacking the philosophy of Sangh Parivar, asserted that the Congress recognises the cultural "diversities" of the "social inclusiveness of one nation, many cultures and many ways of life", instead of "one nation, one culture, one people"—which happens to be the ideological doctrine of the believers of *Hindu Rashtra*. Mr. Vajpayee has taken a public position that his Government, whether at the Centre or in Gujarat, is committed to the maintenance of law and order. On Mahavir Jayanti, he repeated his commitment to Indian pluralism and secular traditions of India. These statements from the two have initiated a serious public debate on: Who is a secularist? What is the meaning of Indian nationalism? Who is an actual believer and practitioner of cultural pluralism? The Sangh Parivar has always maintained that the Congress party has practiced pseudosecularism, always pampering the Indian minorities. Meanwhile, the Congress has described the Sangh Parivar as anti-minority, because the goal of *Hindu Rashtra* is built on the definition of Hindu India. Golwalkar defined the belief-system of the Sangh Parivar in 1940 in his *What is Hinduism?* by stating that: "The non-Hindus of India must learn to respect and hold in reverence Hindu religion, must entertain no idea but glorification of the Hindu race and culture and may stay in the country while subordinated to the Hindu nation". This idea has been expressed by the RSS Chief, Mr. K.S. Sudershan in March 2002, in Bangalore, that "Indian minorities should win over the goodwill of the Hindus". It is clear that the RSS, from 1925 to 2002, has taught its *Swayamsevaks*, including Mr. Vajpayee and Mr. Narendra Modi, that India consists of Hindus and the "others" are minorities and it is for the minorities to prove their *bona fides* by courting the goodwill of the majority Hindus. VD Savarkar, in *What is Hindutva?* had clearly stated that Muslims and Christians are the "other outsiders" and India is a "*Pitribhoomi*" and "*Pujyabhoomi*" and hence the "*Matribhoomi*" of the Hindus only. This definition of India—as the sole motherland of the Hindus—was opposed and contested by various national leaders, including Gandhi and Nehru. The Congress-led anti-colonial Freedom Movement contested the definition of India as a privileged private property of the Hindus and in the struggle for Indian Independence the Congress and other secular nationalists, opposed Savarkar's Hindu Mahasabha and Jinnah's Muslim League.

After Independence, this fundamental divide has been accentuated with the emergence of the Sangh Parivar as an important factor in Indian public life. Hence, the issue of secularism versus Hindu majoritarian; cultural pluralism versus Brahamanical Vedic Hindu hegemonism; and equality before law versus privileged status of the Hindu has divided and polarised Mr. Vajpayee's BJP and Mrs. Gandhi's Congress.

It is a great tribute to Indian democracy that every autonomous institution of civil society, like intellectuals, the press, television and leaders of the political class, is involved in a grand ideological debate about the definition and the meaning of India. It deserves to be stated that a viewpoint that Indian politicians are always involved in trivial personal issues is false because the Indian political class is actively involved in defining: Who should govern India? Who is capable of defending the social fabric of India? Whom should the voters elect for maintaining social harmony? Which party can be trusted to uphold the basic structure of the Indian Constitution as repeatedly defined by the Supreme Court of India. Are these trivial political issues? Mrs. Gandhi accused Mr. Vajpayee on the floor of Parliament that "he should not succumb to the pressures and dictates of the Sangh Parivar" because the Prime Minister is an upholder of the letter and spirit of constitutional legality.

The country is witnessing an extremely high level of political debate which has clearly polarised the whole country. Mr. Ram Vilas Paswan resigned on April 29, 2002, from the Vajpayee-led Government because he felt, like the Congress leader, that the Government had failed to protect the life and property of the minorities in Gujarat. Albeit Mr. Paswan's other compulsions, he had to publicly project himself as a defender of Indian secularism. Gujarat has compelled public leaders and opinion makers to define their public position and get counted on one side or the other. The clash between Mr. Vajpayee and Mrs. Gandhi has brought every thinking person and "men of conscience" to take sides in politics. The ongoing public debate between Indian votaries of secularism and *Hindutva* has influenced everyone; people are today really involved in defining India and the meaning of Indianness. Mr. Vajpayee observed at Panaji on April 12, 2002, that India was secular even before Christians and Muslims came to India. His claim that the Christians and Muslims of India are to offer prayers in mosques and churches was immediately challenged on the plea that it is not he but the secular, democratic Constitution of India that has provided this guarantee. The public debate between the Prime Minister and the Leader of the Opposition is not confined to abstractions of ideology or history, it has been extended to the actual role of the Narendra Modi Government. Many NGOs, citizens groups and the press have castigated the Modi Government for being biased and prejudiced towards the suffering Muslims. It has been suggested that a Government trained in anti-minority ideology, cannot defend and protect the minorities. Mr. Vajpayee rejected this notion in Goa. But the critics of the Sangh Parivar-led Government have been engaged in marshalling evidence to provide evidence and substantiate that the Modi Government is partisan. The National Human Rights Commission and the National Minority Commission have come out openly against a 'biased' state apparatus in Gujarat and the Prime Minister has been compelled to defend it in Parliament and in the press. It is a tribute to our parliamentary democracy that the Lok Sabha discussed for 17 hours, on April 30, 2002, the fundamental differences between the Government and the Opposition.

Democracy is a 'countervailing' force in India and it deserves to be defended and strengthened because it provides every opportunity to support or expose and depose a wanted or an unwanted Government of the day. At the level of ideology, that choice has been made. (*May 15, 2002, The Pioneer*)

A Riot of Identities

Veerappan is a bandit, a killer, a smuggler and in his latest Avatar, he is a great champion of Tamilian cause and if any harm is done to Rajkumar, a Kannadiga hero, Veerappan will be happy because anti-Tamilian riots in Karnataka on the emotive issue of Rajkumar shall add to the popularity of Veerappan as a Tamilian hero. It is no secret that Veerappan, a bandit, like Prabhakaran, a Sri Lankan terrorist, has open and hidden political support in Tamil Nadu. S.M. Krishan, the Chief Minister of Karnataka, is caught in a serious dilemma because the kidnapping of Rajkumar by a well-known criminal, has ceased to be a purely legal problem because it has got linked with the emotive issue of identity of the Kannadiga hero Rajkumar and the Tamilian identity of the bandit Veerappan. Any mishandling of the Rajkumar issue will lead to riots on the basis of identity versus identity. If on the one hand, the state government of Karnataka seems to have collapsed before a bandit, on the other, a larger issue of identity versus identity politics has been dramatised because the victim is identified with Kannadiga emotions and the criminal has been fully identified with Tamilians emotions. In the process the state government is standing as a helpless spectator in the ongoing drama. A few more facts may be mentioned to substantiate the argument that the politics of identities, if not handled with sensitivity, has always led to violence and killing in society. The Congress was eliminated by Dravadian parties in Tamil Nadu because the Congress could not mobilise Tamilians on the basis of their exclusive identity.

The Dravadian movement has been built on the basis of a mythical and false history of Aryans versus Dravadians, and Dravadian parties have gained in political strength only by playing on the sentiments of the Dravadian identity. Since the Congress was an all-India socially "inclusivist" party, it was confronted by a militant "exclusivist" Dravadian party whose leaders had always told Dravadians that they were different from the others. The roots of the Congress decline in Tamil Nadu lie in the fact that the Dravadian parties succeeded in playing on the emotions of the Tamilians on the issues of language and culture which were made to seem threatened by Brahmans and the Aryan race of North India. The self-immolation of Tamilians in 1965 on the issue of the Hindi language brought into sharp focus that identity politics is always built on the basis of an enemy and this enemy in 1965 was represented by the forces represented by the Central Government which wanted to impose Hindi on the Tamilians. Tamil versus Hindi and Tamil Nadu versus the "other India" has become a permanent benchmark of politics in Tamil Nadu. Every identity-based politics in a multi-identity, plural society, is built on the premise that any identity-based parties are promoters and defenders of identity and others are enemies. This fact came to the public notice once again when Tamilian leaders publicly demanded the partition of Sri Lanka and the creation of an Independent Tamil Homeland as demanded by the terrorist Prabhakaran. The Union Government was put into an awkward position on such a public stand by the Tamilian parties which are also alliance partners of the NDA coalition government. Tamilian parties as champions of Tamil identity, could not but take a public stand in defence of Tamilians wherever they happen to be living.

While the whole of India is a great social and cultural mosaic of multiple identities, the seven sisters of North-East Indian are caught in the vicious circle of identity versus identity and sub-identity versus sub-identity competitive and violent politics. The Naga problem is not confined to only the state of Nagaland but it has become extremely complicated because the Naga militant leaders want a greater Nagaland which should consist of all districts of the Naga population of Assam and Manipur.

The champions of Naga identity, like their counterparts in Tamil Nadu, claim to represent the interests of all Nagas irrespective of the fact that their place of birth may be in Assam or Manipur or anywhere else. The Akali Dal of Punjab claims to be the sole spokesman of the Sikh community, and this Sikh-party was championing the cause of Sikhs residing in Udampur district of Uttar Pradesh on the basis of the same logic of the practitioners of identity policies that they are custodians of "identity interests" irrespective of the principle of territoriality and boundaries of the various states of India. Further, every major political party of India fears that if Kashmir valley secedes from India, a Hindu backlash will take place in the country. The upshot of this discussion is that in a multi-identity country, the politics of identity and identity-based parties can willingly or unwillingly become the source of violent conflicts and social discord.

Unfortunately, the decade of the 1990s witnessed the emergence of exclusivist identity politics in a big way around the politics of Mandal and Mandir (Temple) and was a decade of social violence and discord. Purely caste-based parties, like the Bahujan Samaj Party of Mr. Kanshi Ram or the Samajwadi Party of Mr. Mulayam Singh Yadav or the Rashtriya Janata Dal of Mr. Laloo Prasad Yadav or the Samata Party of Mr. Nitish Kumar, have led to the total social fragmentation of Uttar Pradesh and Bihar and caste wars have become the order of the day. Similarly, a Hindu religion-based party has served notice on religious minorities like the Muslims and the Christians that the state functionaries will practice discrimination on the basis of religious identities. An exclusivist identity politics is logically "discriminatory" because the patrons of identity-politics thrive on identity animosities and identity divisions. Mr. Ram Prakash Gupta of Uttar Pradesh and Mr. Keshubhai Patel of Gujarat have given a message that their state government is of the Hindus, by the Hindus and of the Hindus. Mr. Laloo Prasad Yadav of Bihar says that he represents Yadavas and Muslims and the state government of Bihar under RJD is a government of the two main identity groups of Bihar.

The "caravan" of identity politics is moving because small states like Chhatisgarh or Uttaranchal or others will continue to be created. This is because political leaders, having exhausted the potential of ruling over large arrears, will continue to manipulate sub-identities to become Chief Ministers. It is not surprising that Mr. Shyama Charan Shukla and Mr. Vidya Charan Shukla, the sons of the famous Ravi Shankar Shukla, consider the whole of Madhya Pradesh as their private property, and if these two brothers have been dispossessed of their whole MP, then they are claimants to the Chief Ministership of the newly created Chhatisgarh with a slogan that a tribal need not be leading the so-called tribal state. The story does not end here.

Identities and sub-identities are being manufactured and manipulated by political leaders for political benefits, cultural identities are picked up by political leaders who identify themselves with their community by the accident of birth and they transform it into a road towards political power. Mr. Bal Thackrey of the Shiv Sena came into prominence in the 1960s by claiming to be the champion of the Maharashtrians. He launched a cleansing process in Bombay where non-Maharashtrians were physically targetted. Identity politics leads to the terrorisation of minority cultural groups and also their physical liquidation, if politically profitable. The riot of identity competition in India actually leads to "riots" and killings whether in the name of religion or caste or language. If India is not to be involved in a million mutinies and mini civil wars, socially inclusivist parties should confront local, exclusivist parties, otherwise, a multi-cultural Indian will remain burning. It has been observed that religionising politics tempts politicians to messianic delusion, and politicising religion cheapens and corrupts the spirit. In the Indian context any cultural identity-based politics leads to confrontation because leaders of cultural exclusion are always fanatics about their opinions and views. Broad social and political fronts cutting across parochial identities should emerge in politics and pursue the goals of purposeful nation-building instead of the present politics of identities which is leading to destruction. (*November 20, 2000, The Pioneer*)

Why the Bullet is Ruling Over the Ballot

The ongoing debate of the need for a new law to tackle the problem of terrorism in India has become polarised between the defenders of the Prevention of Terrorism Ordinance/Act and its opponents and critics. An important question that has been side-tracked in this emotive debate is 'Why does terrorism take birth in a democracy?'. Why do groups in a society feel the need for taking refuge behind the politics of bullet in preference to the politics of ballot? An opposite proposition is that terrorist groups emerge in totalitarian, authoritarian and military-bureaucratic regimes because these dictatorial state systems are repressive, oppressive and coercive. Since they do not provide any public space for dissent, a section of society is compelled to take recourse to guns to confront the guns of anti-democratic coercive regimes.

The colonial state of India oppressed all anti-colonial struggles but they made a distinction between Gandhi-led Satayagraha and "extremists/terrorists". The revolutionaries of Bengal or leaders like Balgangadhar Tilak, or young progressive fighters like Shaheed Bhagat Singh were victims of ruthless oppression indulged in by the colonisers. Even Satyagrahis like Gandhi or Nehru were put behind the bar on the charge of "law breakers". During colonial rule, Indians debated the strategy of powerful Gandhian Satyagraha versus the power of bullets to win freedom for India. The upshot of this illustration is that an important section of Indian leadership opted for the politics of gun because they were convinced that the colonial state apparatus could not have been destroyed without armed struggle.

While Satyagrahis also suffered great brutalities at the hands of the oppressive colonial state, they preferred to follow the Gramacian path of "passive revolution" under the leadership of Gandhi. It is not without reason that the British rulers, while adopting apparently two different approaches when dealing with Satyagrahis and revolutionaries, believed in "suppressing both".

Why the politics of the bullet today in a society that very successfully practices the politics of the ballot? It will be helpful to categorise groups which have taken to guns in preference to ballot in the post-independence period of democratic India.

Agrarian India has given birth to some of the practitioners of the politics of the bullet. Further, some regions where such groups emerged around the "land question" and "agrarian injustice", politics of bullet still continues while in some regions where such groups emerged in the 1960s or 1970s, are no more in the picture at all. The reference here is to the various Naxalite groups like People's War Groups or Liberation Groups or Moist groups. It is worth mentioning that they do not have an all-India presence. Further, some of them like late Vinod Mishra who began with politics of bullet for agrarian restructuring, later on opted for politics of ballot. West Bengal in the 1960s and upto the late 1970s witnessed the powerful Naxal struggle and the state response was equally powerful repression. Naxal movement in West Bengal is a thing of the past because the Left Front government caught the bull by its horns and plunged into the task of land reforms. The breeding ground of social discontent and anger in West Bengal was politically identified, but Siddharth Shankar Ray responded to the socially discontented groups by practising the violence of the state. The Left Front government on the other hand, understood the social roots of social violence and addressed itself to the task of social reconstruction.

The moral of this story is that Congress or Telugu Desam in Andhra Pradesh are depending on the power of the state to deal with agrarian resistance groups; and L.K. Advani, the Home Minister of India, announced at the Inter-State Council meeting on November 17, 2001 that in three years from 1998 to 2001, the central government has increased the assistance for the modernisation of police forces in the state from Rs. 98 crore to Rs. 1,000 crore. Why is it that in the south of India, only Andhra Pradesh wants more money for the modernisation of police forces. Do we need POTO in Andhra Pradesh to confront fighters for social justice in rural Andhra? A telling example from Andhra Pradesh is the abduction of Mr. Chandi Marthanda Rao, a brother of Vidyasagar Rao, Union Minister of State of Home Affairs. He was abducted on October 26, 2001 and released on November 2, 2001. What is the social profile of this abducted Rao? He is a rich peasant who owns more than one hundred acres of land, besides gardens, orchards, etc. and he is also a big contractor who always threatens smaller contractors. Does every rural household in Andhra Pradesh own such an area of land? Similarly, some Naxal groups have penetrated Tribal areas of Madhya Pradesh because exploited and oppressed tribals listen to the advice of the Naxals.

Another important category of practitioners of politics of gun exists in 'border areas' where politics of ethnicity and identity is not sensitively tackled in a democratic-manner. It deserves to be mentioned that India has great success stories in tackling ethnic-identity movements in some of the North-Eastern states and it deserves to be noted that all the seven sisters in North-East India have gone through troubled situations but slowly and gradually, the parliamentary democratic system has taken roots in an extremely complex and volatile society. If democratically elected leaders are insensitive to the genuine feelings of deprivation and alienation of some groups of society, the choices for such groups become very limited. Indira Gandhi imposed an election on Assam when very powerful All Assam Students Union and Asam Gana Parishad movement had given a "boycott" call; their main demand of protecting the Assamese identity from the invasion of the Bangladeshis was not fully responded to by the Indian State. The massacre in Nellie that followed decisively proved the point that the Centre's policy of dealing coercively with mass movements is counter-productive. Similarly, in Punjab, the manipulative politics of the Akalis and a faction-ridden Punjab Congress Party, queered further by Indira Gandhi's machinations, created a Frankenstein in Punjab.

India has to do a lot of soul-searching in answering the question: How many so-called terrorist groups or practitioners of the politics of gun have been patronised or created or encouraged by democratically elected governments? India is not ungovernable because of the so-called "terrorist groups", but because a large number of violence-based groups in the country, except J&K, are primarily the product of indigenous social reasons.

The most important danger in the ongoing debate on "terrorism" is that an umbrella law is being enacted for dealing with a motley crowd of the so-called terrorists without identifying their genesis or social goals. The coloniser categorised every freedom fighter as an enemy of the state. Nelson Mandela has stated that "The very people (US) who had referred to us as terrorists earlier are now referring to us as members of a responsible government".

An umbrella definition of a "terrorist" is full of dangers because it will provide legitimacy to coerce any social group which is dissatisfied with mainstream democratic politics. While the task is to bring every group under the benign and benevolent umbrella of participatory democracy, the real culprits are not only gun-wielding groups, but politicians responsible for eroding democratic spaces. Democratically elected politicians should answer a question: What has been their own role in creating social dissatisfaction and alienation among many groups in society? Save Kashmir, the only way to win over the disaffected is better governance to deal with genuine aspirations. Theoreticians of democracy have attracted our attention towards "*democratic deficit*" as different from "*fiscal deficit*". If democrats do not care for the marginalised or socially dispossessed and disempowered groups, democracy itself cannot serve as a safety valve. (*November 29, 2001, The Pioneer*)

Coalition Dharma in the Age of Region

The Sangh Parivar defines India as "one nation, one language, one culture"; but the BJP-led NDA coalition of 24 parties says India is diverse, plural and socially and culturally at competition with itself—and that, for India to cohere, we have to accept multi-cultural regional identities. These identities cannot be harmonised by believers of overarching Hindu Rashtra. Mr. Atal Bihari Vajpayee and Mr. L.K. Advani have asserted many a time that the success of the NDA is due to the BJP's practice of coalition *dharma*. If so, why could the practitioners of coalition *dharma* not save their Government in 1998?

The Vajpayee Government was defeated in Lok Sabha by one vote because Ms. J. Jayalalitha withdrew support. The collapse of the short-lived coalition was owing to serious conflicts between Tamil Nadu's political compulsions and the all-India politics of the Vajpayee-led dispensation. DMK's M. Karunanidhi continues to support the Vajpayee-led Government because he thinks that the Centre is his only protector against a vindictive Chief Minister. Regional ground realities play a decisive role in the DMK-AIADMK relationship and their approach to the Vajpayee-led Government. Both are determined by the compulsions of local level issues, and not on the basis of any all-India considerations.

Recently, Ms. Jayalalitha embarrassed the Vajpayee Government by arresting the MDMK leader Vaiko under POTA. The BJP is at wits' end because Mr. Vaiko's group backs the NDA. Ms. Jayalalitha, on her part, had an irrefutable argument against Mr. Vaiko. He was guilty of supporting the LTTE, a terrorist organisation. The Jayalalitha story does not end here. Not only did she arrest Mr. Vaiko, she applied POTA on Tamizhar Desiya Iyakkan President Nedumaran, another LTTE supporter.

The Chief Minister's actions have brought into sharp focus the issue of terrorism in Indian politics. The BJP claims the Centre's primary task is to fight cross-border terrorism. The Centre has time and again ruled out negotiations with Pakistan till cross-border infiltration stops. Ms. Jayalalitha is merely asking the self-proclaimed anti-terrorist Central Government to fight against supporters of terrorism in Tamil Nadu. The question she poses is: Sympathisers of terrorism are State politicians on whose support the Vajpayee-led coalition depends. How can such a Government be honest and sincere in its crusade against terrorists?

The BJP, *Hindu Rashtra's* political face at the Centre, has to reconcile the political contradiction posed by fighting terrorism in Kashmir and absolving LTTE supporters in Tamil Nadu. Does the Vajpayee Government's anti-terrorism apply to the whole of India, or is it confined to infiltration in Kashmir? It would seem Tamil Nadu's regional compulsions cannot be accommodated by the votaries of *Hindu Rashtra*.

Trinamool Congress Chief Mamata Banerjee also recently challenged the BJP-led Government. She wanted it to resolve the conflict between Bihar and Bengal on the issue of railway bifurcation. Ms. Banerjee has not hesitated in making Mr. Nitish Kumar the villain of the piece, who abused his power as Railway Minister to favour his own State, Bihar, at Bengal's cost. Has *Hindutva* ideology any sensible solution to the disputes between Bihar, Bengal, Orissa and so on?

Why is the BJP finding it impossible to deal with regional confrontations? The answer is that it has never considered the significance of multiple regional identities that have gone into the making of a rich, diverse and plural India. Believers in unifying ideology are witnessing the falsification and invalidation of their definition of *Hindu Rashtra*. Ms. Banerjee, Ms. Jayalalitha or Dr. Farooq Abdullah are reminding monopolistic *Hindu Rashtrawalls* that India consists of multiple overlapping identities. Hindu identity is not the sum total of Indian reality.

During the past four years, the concept of a unified *Hindu Rashtra* has been challenged time and again. It can be maintained that regional leaders backing the national Government are opportunists, who raise parochial issues to secure concessions from a weak Centre. It can also be suggested that it is wrong to say Mr. Vajpayee leads a "coalition government', given that in reality the NDA is a marriage of convenience among disparate birds of passage.

Regions in India have divergent histories. Tamilian identity was formed long before K.B. Hedgewar, M.S. Gowalkar or V.D. Savarkar came on the scene with the imaginary concept of *Hindu Rashtra*. Telugos revolted against the idea of a common Madras Presidency, and the Nehru Government was forced to establish a States' Reorganisation Council which led to the formation of Andhra Pradesh. Gujarat and Maharashtra fought big battles when Bombay was declared the common capital of the two States, following the reorganisation of States. The Samyukaa Maharashtra Samiti spearheaded a movement for a united Marathi State.

Even before independence, Bengal burnt when Lord Curzon partitioned Bengal in 1905, which had to be annulled in 1911. Orissa and Bihar emerged as separate States much before the votaries of *Hindutva* were even born. Oriya cultural identity has been a driving force for the formation of a united Orissa. Despite partition, poets like Rabindranath Tagore and Nazrul Islam inspire Bengalis on both sides of the border.

M.A. Jinnah laid the foundation of a separate Bangladesh when announced in 1948 in erstwhile Dacca that Urdu would be Pakistan's national language. How could East Bengal accept Urdu as its language in preference to its mother tongue, Bengali? Jinnah and Savarkar were completely off the mark in thinking that Muslim or Hindu identity could be the only unifying factor in South Asia. Sri Lankan Tamils fought a civil war against Sinhalese Buddhists in defence of their identity in a bilingual society. The RSS is also blindly following the agenda of *Hindu Rashtra* by advocating the trifurcation of Jammu & Kashmir to ostensibly accommodate Hindu Dogras, Buddhist Ladakhis and Muslim Kashmiris. India as a Hindu country is a figment of the Sangh Parivar's imagination. The notion is in contradiction with the complex, plural society that is India.

The Vajpayee-led Government is cornered not only by the Opposition, but also by its own allies which represent regional realities and aspirations. The Congress faltered in 1965 when it failed to respect India's linguistic diversity. When Hindi was imposed on the whole of India by the Lal Bahadur Shastri Government, Tamil Nadu burned. Tamilians felt humiliated by Hindi chauvinists. The Sangh Parivar is repeating the mistakes of the Congress by promoting the concept of Hindu and Hindi-based '*rashtra*'.

If creating communal divisions is one part of the Sangh Parivar's agenda, the other is regional suppression by a monolithic Hindu reality.

Yet India cannot be browbeaten into uniformity—it has multiple regional aspirations that demand "autonomous" political space. If "regions" need the Centre to resolve inter-regional and intra-regional disputes, only an honest umpire can help find solutions. *Hindutvavadis* cannot even respond sensibly to water disputes, such as the Cauvery river water dispute between Karnataka and Tamil Nadu.

The essence of Indian nationhood is its heterogeneity. Only by fulfilling regional aspirations can a truly federal, democratic and secular India prosper. The Vajpayee Government knows by now that national interest is to be reconciled with regional compulsions. Ms. Banerjee and Ms. Jayalalitha are Hindu but they also seek, respectively, to protect Bengali and Tamil identity and interests. The moral of the story: Unity in diversity cannot be replaced by *Hindu Rashtra*. (*15th August, 2002, The Pioneer*)

Goodbye Consensus, Hello Conflict

The July-August, 2002 Monsoon session of Parliament had to be adjourned *sine die* because Opposition parties were in no mood for the legislative programme and issues that the ruling alliance wanted debated and approved. Since "deadlocked" sessions have become a norm, a few facts may be mentioned about parliamentary behaviour in general to substantiate the argument that consensual democratic politics is gradually being replaced by a confrontational political process.

The Government and the Opposition have clearly-defined roles in a parliamentary democracy based on a multi-party system. A majority party or coalition has the right to govern because the electoral verdict is in its favour. Opposition parties and groups have the right—even the obligation—to oppose, expose and depose the existing ruling party or alliance of parties. While the legitimate rights of both are considered the pillars of the democratic system, doubts have arisen in public mind about the behaviour of parliamentarians while conducting the business of Parliament.

If every Parliamentary session gets immobilised and faces premature death because Government and Opposition parties cannot follow rules of conduct, people will ponder the fate of democracy in India. The Monsoon session came to an abrupt end because the Opposition demanded the resignation of Petroleum Minister Ram Naik due to the alleged misuse of power in the allotment of petrol pumps on the basis of the political affiliations of the allottees. The Government maintained that "procedures" were followed, and hence Mr. Naik was not expected to quit simply because the Opposition asked for his head.

Similarly the Lok Sabha budget session had come to a standstill because the Government was accused of not taking the Narendra Modi dispensation in Gujarat to task for its inability to protect minorities during the communal holocaust in the State. Gujarat overshadowed the budget, and financial and economic issues of concern to the country could not be discussed. Neither the Government nor the Opposition was willing to concede space to the other.

Not only this. For the first time in the history of the Parliament, the Opposition is not ready to engage in any legislative business with the Defence Minister of India. This is a historic situation — a Cabinet Minister being ostracised by the Opposition.

It could be argued that the acrobatics between Government and Opposition in both Houses of Parliament are a sign of the maturity of Indian democracy. A vigilant Opposition is compelling the Government to be transparent. It can be suggested that an alarmist view of the Government-Opposition rift is uncalled for. Significant issues may cause a sharp divide between their view-points and approaches.

The Jawaharlal Nehru Government between 1947 and 1964 faced many political battles in the Parliament. Public issues of national importance were debated in a normal manner, but deadlock between the Government and the Opposition occurred in 1962 on the issue of the resignation of Krishna Menon, the then Defence Minister. The Opposition held him responsible for the debacle related to the India-China border dispute. It levelled a serious charge against Menon for "politicising" army appointments and playing "favourites" with military generals. It was alleged that a "divided Indian army" could not meet the challenge posed by the Chinese army. This was an exceptional case in India's history and the Government-Opposition confrontations were legitimate.

The Indira Gandhi dispensation and the Opposition were always at loggerheads. Another issue arose in 1986 when Rajiv Gandhi, the then Prime Minister, was accused of accepting "bribes" from foreign suppliers in the Bofors gun deal. This too was an "exceptional" situation. The Opposition carried with conviction the public opinion that the highest authorities were involved in dubious dealings in defence purchases. Despite the fact that its allegations about the personal involvement of Rajiv Gandhi have not been proved till today, the Opposition succeeded in delegitimising the Prime Minister. Mr. V.P. Singh took over in 1989, thanks to his crusade against corruption. Public perceptions of a leader's conduct is important in any democracy. The Opposition had succeeded in projecting Rajiv Gandhi as a tainted Prime Minister.

Similarly, during the budget session of March 2002, it was the Opposition's duty to confront the Government on the issue of communal riots. The Modi regime in Gujarat and the BJP-led Government at the Centre were in the dock. Home Minister L.K. Advani is, after all, constitutionally accountable for communal carnage in any State, and even more so in a State with a Government led by Mr. Advani's own party.

Opposition parties do not have to wait for elections to confront the ruling party if "exceptional" situation arises. They can immobilise the Parliament if the ruling group in power is seen as abdicating responsibilities. But if every Parliament session is dead-locked, the Government and the Opposition must explain their conduct to the public.

What explains the growing schism between the ruling dispensation and the Opposition starting from the Nineties? If, on the one hand, India is moving towards national polarisation between the BJP and the Congress, on the other, parties with sectarian, caste and religious agenda are multiplying. Every small group or leader of a pocket borough wants to enjoy the power of patronage. The BJP-Congress contest is not merely for power, but for ideological dominance. It is simplistic to say that politics is a site for self-aggrandisement. Corruption is one face of the political class. The other is the contest between *Hindutva* politics and Congress politics and there is no meeting point between the two.

The Congress is thus compelled to attack the BJP and the Government on every public issue as preparation for the 2004 Lok Sabha elections. The BJP itself had always targeted the Congress as the fountainhead of corruption. Now the Congress is hyperactive in exposing the BJP's corruption, because it has to demolish the BJP's claim to being a "party with a difference".

Further, the media has become a "centre of power" which does not allow any ruling party or coalition to get away with mis-governance. It will not be wrong to say the media is leading the political class, providing parties with material to attack each other. Every scam is getting huge publicity. The media tasted blood during the Bofors kickbacks controversy and it has not looked back since. It exposes politicians, whether of the ruling party or the Opposition. Its power increases when parties seem unable to mobilise public opinion on any issue of national concern. Also, walk-outs and deadlocks in the Parliament give publicity to political actors. If they cannot rally voters on genuine issues, noises in the Parliament and their exposure in the media become a substitute. Hence significant or insignificant political issues are taken up on the floor of the House as a means of maintaining links with voters.

The growing bi-polarity between the BJP and the Congress, the multiplicity of sectarian and personalised groups and the support which politicians get from the mass media are leading to an erosion of the sanctity of the Parliament as a forum for democratic debate and dissent. This is cause for concern. Mr. Advani's recent protest that the Opposition waned to destabilise the BJP-led coalition Government was simplistic. The reality is that the Government and the Opposition are not able to arrive at a consensus on issues of public concern. Hence the politics of confrontation. (*24th August, 2002, The Pioneer*)

Hindutva: Place of Birth Pangs

Ms. J. Jayalalitha, Mr. P.A. Sangma and others have questioned Congress President Sonia Gandhi's eligibility as future Prime Minister. Mr. Sharad Pawar, Mr. Sangma and Mr. Tariq Anwar had earlier broken with the Congress because they were marginalised in its new power structure. The split had to do with an unstated leadership dispute between Ms. Gandhi and Mr. Pawar. The latter's ambitions were disguised as concern over Ms. Gandhi's Italian roots, which made her unacceptable as party President to a faction led by Mr. Pawar and others.

A power struggle pure and simple was thus given an alibi by the splinter group. This was the reason the Atal Bihari Vajpayee Government made Mr. Sangma part of the 11-member Constitution Review panel. The NCP leader's one point agenda suited the Sangh Parivar. As does Ms. Jayalalitha's tirade. The latter wants to build bridges with the BJP-led Central Government with a view to arming herself against political adversaries led by DMK leader M. Karunanidhi.

Mr. Pawar, Mr. Sangma, Ms. Jayalalitha, Mr. Chandrababu Naidu and stray Janata Dal-type socialists have political reasons to raise the issue of Ms. Gandhi's Italian roots. By contrast, the Sangh Parivar has an ideological position. It does not accept Muslims and Christians as indigenous because neither have their most venerated places of worship in India. Christians look towards the Pope and Muslims towards Mecca and Medina. The Sangh Parivar feels these two "alien" religions cannot be accepted as truly Indian.

While one group would like to form a third front, the other wants to establish *Hindu Rashtra*. The BJP represents Hindus and its leader in Gujarat, Mr. Narendra Modi, spoke the language of the Sangh Parivar by referring to Ms. Gandhi as "*Italy ki beti*" in his first round of the Gaurav Yatra. He sought to appropriate Mahatma Gandhi's legacy when he said the Congress's ploy to foist Ms. Gandhi as PM on the country was "an insult to the Mahatma" who had fought against the rule of white-skinned people.

The Gujarat Chief Minister and others in the Sangh Parivar forget that Mahatma Gandhi said he was against British rule but "not against the British people". It was in keeping with this tradition that the Congress accepted Annie Besant and post-Independence India appreciated the contributions of Mother Teresa, a Catholic nun.

Mr. Modi also remarked on Ms. Gandhi's religion during the Gaurav Yatra, and cleverly mentioned the Pope. These remarks were not accidental. He had earlier attacked CEC J.M. Lyngdoh, insinuating that his decision to delay the Gujarat polls had something to do with the fact he belonged to the same religion as Ms. Gandhi.

My purpose is not to defend the Congress or its present crop of leaders. Today's Congress is completely de-ideologised. It is guilty of making every kind of political compromise in public life. The party as well as its splinter groups have nothing to do with Nehru's Congress, which was firmly based on the ideology of a democratic, secular and federal state that was to promote the welfare model of development. The Congress today has abandoned the ideological moorings of yesterday's freedom fighters. Its leadership, like that of regionalist and subregionalist parties, is guided by lust for power for the sake of power and electoral victory for the purpose of operating a network of patronage.

Ms. Gandhi talks of "good governance" as the virtue of Congress State Governments. But their "good governance" lacks any powerful social goal and content. The issue, therefore, does not concern Ms. Gandhi's foreign origins. The present level of political debate in India should be of concern to defenders of multicultural democracy, because the quality of democratic governance depends on the quality of public issues raised by political parties. Rhetoric, sloganeering and personal attacks are an acceptable part of electoral politics today. Politics at one level is a dirty activity, in which character assassination is par for the course.

Every political party made, at one time or another, a business of attacking the "dynastic" nature of the Congress. In a manner of speaking, the "anti-dynastic" platform has collapsed like a house of cards, because every party or group has created its own "dynasty". All politicians have accepted the Congress culture, by politically promoting sons, daughters, daughters-in-law, wives and other relatives. "Kinship" with party bosses guarantees a political future. Anti-dynastic politics was never seriously part of the political process, confined as it was to drawing room discussions.

Leaders raise minor, emotive or tasteless issues for political mobilisation and during electioneering. But the issues raised by the Sangh Parivar about Ms. Gandhi deserve serious analysis. If the politics of religion and nativity becomes an "agenda", it can prove dangerous for India's multicultural social fabric. If elections are fought on the basis of the "foreignness" of Ms. Gandhi, the matter will not stop there. Nativity has been a factor in regional politics and its consequences have been quite disastrous.

Shiv Sena leader Bal Thackeray had once said Maharashtra was for Maharashtrians only. Malayalees and other South Indians working in what was then Bombay were targeted by Shiv Sainiks, even though these non-Maharashtrians happened to be Hindus. The students' movement in Assam in the early Eighties targeted Bengalis, irrespective of the fact the AASU leaders were only against foreigners (Bangladeshis). The Northeast has always faced social strife due to the politics of 'insiders' versus 'outsiders'. The Sangh Parivar too has a world view of 'us' (Hindus) versus 'them'. Such antagonism towards the demonised 'Other' showed its terrible face in the Gujarat riots from March to June this year.

Communal riots and violence are a direct consequence of the ideology which pits the 'native' against the 'foreigner' or the Hindu against the Muslim or Christian. If electoral politics revolves around the religion or place of birth of Indian citizens, we are bound to institutionalise social divisiveness.

Another dangerous fallout of the Sangh Parivar's ongoing political mobilisation in the context of Gujarat is that emotive issues of religion and nativity have pushed out the basic issues of nation-building from the agenda of all-India parties. It has been said that regional parties contest polls on regional and State-specific issues whereas national parties focus on nation-building. How is a citizen's religion helpful or harmful to the latter? The Sangh Parivar has spelt out that nation-building is the task of Hindus. Its politics is limited to issues concerning one favoured religious community. Are we to assume that Mr. Modi is contesting elections as a custodian of Hindu interests only? Consider also the fact that Hindu symbols and places of worship have assumed 'special status' in the *saffron* politics. If mobilisation and elections are focussed on the Hindu "votebank", any government formed on such a mandate will serve Hindu interests alone.

In brief, politics is getting polarised around "emotive" and socially divisive issues. Socio-economic problems—the real issues of nation-building—are being sidetracked. Mr. Modi is the representative articulator of majoritarian identity. His attack on Ms. Gandhi shows the real all-India agenda of the *saffronites*. Through the assault on a person's faith and her political rights by virtue of her citizenship, the Sangh Parivar is attacking the Constitution. The real message, as articulated by Mr. Modi, goes beyond Ms. Gandhi's roots. It communicates an ominous ideological position against the "Christian Sonia", based on the premise that all minority communities are outsiders. Every defender of India's pluralist ethos, therefore, has cause to worry. (*27th Sept., 2002, The Pioneer*)

3

Uttar Pradesh Politics: Headquarters of Intense Social Struggle

Uttar Pradesh: Caste Aside

The forthcoming UP Assembly elections are critical for the BJP because for obvious reasons the outcome will have a direct impact on the leadership of Prime Minister Atal Bihari Vajpayee and the NDA Government at the Centre. Mr. Vajpayee has himself conveyed the message to the members of the Sangh Parivar that the future of his NDA Government is linked with the outcome of UP Assembly elections. BJP's Chief Minister of UP, Rajnath Singh, has already put forward a new scheme of "reservations within reservations" and "jobs within jobs" for the Dalits and the backward castes by slicing (from 'slice') the quotas around Backward Castes, the Extremely Most Backward Castes, and the Muslim Backward Castes. By opening a Pandora's box of "socially backward versus other socially backward castes", Mr. Singh has posed a potent political challenge to the caste-based Bahujan Samaj Party of Mr. Kanshi Ram and Ms. Mayawati, and the Samajwadi Party of Mr. Mulayam Singh Yadav.

It deserves to be stated that political compromises made by the Congress in UP have led to a situation where it is not at all in the reckoning and now the political triangle consists of the BJP, BSP and Samajwadi Party. This is the reason that the BJP is playing a "caste card in politics" because its two main political rivals have strong caste-based social support among the Jatavas or Chamars of the BSP, and Yadavs of the Samajwadi Party. None of these three contenders for power in UP are taking the Congress even as a marginal factor in the forthcoming elections. Mr. Rajnath Singh appointed a Social Justice Committee under Mr. Hukam Singh to look into the 27 per cent quota of reservations of public positions for the backward castes of Uttar Pradesh.

This Social Justice Committee of the BJP State Government has followed the path shown by Mr. V.P. Singh, who played the caste reservation game to protect his temporary prime ministership in August, 1990. Incidentally, Mr. V.P. Singh, the "messiah" of the worst kind of casteist politics in India, proclaimed the acceptance of Mandal Commission Report on reservations in public services in the name of social justice for the backward castes. It is ironical that the worst kind of casteist politicians of UP conceal their activity of vulgar manipulative politics by taking recourse to the ideology of social justice.

The Rajnath Singh Government's new policy of sub-quotas for reservations is based on sub-division of 27 per cent quota into five per cent for the Yadavs, nine per cent for eight most backward castes which also includes Lodhs, Kurmis and the Jats; and the remaining 14 per cent of reservations are for the 70 other backward castes. Further, 22 Muslim castes have been also given benefits of reservations in the category of Extremely Most Backward Castes. This new casteist politics of the BJP has completely rattled Mr. Mulayam Singh Yadav, Ms. Mayawati and other sub-caste leaders, who feel threatened because "quotas within quota" caste policy has directly hit the caste support base of the two leaders. Mr. Mulayam Singh Yadav has jumped into the "new debate" by observing that "we want 11 to 15 per cent of State Government jobs to be reserved for the poor from the upper castes". Ms. Mayawati, while criticising the policy of "reservation within reservation" of the *Manuwadi* BJP, has demanded reservation in the private sector.

Another UP leader Beni Prasad Verma wants "reservation on the basis of caste percentage of Uttar Pradesh population" and Mayawati too wants caste-based census of the State's population for determining the quota for reservations for each caste. The national leadership of the BJP, which is deeply involved in the politics of elections to the UP Assembly, desires that the Hukum Singh UP Social Justice Committee should also find ways and means for five per cent "economically backward" sections among the upper castes.

Why is the caravan of caste and sub-caste based reservations moving forward? Why has the BJP jumped into the caste-based politics of UP? What has been the impact of caste-based politics on the governance of the State? How has politics of caste impacted civil society in UP? These questions about the ongoing drama of casteisation, communalisation, criminalisation and complete marginalisation of secular, progressive forces in UP cannot be answered without contextualisation of the social order in the State.

A few important features of political and socio-cultural profile of UP may be mentioned to properly comprehend its continuing downslide. UP was very important headquarters of the Congress, socialists, communists, Muslim Leaguers and Hindu Maha Sabha-ites, and all these political tendencies were actively involved in political competition during the struggle for freedom. Every major ideological group was found in an active contest in UP and every major ideology had its own active followers and leaders. Every major ideology in the State thus received its intellectual sustenance from highly developed universities and colleges.

The Uttar Pradesh intelligentsia, along with the literati, supported and supplemented contending ideologies in the State. On the eve of independence, UP launched its journey with all the assets and liabilities of this historical inheritance. If on the one hand, UP could boast of its ideological and organisational capital, on the other, Partition of India left the State as a completely fractured society. UP needed a healing touch because its leadership and political formations had not only to fight against the monster of communalism, the Muslim minority too had to be assured that it was absolutely safe in India. Nehru's Congress, Acharya Narendra Dev's socialists and Z.A. Ahmad's communists were very active in providing a socially progressive political umbrella to all communities against communal forces in the State.

The major generalisation from this pre-independence and post-independence social profile of UP is that it started its democratic journey with a good network of party organisations, trade unions, kisan sabhas, student unions and provincial, regional, district, city, town and village level organisational leadership. How was this great asset of politics squandered away? The Nehru Congress at the apex was socially progressive, but Congress leadership in UP was socially conservative and practitioner of caste and soft *Hindutva*. Congress social class and caste alliance in UP consisted of the "twice born castes" with the hegemony of Brahmins, Thakurs, Rajputs, Banias and Kayasthas in this order, and for the winning of an election, the Congress created a powerful social constituency among Muslims and Scheduled Castes.

The political superstructure of UP reveals the social essence of the Congress's leadership. Govind Ballabh Pant, Dr. Sampurnanand, Chandra Bhanu Gupta, Kamlapati Tripathi, H.N. Bahuguna, Narain Dutt Tiwari and V.P. Singh occupied the highest echelons of power in the UP Congress, and the odd man out was Chaudhary Charan Singh, who was looked down upon by the high caste leaders as a rough Jat peasant. Not only this. All the major players in UP politics combined their social conservatism with the practice of soft *Hindutva* and caste-based loyalties. (*October 3, 2001, The Pioneer*)

UP Elections a Repeat of 1996 Farce and Tragedy Rolled into One

Uttar Pradesh is destined to witness the repeat performance of 1996 during the forthcoming state assembly elections of 2002 because society and polity of the state have been completely frozen and immobilised by sectarian casteists, Hindu communalists and corrupt, criminal and completely normless and manipulative political class. A few facts may be mentioned to substantiate the argument that the forthcoming elections are in reality a "farce" and none of the political formations or groups or individual leaders is capable of pulling out Uttar Pradesh from its tragic situation after the elections.

First, Uttar Pradesh has neither a "two party system" like some other states of India, nor a major party which has social presence and electoral power in all the regions of state. The BJP is a party of, by, and for the Hindus and the *Hindutva* politics is challenged by the caste reality of Uttar Pradesh society. Since caste is not a hegemonic construction in society, every important sub-caste has been appropriated by different caste leaders for electoral victories.

Mulayam Singh Yadav's Samajwadi Party, George Fernandes's Samata Party, the Janata Dal (United) of Sharad Yadav, the Lok Janshakti of Ram Vilas Paswan and the Rashtriya Lok Dal of Ajit Singh have established their narrow social base among different castes and sub-castes which are described as "Backward Castes" or "Other Backward Castes" or "Most Backward Castes". It is a misnomer to describe them as political parties. In reality, individual caste leaders have floated their private shops which can be auctioned to any buyer before and after the elections. Similarly, the Bahujan Samaj Party of Mayawati claims loyalty of "Jatav" Dalits. Many other Dalit castes act as "floating" voters and the Bahujan Samaj Party, because of divisions among the Dalits, can not get more than 20 per cent of the voters' support and it can just cross the mark of 50 seats in a state assembly of 403 members. Same is true of Mulayam Singh's "backward caste" vote bank.

Second, the logic of above description is that fragmented social profile of the voters has led to the proliferation of parties or groups or individual leaders who are not bound by any ideology except the lust for political power. The power for the sake of personal and sectional benefits has become the leading normative framework of Uttar Pradesh political class.

The BJP formed its so-called coalition government in the state by bribing and splitting the Congress and the BSP and it was not surprising that the splintered groups like the Loktantrik Congress Party and the Kisan Mazdoor Bahujan Party got a lion's share of power in the Kalyan Singh, Ram Prakash Gupta and Rajnath Singh-led BJP state governments.

It has become crystal clear from the experience of 1996 to 2002 that casteists or communalists can do anything to get into the corridors of power in the state. Uttar Pradesh polity and society are caught in the vicious circle of casteist and communalist led criminal-corrupt and completely immoral culture of politics. This is the background of forthcoming state assembly elections where the BSP, the Congress, People's Front formed by Mulayam Singh Yadav and the BJP with its seven allies are competing for the support of voters during the elections of 2002. A listing of BJP allies will reveal that all its seven allies are paper tigers and leaders with limited caste appeal. Maneka Gandhi's Shakti Dal, Ajit Singh's Rashtriya Lok Dal, Sharad Yadav's Janata Dal (United), Ram Vilas Paswan's Lok Janshakti, Fernandes's Samata Party and defectors like the Loktantrik Congress Party or the Kisan Mazdoor Bahujan Party are all interested in loaves and fishes of power politics by joining the bandwagon of Hindu communalists.

The most telling illustration of completely de-ideologised, immoral and opportunistic politics is provided by the BJP itself which has been described as a "party with a difference". The BJP MLAs were involved in "cross-voting" during the elections of the Rajya Sabha and the Legislative Council seats in 2000 and it has led the BJP not to nominate 40 out of its 158 sitting MLAs for the forthcoming elections. The BJP MLAs were bought for "cross-voting". Not only this. The BJP's unprincipled quest for power led the party of "principles" to accommodate 45 defectors, including well-known criminals, in its Council of Ministers of about a 100. Further, the leaders of the same caste base are fragmenting each other's voters during the elections. Ajit Singh of the Rashtriya Lok Dal and Om Prakash Chautala of the Indian National Lok Dal are competing against one another for the votes of Jats of western Uttar Pradesh and Kalyan Singh of the Rashtriya Kranti Dal is competing for a section of Dalit votes which may support either the BSP or the People's Front. How can such a socially and politically fragmented state provide a viable majority to any party or even a sizable number of seats to an important political group?

Uttar Pradesh is paying a very heavy price for complete sectarianisation and communalisation of polity and society. Sonia Gandhi in her *Maha Parivartan* rallies is correctly propagating that "Uttar Pradesh has suffered very heavily from the sectarian and backward looking politics of casteists and communalists". Economic development and good governance in Uttar Pradesh have become a dirty word in the hands of sectarian casteists and Hindu communalists. The UP Directorate of Economics and Statistics Report tells us that domestic production declined to 3.6 per cent from 7.2 per cent in 1996-1999. During these three years, production in agriculture and services fell from 8.4 per cent to 1.1 per cent, the industrial output fell from 5.3 per cent to 4.6 per cent and the debt burden of the state government in 1996-99 has risen to Rs. 92,000 crore.

Political class is completely engaged only in the politics of winning an election and its worst example is again provided by the BJP. Rajnath Singh announced the creation of "quota within quota" among the backwards and the state government could not find jobs for 40,000 people who were identified as the "other most backward castes". Political leadership of Uttar Pradesh has accepted that it is not possible to govern and develop a large state. Ajit Singh, with the support of BJP, is contesting the elections of 2002 for another division of the state for the formation of Harit Pradesh for Jats of western Uttar Pradesh.

It has been suggested that the society of Uttar Pradesh is witnessing a great social churning and anti-Brahmin backward castes and Dalits are "asserting their social right to live with dignity" under the regime of their own backward caste or Dalit parties and leaders. Since Uttar Pradesh is witnessing a kind of democratic social revolution led by the Dalit and backward caste parties and leaders, any demand for good governance for economic development and social progress is a project of "social status-quoiss". Dalits of Uttar Pradesh are demanding "self- respect" and parties of the Dalits or backwards are guarantors of "dignity for the downtrodden castes". If on the one hand the so-called agenda of "social dignity" is being propagated by proliferating backward and Dalit parties, on the other, the forces of *Hindutva* are spreading the message that Hindu India is in danger and party of the Hindus can defend and protect Hindu India against non-Hindu enemies and terrorists. Elections of 2002 are not being contested on the issues of misgovernance, growing criminality and the breakdown of law and order in Uttar Pradesh.

The electoral agenda of main parties and groups, except the Congress, is a repeat performance of 1996 state assembly elections. The clock has stopped moving in Uttar Pradesh in spite of the fact that we have entered the 21st century. The Congress under Sonia Gandhi is raising important electoral issues in Uttar Pradesh but it is sandwiched between sectarian casteists and communalists and also its own non-existing party organisation. The decade of 1990s brought clouds of darkness over Uttar Pradesh in the form of mandalisation and communalisation of society, and it was expected that the voters who have now experienced the governments of Mulayam Singh Yadav or Mayawati or the three Chief Ministers of the BJP will learn appropriate lessons and opt for progressive and developmental secular platform of the Congress. This hope for Uttar Pradesh's bright future has no takers because fragmented voters and vulgar power manipulators have captured "segments" of society where elections will be a farcical repetition of 1996 and the tragedy of backward Uttar Pradesh will continue till caste and *Hindutva* brand of politics is not completely rejected by the voters. In the 21st century a society which is engaged in fighting against the "cunningness of the past" cannot have any future in spite of regular democratic elections. (*January 26, 2002, The Tribune*)

Uttar Pradesh: Verdict for a Social Bloc

The electoral verdict of the February 2002 Uttar Pradesh Assembly elections has been nullified by the Presidential proclamation of March 8 and the Assembly placed under temporary suspension. The Governor Vishnu Kant Shastri's recommendation to the President for imposing Central rule was based on a mechanical criterion relating to the arithmetic of the "number of seats" as a determining factor among the major contenders for power. The Governor's technically correct approach made him conclude that no single party or a coalition of parties was in a position to form a Government because the verdict was completely fractured.

A democratically-elected Government can be formed in Uttar Pradesh if the mainstream voters can learn from a periphery State such as Manipur, and the Samajwadi Party (SP), the Bahujan Samaj Party (BSP), the Congress and Ajit Singh's Lok Dal are prepared to form a "Progressive Secular Front" for managing the State's affairs. The verdict of the Uttar Pradesh voters is fractured but it is decisively in favour of the socially progressive Backward Caste and Dalit parties. The BJP, which secured only 88 Assembly seats polling just 20.07 per cent of the vote, has been rejected. This in spite of Rajnath Singh's "quota within quota" scheme.

The Backward Caste and Dalit voters showed their confidence in their "own" political parties with the SP getting 146 seats and the BSP 98. Further, the percentage of votes obtained by the SP is 26.15 and the BSP 23.17. Both these parties of the Backward Castes and the Dalits have obtained more number of seats and percentage of votes than the BJP.

Why have the Backward Caste and Dalit parties not been able to form a coalition Government though their social constituencies decisively supported them? Is it only an "ego" problem between Mulayam Singh Yadav and Mayawati? Any clash of personalities cannot be ruled out as an important cause for keeping natural allies apart. The conflict of interests between the SP and the BSP is reflective of the divisions among their social constituencies. The "other backward caste" middle peasantry represented by the Yadavas comes into conflict with non-land owning Dalit castes and this division is reflected in the emergence of many parties of the Backward Castes and the Dalits.

The logic of power for its own sake can be offered as an explanation for the continuing splits among the parties whether of the high castes or the middle castes or the Dalits. It will be simplistic to say that the same caste group gets divided among many parties or leaders because of "opportunism" in politics. A deeper explanation for the emergence of more than one "claimant" for the same caste or sub-caste constituency is the fact that a homogenous "backward" or "Dalit" caste is an artificial political construct because different groups among the hierarchy of the Backward Castes and the Dalits have serious inter-caste and intra-caste clash of interests.

A telling example is provided by Kalyan Singh, erstwhile Uttar Pradesh Chief Minister, who after walking out from the BJP floated his own party banking on his "Lodh" caste. The Rashtriya Kranti Dal of Kalyan Singh, D.P. Yadav's Rashtriya Parivartan Dal, or Apna Dal etc. are being floated in the State not only because of 'personality clashes' but also because segments of castes provide "support" to their own leaders. The observable fragmentation of parties in Uttar Pradesh is a clear reflection of the "divisive" character of pure casteist politics. The decade of the 1990s is remembered for caste wars and caste versus caste politics in Uttar Pradesh. This is one part of the story of the State's electoral politics.

The question is: can a 'secular social bloc' be formed in Uttar Pradesh where the BJP stands on one side of the political divide and the SP, the BSP, the Congress and Ajit Singh's Lok Dal as natural social allies on the other? Can the State be polarised between the defeated high caste party of the Hindus, and other social forces which stand against the Brahamanical-Hindutva rule of the BJP?

The meaning of the Uttar Pradesh elections is very clear. The BJP has been completely rejected by the voters and the Government should be formed by anti-BJP social and political forces represented by the SP, the BSP, the Congress, and Ajit Singh's Lok Dal. Who will bell the cat and bring these formations together under the umbrella of a "Progressive Secular Front"?

Can the CPI(M) play the role of facilitator for formation of such a front of major anti-BJP victorious parties and social groups in Uttar Pradesh? On the occasion of his party congress in Hyderabad on March 25, the CPI(M) general secretary, Harkishan Singh Surjeet, said a decisive battle had to be launched against the BJP, which is a "grave threat to the country's unity". The CPI(M)'s People's Front can be actualised and concretised in Uttar Pradesh where a specific situation has been created as a result of the Assembly elections. It is neither necessary nor desirable to project Mr. Mulayam Singh as the sole contender for power and as the only pillar of the People's Front. Further, his claim as the sole spokesman of the State's Muslims lies shattered because Muslims have voted for the SP, the BSP, the Congress and other small secular outfits.

Since the Uttar Pradesh vote is divided among the anti-Brahamanical social forces, it is essential to bring them on one platform on the basis of a common agenda for governance. A great advantage of a progressive anti-BJP "social bloc" represented by Mr. Mulayam Singh, Ms. Mayawati, the Congress and Mr. Ajit Singh is that "pure casteist politics" will be "neutralised" when representatives of Yadavs, Kurmis, Koeris, Pasis, Jatavas, Muslims and other groups are brought together in a coalition.

A great advantage of bringing these 'conflicting castes' under the umbrella of a 'social bloc'-led Government is that it will provide caste-based checks and balances within the Government. If the BSP alone forms a Government in Uttar Pradesh, the Yadavs and other land-owning peasant castes will follow a path of opposition and confrontation with the State Government because the BSP caste-social base is absolutely opposite to that of the Yadav caste-based SP. The story will be repeated if Mr. Mulayam Singh alone forms a Government. The choice before the major anti-BJP parties of the backward and deprived social castes and classes is to form a joint anti-BJP front and launch a developmental agenda for the State or launch a Hobbesian war of "all against all" which will be nasty, poor, brutish and short because money and muscle power will rule.

The people of the State have suffered because of the complete casteisation and communalisation of politics where the agenda of development is conspicuous by its absence. Any revival of hope in Uttar Pradesh depends on creating a 'federation' of anti-high caste Backward Castes, Dalits and Muslims who would operate their own internal checks and balances to keep away the malice of casteist politics. A People's Front means a non-BJP coalition Government of the SP, the BSP, the Congress and the Lok Dal. This is the real meaning of the vote of the Assembly elections. And only this arrangement will bring back the 'agenda of development' to the centre stage of that unfortunate State. (*April 5, 2002, The Hindu*)

State Assembly Elections: Needed A Broad-Based Coalition

While the state Assembly election verdict in Punjab and Uttaranchal is clearly in favour of the Congress party for governance and the Akali Dal and BJP for playing the role of opposition in these states, the voters of Uttar Pradesh and Manipur have not given any clear verdict in favour of any party or group or leader either for the purposes of governance of their states or for performing the role of the opposition party. Further, the Congress has gained support of the voters in Punjab, Uttaranchal and Manipur but in Uttar Pradesh its performance has gone down as compared with the state Assembly elections of 1996. The focus of the analysis of Assembly elections is on the performance of the BJP. The other important issue of analysis is to understand the emerging trends of politics in Uttar Pradesh where the voters have neither completely supported the regional formation like Samajwadi Party and the BSP or an all-India party like the Congress.

Not only this. In the decade of 1990s, the BJP had emerged on the national scene with the full backing and support of large sections of Hindus' of Uttar Pradesh but during these elections it has been reduced to the third level in terms of seats in the Assembly of 403 members. Why has the BJP been decimated in Uttar Pradesh which gave birth to its agitation for the Ram temple? Why has BJP lost in Uttaranchal, which is its own creation? Why have urban Hindus in Punjab rejected a party which claims property rights over Hindu votes? The BJP bubble has burst because the myth of Hindu votes constructed by the party has been completely exposed and BJP is biting the dust. It deserves to be emphasised that there is nothing like a Hindu vote bank and the BJP has not been authorised by the Hindus to act as a sole spokesman of this religious community.

The BJP had garnered Hindu votes in Uttar Pradesh by raising the emotive issue of the Ram temple and when its state government was dismissed on December 7, 1992 for actively participating in the destruction of Babri Mosque at Ayodhya, the voters punished the BJP in the state Assembly elections of 1993 by voting out the BJP in UP, along with Madhya Pradesh and Himachal Pradesh. BJP wanted Hindus to reward the party for its misadventure on December 6, 1992, but the Hindus did the opposite. Even in the UP Assembly elections of 1996, the so-called Hindu voters did not give a clear verdict in favour of the BJP. The elections of 2002 have brought only 88 seats to the party in an Assembly of 403 members. What is the explanation for the failure of BJP to mobilise the Hindu voters? While Uttar Pradesh has not given the verdict in favour of any one political formation, the social bloc of backward castes, Dalits and Muslims has displayed its preference for the Congress, the Samajwadi Party and the BSP. The verdict is not only against *Hindutva* but it is also a clear expression of preference for the non-high caste social bloc of parties.

The voters verdict is against Hindutva but it is also a clear expression of preference for the non-high caste social bloc of parties. Congress is a secular party which is not identified with any one caste or community.

Congress is a secular party which is not identified with any one caste or community. Mulayam Singh Yadav represents an important social constituency of Yadav, backward castes and Muslims. Mayawati is an authentic representative of upwardly mobile Dalits, Jatavas and Muslims. The BJP's ideology is reflective of the *Brahamanical* social order. The meaning of UP verdict is that all those social groups which are against this order and its political representative like the BJP, prefer a rule by the Congress, Mulayam Singh Yadav or Mayawati because they represent the majority of the social bloc. The point to be emphasised is that the BJP emerged on the scene by exploiting emotions of a section of Hindus and manipulating their vote. Elections bereft of emotive issues have exposed the BJP completely because there is nothing like a Hindu vote bank. Further, Congress, SP and BSP should do a lot of self-introspection to realise their own follies which brought the BJP on the scene.

Uttar Pradesh has suffered because the politics of social development of the whole state was abandoned in the decade of 1990s. Casteist leaders created a situation where Uttar Pradesh did not have a state government for the whole state. Mulayam Singh Yadav's government brought the Yadav caste into the corridors of power, and Mayawati's two tenures as the chief minister witnessed upwardly mobile Dalits occupying the seats of power and decision-making. The BJP does not even pretend to be a party of all the communities and social coalition which has expressed a clear preference for Congress, SP and BSP. If it does not accept this social reality, Uttar Pradesh will decline further. It is absurd to claim that Mulayam Singh Yadav is the sole representative of secular forces in Uttar Pradesh. Congress and Bahujan Samaj party have impeccable secular credentials and secular coalition of these three political formations deserves to govern the state because this is the meaning of electoral verdict of 2002 in Uttar Pradesh.

The Punjab politics should be observed carefully because the Akali Dal is dangerous in defeat. Parkash Singh Badal has already signaled that he will play the Sikh communal card by announcing the construction of a memorial of the 'martyrs' of the Bluestar Operation of 1984. G.S. Tohra has also alleged that the Akali Dal has been defeated in 2002 because Badal did not promote and protect Panthic interests. The stalwarts of Sikh communalism have not learnt any lesson from the tragedy of the Punjab of 1980s and 1990s. Akalis out of office play an emotional card of 'historic grievances of the Sikhs' and encourage Hindu-Sikh divide and urban-rural divide. The Congress party should also learn from its blunders of the past because Zail Singh had encouraged Indira Gandhi to create a monster called Jarnail Singh Bhinderawale.

To sum up, communal and secular parties have created a piquant situation where the state apparatus gets communalised and castesised. Communalism cannot be fought by caste sectarianism. Hence a social coalition which cuts across all castes and communities should lead the politically most crucial state. (*March 1, 2002, Rashtriya Sahara*)

The Opportunism of Dalit "Elites"

The Sangh Parivar has taken upon itself the responsibility of protecting the Hindu religion from Buddhism or Christianity because many Dalits prefer to walk out of the tyrannical *Brahamanical* social order. Bajrang Dal and Vishwa Hindu Parishad demanded from the Vajpayee government that it should impose a ban on a function organised in Delhi for the conversion of Dalits to Buddhism in November 2001. However, Udit Raj, a senior civil servant, has publicly announced that he will continue to organise such large scale conversions of Dalits to Buddhism. Udit Raj of the Scheduled Caste/Scheduled Tribe Civil Service Organisation is the latest to launch such a movement. Many great leaders have made attempts to reform Hindu religion but some leaders launched movements to end *Brahamanical* hegemony by creating a separate Dalit identity because Hindu religion does not have any capacity for a large scale internal reform of its tyrannical caste hierarchical system. The twentieth century witnessed a very powerful anti-Brahman movements in Tamil Nadu, Maharashtra and in other parts of India with a view to liberate Dalits from Hindu oppression and provide a separate identity to Dalits. Because of Gandhi-Ambedkar efforts, the social agenda of Dalit movements is now fully integrated with the political agenda of democratic governance of India. The issue of Dalits in India has moved away from Hindu religious scriptures to the Constitution of India and from the domain of priestly class to Parliament and political parties. Since *Brahamanical* social order could not be reformed by its inner dynamics, Parliamentary legislation became a necessary instrument for protecting the Dalits against discrimination and humiliation inflicted on them. This merger of social reform movement of Dalits with democratic politics of India has clearly revealed that Dalit reform movement has been infected with all the evils of mainstream politics of the country.

An important question is: Is Dalit politics different from other all-India political parties or regional and sub-regional parties? The Dalit elite who has emerged during the last fifty three years is articulating specific Dalit issues and concerns. How have the Dalit political parties or leaders been able to transform Dalit social life by using power of Central and State governments? A few facts may be mentioned to substantiate the argument that the larger agenda of Dalit movement gets seriously compromised by the Dalit leaders and Dalit political parties because Dalits have not been able to project an alternative political model of governance. Take the issue of reservations for Dalits in public institutions of every kind, *i.e.* from Panchayat to Parliament and from clerk to Cabinet Secretary, has been a common agenda of every political party including the BJP which is a party of high caste Hindus. Further, the issue of reservations for Dalits in public institutions has become a cementing factor irrespective of political divide in India and political leaders like Rajnath Singh of the Uttar Pradesh BJP is worried about the 'most backward castes' and he has instituted a "quota within quota" for real Dalits and many backward caste leaders have been busy in getting different castes like Jats in the reservation lists of the Backward Castes. It can be argued that the contentious issue of reservations for Dalits in public institutions has achieved a national political consensus because of the Dalit social movements, Dalit leaders and Dalit political parties. At the end of the day, reservation is not a special Dalit issue because every political party has consented for its acceptance and implementation. This political consensus was shown in Parliament when the 92 Amendment of the Constitution of India was unanimously approved and Article 16 was amended "to ensure seniority to SCs and STs by virtue of reservations".

Have Dalit political parties pursued any special programme for the real upliftment of the poor and really oppressed Dalits which are basically different from other mainstream all-India or regional parties? The answer to this question is a big no. Mulayam Singh Yadav of Uttar Pradesh, Laloo Prasad Yadav of Bihar and Mayawati of the Bahujan Samaj Party have done nothing to disturb the agrarian power arrangements by undertaking the "unfinished" agenda of land reforms in Uttar Pradesh and Bihar. These Messiahs of Dalit politics have protected the status quo of Bihar and Uttar Pradesh social order by not changing land relations in rural areas. If Dalit parties or leaders had done anything concrete for the uplift of the real poor Dalit, the National Commission for SCs/STs in its report of 2000 AD on the basis of National Crime Bureau record would not have shown that crimes against SCs and STs in 2000 AD were committed against 23,742 Dalits and Uttar Pradesh is at the top of the list where 6,599 scheduled castes were victims of registered crimes which were committed against them. Rulers of Bihar have not been able to check caste wars irrespective of the governmental power being exercised by the Messiahs of Dalits.

Unfortunately, Dalit leaders have not shown any special distinction as a role model of an alternative Dalit politics. Ramvilas Paswan, Sharad Yadav, Mayawati, Kanshi Ram and others have practiced vulgar politics of compromises and opportunism. No mainstream political party is untouchable for the Dalit leaders, parties and groups. Ms. Mayawati became Chief Minister of Uttar Pradesh with the approval and support of its opponent *Manuwadi* BJP and the RJP successfully engineered a split in the USP, and a so-called Kisan Majdoor Bahujan party was formed by "defectors" from the BSP who along with another "splinter" group known as Loktantrik Congress party joined the BJP coalition, and Uttar Pradesh has witnessed that the politics of contradictions between Dalits and *Hindutva* comes to an end when sharing the spoils of office and the benefits of power. The Vajpayee-led Government at the centre is a great testimony to the fact that Dalit leadership is as power hungry as the so-called Manuwadi parties.

Moreover, the cause of Dalit movement has suffered a big set back because of Dalit parties, leaders and groups. Dalit Movement is led by Dalit intellectuals, writers, civil servants, non-government organisations and a lot of Dalit literature is being written to strengthen Dalit social solidarity while the goal of Dalit social movement is to create an all-inclusive Dalit social category. Dalit politicians are engaged in fragmenting the Dalits. A moot question can be asked: Is there an all-India Dalit social category? Leaders of Dalit social movement have projected Phule or Dr. B.R. Ambedkar as leaders of all-Dalits but politics of Dalit leaders is at variance with the goal of unity of Dalit social reformers. The ruling classes of India are quite happy with the ongoing process of fragmentation of parties, castes and groups because an all-India united struggle of the oppressed threatens the social *status quo* and Paswans, Yadavs, Kurmis, Koris, Jatavas, Mohars, Chammars, Dhobis, etc. should remain separate from other Dalit groups because separate and small Dalit pockets can be managed effectively by the ruling classes. Dalit politics has taken a path where its distinctness is under great suspicion.

A Dalit leader has asked the Dalits to "Live like a tiger, not like a goat". Udit Raj, a new-convert Dalit to Buddhism has to answer many inconvenient and difficult questions about the 'model' of politics of Dalit parties. A great achievement of the emergence of Dalit politics in the decade of 1990s is visible in small towns where Dalits are challenging the Hindu domination. A feeling of self-respect and dignity has percolated to Dalits with the emergence of Mayawatis, Kanshirams and Neo-Buddhist movement. Social assertions by Dalits have become an idiom of new democratic politics of India and atrocities against Dalits are getting highlighted and many a time successfully resisted. One of the goals of Dalit social movement has been achieved with the emergence of Dalit parties that Dalits can breathe well with dignity. Mayawati provides a sense of "social respect" to Dalits. This positive achievement of the ongoing Dalit social movement is threatened by the logic of power pursued by Dalit parties. Even leaders of the Dalit Social Movement are gradually getting "co-opted" in the system and the Dalit elite has all the vices and virtues of the Hindu or Muslim elite. It is possible that like opportunistic Dalit politics, Dalit social movement may also get derailed because the real Dalit elite are distancing themselves from the real poor and oppressed Dalits. (*January 12, 2002, The Pioneer*)

Dalit Politics: What India Needs is More Democracy

Chandra Bhan Prasad, in his contribution '50 *years of democracy in reverse gear*' (May 19), has made observations which deserve to be contested. While dealing with post-Independence democratic experiment of India, Prasad has failed to understand the impact which competitive electoral politics based on democratic universal adult franchise has made on the age-old *Varna*-based social order.

A few facts may be mentioned to substantiate the argument that adult suffrage combined with the holding of regular elections in India has played a revolutionary role in reshaping of the inherited "old social order". First, Indian electoral politics has witnessed a great shift away from the early phase of high caste controlled "vote banks" based on "patron-client" relationships, to a large scale participation of the downtrodden castes and classes in the decade of 1990s. Hence, the participatory democracy of the 1990s is a break with the past because of the growing social and political assertions of the downtrodden, oppressed and suppressed caste and classes.

Second, Prasad has not been able to capture an all-India picture because he does not relate regional differences with the levels of participation and assertions of the Dalits. Since Tamil Nadu or Maharashtra had witnessed powerful anti-Brahman social reform movements in pre-Independence India, political changes in these states were felt in the early 1960s as compared to the North Indian states where such social reform movements had not taken place in the twentieth century.

Third, Mr. Prasad has totally rejected power relationships in agrarian India when he wrongly constructs a *Shudra* identity category by constructing a "Non-Brahman-non-Dalits (or the middle castes).

One must note that Indian *varna* is based on socially *Achuta* (untouchable), *Malechchas* (impure) and *Shudras* categories, which convey many different meanings in ancient Hindu texts. It is here the *varna* system showed its real face. It is absurd to bring together Chaudhary Charan Singh in the category of *Achutas* by constructing a category of *Shudras* for Jats or Yadavas or other peasant castes.

Moreover, Mr. Prasad is also totally confused in his analysis because on the one hand he recognises the land owning power of the "middle castes" whom he describes as *Shudras*, and on the other, he has abruptly concluded that *Shudras*, the land owning peasant castes, "are turning (Indian democracy) into reverse gear." Does he mean to convey that

Dalits along with Brahmans are better defenders of democracy than the backward castes, or perhaps that the backward castes are not capable of leading the country towards progress unlike their upper caste counterparts?

Therefore, while Dalit intellectuals and political leaders like Mr. Kanshi Ram and Ms Mayawati are not helpful in the analysis of changing caste realities of India, it must be realised that under the powerful impact of universal franchise the construction of identity like Dalits, or *Shudras* or Bahujan Samaj for that matter, is at best, arbitrary and at worst fanciful. Dalits or *Shudras* or Bahujan Samaj has its own hierarchy and a scavenger caste (sweeper) or *Chamar* is inferior to *Dhobi* (washerman) and *Nai* (barber).

In this jungle of Indian caste system, it is false bravado to pit Ambedkar against Gandhi by maintaining that Dalit category is more meaningful and nearer social reality than Gandhi's *Harijan*. It is this that leads Mr. Prasad to make *Shudra* category as applicable to all middle caste peasants. Do the Jats of Uttar Pradesh or Haryana or Rajasthan consider themselves *Shudras*?

Not only this. In Gujarat, Jats have migrated to higher caste of Rajputs. Upward caste mobility is as important a reality of Indian society as caste-*varna* hierarchy.

The upshot of above argument is that Mr. Prasad has not grappled with the phenomenon of social and political change in contemporary India. The traditional land owning high castes have been challenged and replaced by the backward caste middle peasantry. The Mandal Commission recommendations were implemented to satisfy the "new power caste elite" of the backwards. If Mr. Prasad had analysed these social and political shifts in India, he would not have concluded that democracy is in reverse gear. Social dialectics of India has many contradictory faces and an interplay of negative and positive factors in society is observable.

Displacement of powerful social groups cannot be a smooth affair. It is a tribute to Indian democracy that the socially neglected castes and groups are heard in the corridors of power. Fenon's *The wretched of the Earth* are provided with a powerful weapon of "vote" and during the last 55 years, the power of the vote has shown many positive and negative social results. India needs "more democracy" because democracy has its own cleansing mechanisms. (*June 3, 2002, The Pioneer*)

Why is Mulayam Singh Angry?

Mr. Mulayam Singh Yadav has been lionised by communist parties and liberal-progressive intellectuals on the basis of his secular credentials. But this leader of the Yadavs in Uttar Pradesh is unhappy not only with his Marxist friends, but also quite agitated by the fact the UP Chief Minister's office is out of reach. BSP leader Ms. Mayawati has formed an alliance with the BJP to keep him out of power. Hence, of late, his every action is conditioned by his political frustrations.

He had walked out of the People's Front when he decided to support the presidential candidature of Dr. A.P.J. Abdul Kalam against Left nominee Lakshmi Sahgal. A few days before he backed the NDA candidate, Mr. Mulayam Singh had agreed to an Opposition's plan to support Mr. K.R. Narayanan. Since the latter did not agree to contest the elections, he parted company with the Left.

Yet, on August 24, the Samajwadi Party leader castigated Dr. Kalam for returning the Ordinance on electoral reforms to the Atal Bihari Vajpayee Government. He described the demand for a re-look as a "matter of grave concern", since the Ordinance reflected "political consensus". He said that by, "questioning the Government's sagacity", Dr. Kalam had acted "against the true spirit of the Constitution". During his uncalled for "outburst" against the Head of State, he warned the latter against being "guided by some intellectuals" who were "ignorant of the ground realities of Indian politics". The SP supremo also did not attend Mr. Somnath Chatterjee's dinner to cement "Opposition unity" on August 27.

Mr. Mulayam Singh is also angry with the Congress. He refused to support Ms. Sonia Gandhi in April, 1999, when the then President, Mr. Narayanan, had to find an alternative Prime Minister because the Vajpayee Government had been defeated by one vote in the Lok Sabha on April 17. He also was livid with the Congress in 2002, when after the UP elections, it kept aloof from the Samajwadi Party, due to which the BJP, BSP and the National Lok Dal alliance was able to take over. The Congress avenged in 2002 his refusal to back Ms. Gandhi in 1999.

Mr. Mulayam Singh's political ambitions and frustrations have a bearing on UP politics and also on future coalitions at the Centre. What kind of leader is he? Does he have any progressive social philosophy? How did he conduct himself as Chief Minister? What is the nature of his social constituency?

The SP leader claims to be a follower of the socialist leader, Ram Manohar Lohia. Lohia's socialism was flawed and his attempt to construct a new model of Asian socialism for agrarian societies was mere kite-flying. His great revolutionary hope was the middle peasantry—in the concrete context of India's agrarian society, the OBC middle peasantry. UP's Mulayam Singh and Bihar's Laloo Prasad Yadav are 'socialist revolutionaries', testifying to Lohia's ideological bankruptcy.

Lohia's Yadavs, Koris, Kurmis and other backward *jatis* are the new "oppressors" in North India's rural society, as the new land-owning, surplus-producing castes and classes. Mr. Mulayam Singh's attitude towards Ms. Mayawati is conditioned by the caste-class hierarchy pitting Yadavs against Dalits. It is not by accident that a Dalit party formed an alliance with practitioners of Brahminical *Hindutva* and not with the Yadav-led SP. The "grassroot reality", to which he referred while chastising Dr. Kalam, is his own championship of this class of oppressors versus Ms. Mayawati, the 'oppressed'. Neither Lohia nor his disciple can resolve this social antagonism.

Lohia's ideological woolly-headedness did not end there. He identified English-speaking minority castes and classes as enemies of his brand of socialism, and wanted English replaced by Hindi. He felt this would empower the oppressed non-English speaking Indians. If this logic is extended to the whole of India. Lohia's socialism will remain confined to the backward States of UP and Bihar. Mr. Mulayam Singh is a fanatical supporter of Hindi as the so-called national language. This has led to his political confinement in UP. He is thus a parochial leader of a particular backward State, and has nothing to do with any kind of socialism.

Lohialites like him have always opposed the Congress's 'dynastic politics'. Yet Mr. Mulayam Singh has no problem making his own son an MP. His political shop has luminaries like Mr. Amar Singh and he hobnobs with Mr. Amitabh Bachchan and Mr. Anil Ambani. With the help of these privileged friends, he aspires to usher in socialism. All of it clearly proves the SP leader seeks power in UP to promote a network of patronage so that he or his son can be the Chief Minister in UP or Ministers at the Centre.

Which brings us to the 'reality' of today's political processes. The emergence of coalitions at the Centre, the gradual decline of the all-India Congress and its replacement by regional forces was celebrated. It was expected to transform the quality of politics by ending the four decades of the 'corrupt' Congress's dominance. The euphoria has proved short-lived. Alternatives to the Congress have imbibed the very culture they accuse it of. The Congress's replacement by casteist/regional forces has neither ended corruption nor thrown up an alternative model of governance.

Corruption in public life has multiplied. Parties and groups contesting national and State elections collect funds via a system of "cash-for-contract". Why does Mr. Mulayam Singh need Mr. Amar Singh, a lobbyist for big business? Why does Shiv Sena supremo Bal Thackeray want Mr. Suresh Prabhu removed as Union Power Minister? Besides, regional parties need to be evaluated on the basis of their performance. Did Mr. Mulayam Singh project any new picture for UP that was fundamentally different from that of much-maligned Congress Chief Ministers?

The Nineties witnessed the emergence of 'regionalists' who are now busy creating new sub-regional States to occupy chief ministerial office. The creation of Uttaranchal, Jharkhand or Chhatisgarh or a proposed Vidharbha or Telengana are the result of the growth of regional, inter-regional and intra-regional competition and conflict. If regional leaders like Mr. Mulayam, Mr. Laloo Yadav, Mr. M. Karunanidhi and Mr. N. Chandrababu Naidu were lionised as challengers of the corrupt Congress, regional and sub-regional competition was accentuated, since coalitions at the Centre were dependent on regional/sub-regional leaders.

Mr. Ajit Singh supports any and every coalition at the Centre because he wants to be Chief Minister of a new state Harit Pradesh, carved out of UP. If Uttaranchal could be thus created, why not a State for Ajit Singh? Regionalism has not brought a new style of governance. Every political group in the Vajpayee Government, including the BJP, pursues its own agenda. Instead of bringing any coherence in the Government, coalitions are marked by the chaos created by mutually antagonistic groups.

Ms. Mamata Banerjee attacks Nitish Kumar, Mr. Thackeray humiliates the Centre by demanding replacements of individual Shiv Sena Ministers, and the BJP pursues *Hindutva*. When Mr. Mulayam Singh was Defence Minister in the short-lived H.D. Deve Gowda and I.K. Gujral dispensations, he was busy in promoting his own interests in UP.

Like any other regional satrap, Mr. Mulayam Singh lacks an all-India vision. Hence he is angry. He is out of power in his own State and he has no interest in national issues when out of power. All regional leaders like him represent segments of a caste, which compels them to form coalitions in their own respective States. The examples of Maharashtra, Orissa, UP and Bihar amply illustrate this truth. (*7th Sept., 2002, The Pioneer*)

4

Bending the Constitution and Federal Relations

A Living Constitution

During a special session of the Indian Parliament held on January 27, 2000, the President K.R. Narayanan, and the Prime Minister, Atal Bihari Vajpayee, found themselves in opposite camps while celebrating the completion of fifty years of the Republic and the Constitution of India. While the President unequivocally defended the working of parliamentary constitutional democracy of India, the Prime Minister took a position in favour of a comprehensive "review of the Constitution" by a Review Commission.

While the BJP-led National Democratic Alliance has stated in its election manifesto that the growing political instability is harmful and dysfunctional for economic development of the country, the President has argued that "accountability and transparent behaviour" of the elected political representatives is more important than the search for political stability through the mechanism of review of the Constitution. The essence of the debate between the President and the Prime Minister lies in their approach towards the existing parliamentary democratic system as it is, or some kind of amendment of the system which combines some elements of presidentialism along with the parliamentary system. Vajpayee has made the plank of "political stability" as the crux of the issue and constitutional review is perceived by him as an effort to ensure the elected political representatives a fixed term of five years. This fixity of tenure of elected political executive is an essential feature of presidentialism and not of the parliamentary system of democracy. The upshot of this debate on Constitution is between parliamentary and accountable democracy or fixed tenurial rule by an elected political executive like the presidential system of the USA or the chancellor system of Germany. Every other argument for the need of constitutional reviews is linked with the basic issue of relevance or irrelevance of parliamentary or presidential system for an effective governance of India with a view to achieving political stability. Hence, the President and the Prime Minister have fundamental differences on the capacity of the system of governance as provided by the Indian Constitution. Incidentally, during the Emergency regime of Indira Gandhi in 1975-77, such a demand for a fixed term for an elected and powerful chief executive was articulated by some supporters of the Emergency regime because political stability was the slogan of Indira Gandhi and it was strongly opposed by the present political ruling group.

The central issue is that the parliamentary system of democracy has stood the test of time and it has achieved these goals of governance for which the constitution makers preferred the parliamentary over the presidential system for India.

Why is the parliamentary system of democracy appropriate for the governance of a diverse, pluralist and continent-sized country like India? India has every conceivable diversity and every group expects to be represented in the government.

Parliamentary democracy ensures that different multiple groups can be accommodated in the system of governance by providing them with an opportunity to participate in governance and also feel that they are as important as any other linguistic or cultural or religious group of the country. India has multiple kinds of majorities and minorities and they get a feeling of "togetherness" by participating in the Indian system of governance. Parliamentary system has achieved national integration by providing representation to the diverse peoples of South, North, North-West and North-East India.

And it is only in such a system that people from Arunachal Pradesh to Jammu and Kashmir can get involved in the sharing of political power for governance. Political unity of a diverse and pluralist country like India cannot be taken for granted unless every region or every cultural group is involved in the governance of the whole of India. This concept of the whole of India is acceptable to all if they have a right to enter Parliament, and become a member of the council of ministers.

Further, the Central Government of India has to be collectively accountable for the governance of the whole country, but regional or group representatives in the council of ministers act as a link between their social constituency and the Central government. Parliamentary system of democracy during the last fifty years has ensured horizontal and vertical accountability of the political executive of the Centre.

Democratic political system has stood the test of times not only because multiple groups have developed a feeling that "it is our government" but also because "we have our minister" in the government. It is worth mentioning that every state of the Indian Republic has multiple social groups and inter-state and intra-state imbalances. Parliamentary democratic institutions at the level of Indian states also ensure participation of all regions, sub-regions, dominant groups and multiple sub-groups in the processes of governance.

The Constitution of India has shown enough flexibility and adaptability during the last fifty years and 79 constitutional amendments have made this document a living and dynamic framework for the governance of a diverse country. Parliamentary system has fulfilled the felt social needs of multiple groups.

The upshot of the above discussion is that tinkering with the philosophy and basic structure of the Constitution is fraught with dangers because making the Constitution a subject of public and political controversy will generate unending disputes. (*February 1, 2000, The Observer*)

Casting a Shadow on Development

The political class in a democracy is always responsive to the socially felt needs and aspirations of multiple groups and parties, because organised structures of politics represent diverse and competing interests and the needs of multiple groups in society.

The ongoing controversy on the need and rationale for the National Commission to review the Working of the Constitution by the BJP-led Government is a sign of the health of Indian democracy because both the supporters and opponents of a constitutional review have joined the public debate. That the Head of the State and Head of the Government are actively participating on issues raised by the "Consultation Papers" issued by the commission should be welcomed.

The central issue raised by the President and the Prime Minister which has evinced conflicting responses concerns the stability of the Union Government. While the Prime Minister has attracted the nation's attention to the need for "political stability for good governance", the President has suggested that there is no need to overemphasise the importance of stability and uniformity. He has also pointed out that the founding fathers of our Constitution had the wisdom and foresight not to over-value stability and had preferred more responsibility.

There is actually no need for a review to ensure stability, because constitutional legality for a fixed term of five years can prove to be dangerous for the functioning of parliamentary democracy. The sources of political stability lie in the political process, and correctives will also emerge only from the democratic-electoral process itself. Further, our fixation on political stability and instability of elected government is completely off the mark because in almost all states of India, elected Governments have continued to complete their full term.

Also, the present defenders of the need for political stability have been vocal critics and opponents of the forty years of the dominance of the Congress.

The main argument of anti-Congress political groups was that the culture of political corruption was born because of the Congress's monopoly of power. Congress Governments were castigated for every evil in the body politic and movements were launched to remove the Congress from power.

Jayaprakash Narayan launched movements in Gujarat and Bihar in 1974-75 on the issue of corruption in public life and the participants in the J P movement had demanded resignation of Congress ministers even before they completed their full terms.

The moral of this story is that stable Congress Governments were equated with corruption and it was felt that the people had to be saved from arrogant and corrupt politicians who misused and abused their power because they were in place for five years. A section of the Indian political class has always articulated the opinion that stability not only makes elected representatives corrupt but also desensitises them to the changing needs of society.

The opponents of Congress domination were not far from the truth when they thought that political stability had given birth to corruption in public life. Further, the quality of governance does not depend on the stability of legislatures for five years.

Mr. Laloo Prasad Yadav of Bihar and his wife, Ms. Rabri Devi, have given great political stability to Bihar alongwith "Goonda Raj". And is the BJP satisfied with the performance of its own State Government in Uttar Pradesh? They have had to try out three Chief Ministers during the last four years.

Actually, a Government's stability is a "neutral factor" as far as quality of governance is concerned. Good governance is closely linked with a perspective on economic development. A stable government can be "status quo-ist" and socially regressive. At best, political stability may be necessary but it can never be a sufficient condition for good governance.

Moreover, the issue of "stability" cannot be delinked from the issues of politics which emerged in a big way in the 1990s. The implementation of the Mandal Commission recommendations by Mr. V.P. Singh in August 1990 came as a bombshell for the States in the Hindi belt where caste equations collapsed.

The backward castes emerged as a powerful force because Mr. V.P. Singh clearly recognised that the socially assertive backward castes would challenge the social power of the upper castes.

Caste politics gave birth to multiple political formations in Uttar Pradesh and Bihar because every sub-caste was led by its own leader. If Mr. Laloo Yadav emerged as a leader of the Yadavs, Kurmis looked towards Mr. Nitish Kumar. Many Janata Dals emerged in the 1990s because peasant castes cannot create a cohesive social coalition for the simple reason that caste identities are divisive. It is very simplistic to suggest that Janata Dals have split because of the clash of personal ambitions.

Politics is reflective of social dynamics in the Hindi heartland where confrontational caste identities are determining electoral verdicts in a highly fragmented manner. This on-going process of social-caste fragmentation is the cause of the emergence of multiple groups in politics. Political competition in reality has become competition among castes and sub-castes and a constitutional review commission should not be allowed to suggest any legalistic remedies to deal with specific social processes generated in post-Mandal North India.

The BJP is finding it extremely difficult to combine its politics of *Hindutva* with the caste reality of Hindu society. Coalition Governments at the Centre are a consequence of the process of social change and NDA leaders are a product of this process. Illogically, the NDA wants stable government in a situation of socially unstable caste competition. It is possible that North India will settle down when caste fatigue sets in. Politics and real issues of development will then occupy the centre stage.

It is essential to allow caste politics to come to an end because only then will the masses and leaders realise the futility of using caste to mobilise. The upshot of the above description is that caste politics has to exhaust itself before the agenda of development again becomes the real concern of people, parties and leaders.

The voters should be allowed to learn through their own experience that neither the issues of caste nor the construction of a Ram Temple can provide answers to their basic needs; and this new learning process is quite observable in North India.

Any artificial intervention to prevent this process of self-learning will be extremely counter-productive to the growth of Indian democracy because the major premise of democracy is that the people find their own answers through a process of trial and error.

The constitutional review commission should be abolished because answers to political questions will be found only through the political process of representative democracy. The politics of caste and religion will be weakened only when the politics of "*rozi-roti*" (jobs and bread) finds some serious takers. (*February 14, 2001, The Pioneer*)

Political Stability has its Price

The Prime Minister, in his address on May 13, 2002 on the occasion of the Golden Jubilee of Parliament, reaffirmed his Government's resolve to protect and preserve the "basic structure of the Indian Constitution". Why did Mr. Atal Bihari Vajpayee feel it necessary to reiterate this commitment? Is there any doubt in the public mind about the BJP-led Government's intentions vis-a-vis the basic foundational principles and institutional arrangements of the Republican Constitution of India?

The NDA Government raised unnecessary controversy through its appointment of a National Constitutional Review Commission to examine the so called inadequacies of the Constitutional framework, as provided by India's Constituent Assembly. Despite the fact that Justice M.N. Venkatachaliah finished his work of constitutional review on March 31, 2002, a vocal section of opinion-makers—rightly or wrongly identified with the Sangh Parivar—continues to argue that the parliamentary system of democracy needs fundamental restructuring to maintain political stability.

Since the plea to reform the parliamentary system, to ensure stable governance for five years, has been made by important NDA leaders, it merits serious analysis and scrutiny. The Constitutional Review Commission, the 11 members of which were Government nominees, has tried to find some remedy whereby stability may be achieved in the coalition era. However, India is unlikely to achieve stability at the Centre in the foreseeable future. Neither can any party get a majority of seats nor can proliferating parties or groups be stopped from contesting elections. Hence the champions of stability have tried to build a strong case by suggesting fundamental amendments to the Constitution.

The Constitutional Review Commission, after studying some Constitutions of Western democracies, suggested that the prime ministerial candidate be elected by the elected members in a formal Lok Sabha meeting. It said the Prime Minister should not be removed by a vote of no-confidence unless the Lok Sabha nominates an alternative. The essence of this procedure lies in ensuring a five-year term for the Prime Minister. The present system, whereby a leader who loses his parliamentary majority quits prime ministerial office, is to be replaced by the so-called new method of "constructive vote of confidence".

However, the German model of a "constructive vote of confidence" for the removal of the Chancellor has nothing to do with the letter and spirit of parliamentary democracies like the UK, Australia or Canada. The most harmful implication is that the Prime Minister should become a permanent functionary, as under the American or French presidential forms of Government. The German system combines elements of the US presidential system and British parliamentary democracy. The Chancellor is accountable to the elected legislature, but he is assured a four-year tenure because he can be removed only after Parliament has approved an alternative candidate.

Incidentally, the German system is not stable because of the 'constructive vote of confidence', as understood by the Indian constitutional experts. Stability is due to competition between the two major parties of the Socialists and the Christian Democrats, between whom the chancellorship has alternated, supported by a few small parties. The moral of German story is that stability owes to the party system, not Constitutional provisions.

Another fanciful idea is the French model of presidential elections. In the first round of elections in France on April 21, 2002, three candidates—Mr. Jacques Chirac of the Centre-Right, the Socialist candidate, Mr. Lionel Jospin, and the far right National Front's Jean-Marie Le Pen—emerged as contenders for power. Since the socialist candidate secured third place, he was automatically eliminated from the competition, as required by the French Constitution. During the second round on May 5, 2002, Mr. Chirac won because the majority of voters swayed in his favour. The champions of 'second round' elections on the French pattern are repeating the same mistake as they did with the German Model. France has a Presidential system, in which the occupant is not accountable to Parliament.

The makers of the Indian Constitution had opted for full-fledged parliamentary democracy, as existing in Commonwealth countries. The

Council of Ministers led by a Prime Minister is an integral part of the Parliament. Only MPs can be ministers and Prime Minister, remaining in office as long as they have majority support in the elected lower house.

The parliamentary system combines the principle of majority support to the Prime Minister and full acceptability to the elected House of Parliament. It does not accept the principle of prime ministerial power without a clear majority. The Prime Minister has to quit office if he loses the confidence of the majority of Lok Sabha members. He can be changed mid-stream if the latter so wish, expressing themselves through a no-confidence vote.

The Vajpayee Government was in serious difficulty when the Opposition wanted a debate on Gujarat's communal violence under Rule 184, since discussions would have ended with a formal vote in the Lok Sabha. Since the BJP was uncertain about the support of some 'coalition partners', it was hesitant to accept a debate under Rule 184.

The beauty of the parliamentary system is that a Prime Minister can be held accountable for any serious lapse on the part of his Government whenever MPs feel he must answer to society. If he cannot be removed even after he has lost support, the system of governance ceases to be a parliamentary democracy and becomes a Presidential form of government.

It is sophistry to say Lok Sabha members should not voluntarily move a vote of no-confidence. Elected representatives have a right to support or depose a government on the basis of their own understanding of the changing political landscape. What, after all, is the role of an elected Lok Sabha or state Assembly member with relation to the political executive of the Central and State governments? Should a party or a group of parties be stopped from expressing their lack of confidence in a Prime Minister they supported at one time and who they no longer find up to the mark?

The issue is not stability in the coalition era, but the Council of Ministers' accountability before Parliament. "Constructive vote of confidence" curtails the right of Lok Sabha members to realign themselves and replace the Prime Minister. Parties and groups in Parliament should change their partners and make alternative arrangements for governance if they feel dissatisfied. Even a defeated vote of confidence on the floor of the House provides Lok Sabha members an opportunity to oppose the Government. It is also an occasion for the Prime Minister to defend the latter's actions.

Accountability is a condition of the parliamentary system. It does not become irrelevant the moment a Prime Minister gains the support of the majority of Lok Sabha members. Political instability is a result of social 'transition'. Dalits and other oppressed and exploited social groups actively participate in the electoral process and assert their rights. Further, parties are multiplying because politics is considered lucrative. Greed has destroyed the party system. In this period of social change and political opportunism, artificial constitutional restructuring to impose stability at the Centre is indefensible. The attempt to manipulate voters' choices through a so called constitutional reform (by invoking the ghost of instability) is clearly directed against the fundamentals of India's parliamentary democracy. The Constitutional Review Commission has made a wrong diagnosis of the causes of instability. Hence, its prescription is dangerous. (*June 1, 2002, The Pioneer*)

Governance: Cleaning India's Electoral Stables

Every conscious citizen has an agenda for electoral reforms, but political parties, leaders and groups are absolutely unconcerned and indifferent towards them. In fact, every political party or group has developed a great interest in money and muscle power for winning elections, from panchayats to Parliament, and Indians have evolved their indigenous Bharatiya methodology for influencing voters by employing all manner of disingenuous methods with a view to ensure electoral victory.

Every Chief Election Commissioner, without exception, has made constructive suggestions to eradicate specific evils in the Indian democratic electoral process. Electronic machines and identity cards for voters were considered important devices for improving the quality of elections but even these steps have not produced the desired results. The National Commission to Review the Working of the Constitution of India submitted its voluminous report on March 30, 2002 and one detailed set of recommendations deals with the difficult problem of restoring the integrity of the electoral process in the country.

For the sake of public record, MPs have shown great interest for remedying the evil of money power in elections and they have pleaded that the "state funding of elections" will help reduce the dependence of political parties on fund providers. They argue that parties need money for contesting an election and thus funds should be legally provided by the Government. Further, it has been maintained by public actors that "fund providers should be legally allowed to donate for elections", else parties will have to accept funds in a clandestine manner. Since MPs are extremely 'committed' to 'electoral reforms', the Election and Other Related Laws (Amendment) Bill 2002 was introduced in the Lok Sabha on March 19, 2002, with a view to change some of the provisions of the Income Tax Act, 1961, the Representation of Peoples Act, 1951, and the Companies Act, 1956. The sum total of these amendments is that "political parties are allowed to accept donation from any person or company" and the "quantum of such donations" will be declared in public and audited by the Comptroller and Auditor General of India. The greatest virtue attributed to this Amendment Bill is that "donations to parties will become transparent". It rectifies the mischief done by Indira Gandhi, who had legally banned donations from the corporate sector, the consequence of which was that the Congress party became the sole recipient of clandestine funds. It was projected as the fountainhead of corruption in public life and this led Jayaprakash Narayan to launch a movement in Gujarat and Bihar in 1974-75 for the dismissal of the Congress-led State governments. It was alleged that they had won the elections on the basis of corrupt practices.

The essence of the JP Movement was to restore "legitimacy to democracy" by cleansing the body-politic of electoral illegitimacies. Even after about three decades of public debate, the issue continues to remain unresolved. It is essential here to refer to a few new developments in party politics with a view to substantiate the argument.

The Indian political scenario has witnessed a sea change as a consequence to the continuing decline of the Congress's dominance over the country. Every major party or group is either in Government or in Opposition. Not only this, today's ruling party may be in the Opposition tomorrow and *vice-versa*. Changing loyalties has become a rule and has ceased to be considered an exception. The V.P. Singh Government remained in office for 11 months in 1989-90, the Chandra Shekhar Government enjoyed power only for six months during 1991-96 and the P.V. Narasimha Rao Government survived by winning over groups like the Jharkhand Mukti Morcha and Ajit Singh. The story of the "temporariness" of Central governments continued under the leadership of H.D. Deve Gowda, I.K. Gujral and the Vajpayee-led BJP's first two attempts.

Every non-Congress Prime Minister has been involved in a struggle for survival. What are the causes for this instability? What can be the prospects of any meaningful electoral reforms in the new context of proliferation of parties in India? More than forty parties and groups are represented in the Lok Sabha. In the Lok Sabha elections of 1989, 1996, 1998 and 1999, not a single party could reach 200 seats. The Congress party could get only 220 seats in the 1991 Lok Sabha elections and Mr. Vajpayee's party could not get more than 180 seats in the 1998 as well as the 1999 elections. The mushrooming of parties and splinter groups is not confined to the Lok Sabha elections. Bihar and Uttar Pradesh State Assembly elections are contested by dozens of parties. The State Assembly elections of Uttar Pradesh in 2002 featured 15 different political parties, besides sundry independents, and the result is there for all to see. Even the Lok Sabha results from Uttar Pradesh are getting fragmented.

The upshot of the above description is that electoral reforms cannot have any meaningful impact on the electoral process because a viable party system does not exist at present. Can there be any "funding of elections by the state exchequer" when more than 45 claimants are found in the Lok Sabha? Further, states like Uttar Pradesh, Bihar and Manipur have more than a dozen claimants. Any desire to get rid of "money power" in elections is utopian as political players have a view of maximising their personal benefits. Every regional party is the private shop of a leader. Any state funds for elections will have to be given to these 'party dictators'.

The first meaningful step in reforming the Indian electoral democracy is to prohibit any 'independent' contestants in elections. Parliamentary democracy is a system of government where elections are held to elect a majority party for forming the Government and an Opposition to hold the majority accountable for governance. In this scheme, an individual independent candidate has absolutely no place. Further, Lok Sabha elections are held for forming a Government at the Centre. In India, the parliamentary system of democracy combines with a federal system of governance and thus every federal 'unit' or 'state' should be legally represented in the Upper House of Parliament. The Rajya Sabha should be restructured and the representation for every state should be considered a right. Even Rajya Sabha elections have achieved notoriety. The most important comment on Indian legislators is that they are not trustworthy in a secret ballot. A demand has been made to have an "open ballot" for the Rajya Sabha elections. This fact clearly shows that money has great power in Indian democracy. While the Rajya Sabha should have representation of every state, the Lok Sabha should be insulated from political operators who float across parties. A party that has not contested three consecutive Lok Sabha elections or has not secured 10 per cent of the national vote in more than two states should be debarred from contesting elections.

A purely political shop for state level operations should be eligible only for that State's Assembly elections; and only a party that cuts across atleast two or three states and secures a reasonable percentage of votes in the Lok Sabha elections should be listed for all-India elections. In summation, it may be mentioned that the Election and Other Related Laws (Amendment) Bill 2002 for allowing corporate houses for funding parties or Constitution Review Commission Recommendations on Electoral Reforms have ignored the reality of proliferation of parties and political shops. Electoral reforms cannot take place without curbing the birth of 'weather-cock' political groups. Electoral reforms are integrally linked with an Amendment for categorising parties for State Assemblies and parties for the Lok Sabha and only this exercise will ensure legal control over the growth of private shops known as political parties. (*April 27, 2002, The Pioneer*)

Uneasy Federal Relations

The phase of highly-centralised Federal system wherein the States were reduced to the status of "glorified municipalities" had ended long ago, and the '90s had opened a new Pandora's box of problems for the Indian federal system as all the Central Governments led by V.P. Singh, Chandra Shekhar, Narasimha Rao, Deve Gowda, Gujral and Vajpayee had been politically weak, vulnerable and unstable. This weakness of the Centre made every prime minister to respond to demands of any state on the basis of political calculations, thereby forcing it to resort to adhocism. This had created a situation where serious problems of the states remained unresolved and inter-state and the Centre-States conflicts kept on increasing. The end-result is that the Centre has been unable to set up an institutional mechanism where such disputes could have been resolved amicably.

Recently, Rajasthan Chief Minister Ashok Gehlot and Andhra Chief Minister Chandrababu Naidu held separate conclaves of Chief Ministers to deal with the Centre in a collective manner on the financial implications of the Eleventh Finance Commission (EFC) report. It is ironical that some of the coalition partners of the Vajpayee regime had also attended these meetings. Not only this. The EFC award have sharply divided the states, and unfortunately, different States are in a confrontational mood, as Naidu had maintained that "performing and reform-oriented States have been disadvantaged" because of the "non-performing, non-developmental backward States." On the one hand, this has created a sharp division among the 'performers' and 'non-performers', on the other, Laloo Prasad Yadav, Ashok Gehlot and Digvijay Singh have not only defended the EFC report, but also vigorously questioned Naidu.

Another important evidence of the erosion of the leadership role of the Centre in resolving inter-state disputes is the Cauvery dispute. Despite the existing constitutional provisions and institutional mechanisms for resolving water disputes between the states, the Centre has been resorting to adhoc mediations on the issue, as it has been lacking in requisite political strength to take a bold position. Even the neutrality of the Centre had become a bone of contention to the disputants during the '90s. How could Tamil Nadu agree with the Centre's judgement on the Cauvery dispute when Deve Gowda was the prime minister? The same is the position of Karnataka now as the DMK is an important coalition partner of the Vajpayee regime.

This doesn't mean that during the Congress dominance in the Centre, the Centre-States disputes were unheard of. There was recurring allegations from the non-Congress State Governments that they were being discriminated against. But even then, the Congress Governments had always showed a political will and capacity to accommodate specific grievances of the States. It was this political will which is seriously lacking now.

The present Vajpayee regime is inherently weak as it is a 24-party coalition with all the partners having different agenda, while some important States like Rajasthan, MP, Bihar are opposed to it. Further, an adverse relationship has emerged among his alliance partners and the non-alliance group of States. It was dramatised when the NDA appointed Bihar Governor came under fire by the RJD as it feared that the Governor was an instrument in the hands of a hostile Centre. Also, the Left Front ministry of West Bengal alleges that the Centre is encouraging Trinamool leader Mamata Banerjee, a coalition partner, against it. As a result, a peculiarly new situation has emerged where the Central ministers are deemed completely 'partisan' by the States which are not members of the ruling coalition. As if this is not enough, the States are fighting among themselves as some Chief Ministers proclaim themselves as 'progressive' and label some States as 'backward'.

Coming back to the EFC. It is ironic that the Vajpayee government took a legalistic and formalistic position by refusing to discuss the EFC award at the inter-State Council. Formally, it was a correct step as the finance commission is a constitutional body with a specific status in the Federal set up as also its report is binding. However, this legal interpretation was based on a complete lack of political understanding of the changing dynamics of Indian politics. Also since some chief ministers questioned the award, it would have been better if the Centre convened the Inter-State Council meeting.

There is an urgent need for institutionalisation of the Inter-State Council as this a forum where the Prime Minister and Chief Ministers can sit together and iron out issues.

In the absence of such a mechanism, Chief Ministers are forced to confront the Centre which in turn is forced to respond in an adhoc manner. The present political climate is a complete break with the first 40 years of Independence. The choice now is between confrontation or consensus, adhocism or credible solution.

The issue of 'progressive' vs. 'backward' States is likely to become quite grave if it is not tackled on the basis of a national perspective. The political expediency of the NDA government is further revealed in the way it went about with the creation of Jharkhand, Uttarakhand and Chhatisgarh States. But the query is whether creation of these States is a remedy to tackle the problems of inter- and intra-regional imbalances? In fact, regional imbalances and disparities among the various regions are a logical outcome of the capitalist path of development, as capitalism cannot ensure equal development in the entire country.

The Planning Commission and NDC should be involved in the development of underdeveloped regions. The so-called developed States developed not just due to the good performance of their Chief Ministers. Once this fact is recognised, the Indian State will be able to evolve appropriate policies and strategies for tackling specific problems of various underdeveloped regions because the functioning of free market economy without purposeful intervention by the State will lead to centres of development and centres of backwardness. Goal-oriented politics is the real answer to the new issues raised by the new logic of Indian federalism and the politics of adhocism will prove disastrous for the future. (*November 20, 2001, Observer*)

The Leader Must Lead — And Cajole

The controversy between the Central and Chhatisgarh Governments on the privatisation of the Bharat Aluminium Company has once again brought into sharp public focus the multiplicity of contradictions inherent in the day-to-day functioning of India's federal system. The opposition parties in the Lok Sabha castigated the Central Government for disturbing the "delicate balance of power between the centre and the state government" by involving the Supreme Court in a purely political dispute.

The Central Government has alleged that the State Government is "leading the local trade unions" in disrupting the Plant's functioning. The slanging match is significant because some aspects of the New Economic Policy cannot be implemented without the cooperation of the state governments. This controversy could have been avoided if the centre had acknowledged the reality that the Chief Minister of Chhatisgarh belongs to a party in opposition at the centre.

In an era of regionalism, the Centre's economic and political decisions will have to be politically sold to the state governments. Balco is not the only issue. Finance Minister Yashwant Sinha's proposal to decentralise the management of the "food economy" by making the Food Corporation of India a minimal player in procurement and allocation of foodgrains will cause a hue and cry in food-surplus states where powerful farmer's lobbies are active.

If the state governments are assigned the responsibilities of procurement and distribution, the Centre's subsidy bill in fixing the prices of the foodgrains for procurement through the FCI will have to be borne by the state governments. Will they accept this new responsibility because the new situation will create confrontation between powerful Bharatiya Kisan Union leaders and the state governments?

Om Prakash Chautala of Haryana or Prakash Singh Badal of Punjab are class representatives of the surplus-generating peasantry and the existing system of central subsidy for procurement bails out chief ministers who dare not annoy powerful farmers' lobbies. Mr. Sinha has opened a Pandora's box. It has become routine for chief ministers to allege that the Central Government is a great "centraliser of power" and that the states can progress if powers are "decentralised" and the Centre "retreats from many areas of its existing activities". But Mr. Sinha is decentralising procurement, something the state governments will not be ready to touch with a pair of tongs.

The politics of the food economy is integrally linked with the economic interests of the class of food producers. The chief ministers are champions of producer interests and each one wants Central mediation in resolving the conflicts between the politics and economics of foodgrains.

The reform of the state electricity boards has become extremely difficult because most SEBs are moribund. The Prime Minister, in a meeting with Chief Ministers, promised to write off Rs. 26,000 crore which is an outstanding payment to the central utilities like the NTPC and Power Grid. Minister of state for Power Jayawanti Mehta told the Lok Sabha on March 8 that the "net subsidy on account of free/ concessional supply of electricity to the agricultural sector went up from Rs. 19,063 crore in 1997-98 to Rs. 20,232 crore in 1998-99 to Rs. 22,703 crore in 1999-2000". The Minister also provided the 'who is who' of the patrons of subsidy. The chief ministers of Andhra Pradesh, Gujarat, Haryana, Karnataka, Madhya Pradesh, Maharashtra, Rajasthan, Tamil Nadu and Uttar Pradesh have pride of place.

What is the guarantee that after the one-time write-off the state governments will be able to manage electricity tariffs on economic considerations? The state governments, champions of decentralisation and refederalisation, should set their house in order. The SEBs were purely under their control. The NTPC was established for precisely the reason that the SEBs had become sick because they had been made appendages of "free leaders" in the states.

All this is helpful in understanding the complexities and contradictions between the central and the state governments, which have become further accentuated during the era of liberalisation in the 1990s. A few facts may be mentioned to capture the emerging trends in Indian federalism. The central government is expected to provide leadership if any restructuring of economy is undertaken to achieve the goals of the so-called New Indian Economy.

The centre has indeed shown leadership in organising a conference of the chief ministers to implement programmes of reform of the SEBs. The government has also attempted to push the reforms by taking up the responsibility of writing off the arrears of the state governments.

The moral of this story is that the central government can persuade the state governments by arriving at a political consensus among the concerned governments and also extend financial support to the deficit states. A politics of consensus is a necessary condition in maintaining the delicate balance between the centre and states, especially when multiple parties are in power in different states and a coalition government is in power at the centre.

Further, the central government will have to play the role of a "leader" because the 28 state governments are absolutely unequal in their respective levels of development. Indian federal polity is under serious strain because of regional imbalances in the country, and the crisis of regional imbalances will get intensified if the central government is not actively seized of this problem.

Globalisation accentuates regional imbalances and multiplies 'peripheries' because investment flows are very unevenly distributed. The federal political economy of inter-state and intra-state imbalances requires many institutions such as the Finance Commission which can intervene in favour of the backward and underdeveloped regions of the country.

India's federal crisis is deepening because we are not recognising that the central government has to provide appropriate leadership to the many Indias. Market fundamentalists do not have any answers to the problem of dealing with the many Indias and it is only the central government, along with specific state or regional state governments, which can tackle the special problems of neglected and backward regions. The decade of the '90s has dramatised the issue of regional imbalances which has remained brushed under the carpet in the heyday of the system of centralised planning. (*March 17, 2001, Financial Express*)

North-East India: One Country Two Systems

In the past 55 years, every Central government has tried to deal with ethnic conflicts and special group problems in the North East. Despite these efforts, many groups oppose solutions to existing problems. A large number of them have taken recourse to the politics of the gun to achieve their goals. What is the explanation for the continuing inter-ethnic and inter-group strife? Why have the steps taken by Central governments in resolving these conflicts not matched the expectations of warring groups?

The adequacy or the inadequacy of governmental responses to challenges posed by competitive, multiple ethnic groups can be understood by looking at major steps taken by the Central governments while dealing with problems of ethnic identities. First, those living in the North East have bitter experiences of the presence of armed and paramilitary forces. As a result, societies have become psychologically alienated from the State, which is seen as purely coercive.

People's experience at the hands of armed forces becomes a "memory" and the State is considered an "enemy".

Second, the Constitution-makers of India, while dealing with rich diversities, established a complex architecture of governance by harmonising the demands of maintaining the territorial integrity of a newly created Indian state and federal governance of a diverse and plural society. The Constitution-makers took full cognisance of the special problems of multiple cultural groups, and Articles 244, 244A, and part XXI – consisting of Articles 369 to 392 – provided for "special" status to many states including Jammu and Kashmir, Nagaland, Assam, Manipur, Sikkim, Mizoram and Arunachal Pradesh.

Not only this but also the entire Sixth Schedule of the Constitution [Article 244(2) and 275(1)] is concerned with special arrangements for some kind of "self-governance" of tribal areas in Assam, Meghalaya, Tripura and Mizoram. The Central Government "reorganised" some states under the Assam Reorganisation (Meghalaya) Act, 1969 and the North East Areas (Reorganisation) Act, 1971 and converted Union Territories into full-fledged States. Most recently, the Assam government agreed to set up a Bodoland territorial council to meet Bodo demands.

Despite the Centre giving in to demands from different ethnic groups and the creation of multiple units of administration, the North East is plagued by violent conflicts. Even a clash over a village can trigger violence in a fragmented society.

A solution to the intractable Naga question has yet to be found despite numerous rounds of negotiations. The question of a larger Naga homeland remains a divisive issue, rousing emotions ranging from total opposition from majority communities and political parties in Manipur and Assam to support from a large number of Naga tribes and even the Nagaland Assembly.

It appears that every ethnic group has a grievance and the feeling persists, despite constitutional safeguards, that the diverse cultural groups of the North East are "deprived" of their legitimate right to govern themselves.

An innovative strategy is needed to restore confidence among different groups by ensuring that they have a share in power. How can this goal of power-sharing among contending and competing ethnic groups be achieved?

Constitutional provisions provide scope for an innovative approach in dealing with the North East as a whole and not separate parts divided among states, territorial councils *et al.*

The existing arrangements for governance of the North East can be improved and restructured, taking the example of China which has accepted the principle of "one country, two systems" for the governance of Hong Kong. India will have to make many experiments to meet the special needs of different groups for self-governance within the Indian State.

Yet, autonomy for Jammu and Kashmir as provided by Article 370 and for Nagaland under Article 371A is like the Chinese experiment.

It is our proposal that while full cultural autonomy is guaranteed under the Constitution for multiple ethnic groups, the administration of the North East should be the responsibility of a council of elders elected by all major ethnic groups irrespective of their State's territorial status. The council of elders can have 200 members elected by major identity groups cutting across territorial boundaries of the North Eastern States.

After fixing the strength at 200, elections can be held on the pattern of the Lok Sabha where the total number of members is set at 545 irrespective of the size of a constituency or, in the case of an autonomous district council, the size of a community.

The state governments shall transfer those powers to the council which are with the district and village councils and all subjects with regard to the 73rd and 74th constitutional amendments on Panchayati Raj and the municipalities.

The proposal means that the Central government will retreat from its present supra-state role in the North East.

The financial resources for the council of elders will come from the Consolidated Fund of India and it will have the power to preserve, protect, initiate changes, lobby for and represent the cultural rights of various communities. It may press for changes at the regional and national levels, in terms of the Constitution and the local set-up.

The advantage of establishing such a new constitutional authority is to assure every ethnic group that the Centre is committed to non-interference in the "internal, intra-ethnic or inter-ethnic" cultural identity problems. The problem of identity should be delinked from "territory" and the reorganisation of the North East should be stopped.

India cannot be governed from Delhi only and the North East needs to experiment with new forms of self-governance. (*July 13, 2002, The Statesman*)

Verdict on Narayanan: Defender of Democracy

An assessment of the Constitutional head in any parliamentary democracy has to consider the letter and spirit of constitutional provisions regarding the Head of State's role and powers. It can be said that K.R. Narayanan, in office from 1997 to 2002, has competently acted as a guardian of the Constitution. The role played by him during his five-year term was determined by the concrete historical context of the end of the 20th and the beginning of the 21st century.

India is expected to withstand the pressures of the US-dominated unipolar world. Narayanan sternly warned foreign and defence policy makers that unipolarity does not mean the irrelevance of time-tested non-alignment. He was concerned when he felt that, during the visit of former US President Bill Clinton, policy-makers were putting all their eggs in the US basket. Foreign policy, formulated and implemented by Jawaharlal Nehru, had always guarded national self-respect and the relative autonomy of the Indian State while dealing with arrogant Western countries.

Narayanan also defended the Constitution when he turned down the Atal Bihari Vajpayee Governments' recommendation of President's rule in Bihar. By referring back the recommendation to the Government, he not only killed it, he also helped generate a public debate on the use of Article 356 in a situation where a large number of States are ruled by parties opposing the Vajpayee Government. He thus defended the federal system—a pillar of unity in diversity.

He defended the Indian constitution by using the opportunity of addressing the Golden Jubilee session of the Indian Republic. The Sangh Parivar had never accepted the Constitution, which is against the concept of "one nation, one country, one culture". Pluralism is not acceptable to the believers of *Hindu Rashtra*. Constitutional review has been an agenda of the Sangh Parivar, and has nothing to do with the agenda of the BJP's allies in the NDA. Hence, the BJP picked "11 members" to recommend a review of the Constitution. The decision sent alarm signals to Opposition forces which mounted a strong attack on the 'unelected and unelectable members'—unapproved by Parliament—of the review panel.

Narayanan defended the Constitution by asking the political class a question: Who has failed us? The Constitution or the people entrusted with the task of protecting it? The Supreme Court judgements in the cases *Golak Nath Versus State of Punjab*, 1967, and *Keshavanada Versus State of Kerala*, 1973, are relevant: No government can tinker with the Constitution's "basic structure" under the pretext of reviewing its impurities, if any. Constitutions in the Third World have been under threat from political adventurists and India is no exception. Fakhuruddin

Ali Ahmad signed on the dotted line on June 26, 1975, facilitating Indira Gandhi's *coup d'etat*. Giani Zail Singh conspired against a duly elected Prime Minister and vigilant Opposition parties foiled his designs. The review panel's recommendations have been thrown in the dustbin because Narayanan put the full weight of his "office" against the idea of a review.

Narayanan has overseen a phase of social turbulence—one of exploiting ruling classes distancing themselves from 500 million marginalised people. Globalisation, liberalisation, privatisation and 'the retreat of the state' in favour of the free market has made the downtrodden socially orphaned. Narayanan has stressed on social justice, a dirty term for "free market fundamentalists". He has used the prestige of his office to emphasise that social justice is the cornerstone of India's welfare state, and the goal of social equality worth pursuing to maintain social order.

He can be compared only with Rajendra Prasad who, along with Sardar Patel, C. Raja Gopalachari and Govindballabh Pant, represented the Congress Hindu right-wing which opposed Nehru, who led the secular socialist-wing. Rajendra Prasad clashed with Nehru on the issue of religion. The Prime Minister felt the President of a secular republic should not associate himself publicly with the majority community's religion.

Nehru and President Rajendra Prasad confronted one another over the Hindu Code Bill. While the Prime Minister maintained that Hindu social reform was an important Congress agenda the President, leaning towards Hindu right-wing ideology, demanded a democratic verdict on the issue. The President's relationship with Nehru attracted public attention when on November 28, 1960, he raised the issue of presidential powers. Rajendra Prasad and Narayanan, while maintaining the dignity of their office, did not hesitate to express their social philosophy and concerns in public debates.

However, Rajendra Prasad and Nehru had been comrades during the freedom movement. Naryanan and the BJP are ideologically hostile. Yet he confined himself within constitutional limits without sacrificing his role as protector of the democratic, secular, plural, welfare state which is at present under siege. (*July 28, 2002, The Sunday Pioneer*)

Defender of Democracy

The Sangh Parivar is at wits' end because the Election Commission, by exercising its constitutional power under Article 324, has deferred elections to the Gujarat Assembly because "riot victims are still living in fear". The Sangh Parivar stands exposed because the present situation has been created by its own action in Gujarat, beginning from the Godhra incident of February 27, 2002.

The Narendra Modi Government has been wanting elections from April 2002, despite the fact that communal violence was at its peak from March to the end of May. Supported by the BJP at the Centre, it showed an indecent haste to reap the electoral fruits of a communal divide. Governor S.S. Bhandari, an RSS *pracharak*, rushed to L.K. Advani in June, with a demand that elections—due in 2003—be held immediately. Bhandari is on record stating on August 19 that "communal harmony is not complete ... but there is no communal divide." Here is a Sangh Parivar Governor who testifies that communal disharmony exists and still recommends elections!

The EC has foiled the Sangh Parivar's gameplan. This is the reason saffron spokesmen are peeved with the Chief Election Commission who described the situation in Gujarat as "muddy". Modi had himself travelled to New Delhi on June 13, and requested the BJP leadership to permit him to hold elections. His priority was not to crush the rioters but to take advantage of Hindu 'assertion'. K.P.S. Gill was sent by the Centre to Gujarat to assist the Government in dealing with the riots. If the Government machinery could not be trusted to control the situation and if Gill had to do the needful, the same State Government cannot be trusted to organise 'free and fair' elections.

The National Human Rights Commission maintained on June 7 that "despite the measures reportedly taken by the State government ... (its) report of April 12 ... testifies to the increasing numbers who died or were injured ... and compelled to seek shelter in relief camps. The commission has, therefore, reached the definite conclusion that there was a comprehensive failure of the State to protect the constitutional rights of the people." Here is a former Chief Justice of India castigating the Government as late as on June 7 for its failure to defend minorities. The same story is repeated in the EC's report of August 16.

By contrast, Dr. Parveen Bhai Togadia, VHP International General-Secretary, observed on June 6: "While Godhra reflected the '*jihadi*' mentality of the Muslims, the subsequent events ... were proof of the

Hindu awakening." The Sangh Parivar is bent on exploiting this "Hindu awakening". The only stumbling block is the Constitution of democratic and secular India, where all 'autonomous' constitutional authorities have openly maintained that before elections are held, the wounds inflicted on minorities should be healed. The new President, A.P.J. Abdul Kalam, made his symbolic first visit to Gujarat on August 12, because democratic India wanted this gesture of reassurance for the riot victims. Similarly, K.R. Narayanan, former President, observed on August 14, that "I often felt helpless when delegations told me their woes and I could not do anything about it. Gujarat was a major example of helplessness." Gill, on his return from Gujarat, also said that he "did not witness any remorse in Gujarati society". If Modi had nothing to hide, Prime Minister Atal Bihari Vajpayee would not have said on June 6 at Goa that he had decided to ask him to resign but later changed his mind. Why did Vajpayee ask Modi to uphold "*raj dharma*" when dealing with communal riots?

Everything changed on June 6, when the BJP assembled in Goa and Modi was lionised as "Chhota Sardar Patel". Incidentally, the real Sardar Patel had banned the RSS in 1948 because "in practice" RSS members had not adhered to their professed ideals. The difference between Sardar Patel of 1948 and "Chhota Sardar of 2002" is that the former suppressed violence through state power, and the later pretender allowed violence against minorities with a view to achieving "Hindu awakening" to win an election. Why else did the Prime Minister ask Modi not to organise the Gaurau Yatra in July 2002? Was that not clinching evidence of a fear of the 'communal divide' created by the Modi Government?

The EC has defended the Constitution by not holding elections in an atmosphere of "fear" among minority voters. The believers of 'Hindu pride' are crestfallen because their plan to convert Hindu-Muslim hatred into a votebank has been scuttled by an autonomous pillar of the Constitution. Fundamentalists are opposed to democracy of any kind, because multiple checks and balances contain the excesses of violent religious groups. *Hindutva* forces are not able to reconcile their goals with the institutional arrangements of the existing democratic Constitution. The essence of the EC's 40-page document is that it is an 'impartial' indictment of the Modi Government. (*25th August, 2002, The Sunday Pioneer*)

5

Politics of Economics: Confusion and Corruption

A Federal Investigation

Indian federal democracy is facing a serious crisis, given that democratic institutions at the state level are in bad shape. The grand experiment of decentralised democracy may get completely derailed if the working of such institutions is not improved, as per principles laid down by the Constitution. A few facts would substantiate the argument.

How can democracy succeed at the national level if state governments are determined to destroy legal and formal institutional arrangements for democratic governance? First, the bureaucracy in every state has been co-opted by MLAs and ministers and, in the process, has been casteised, communalised and completely parochialised. The former Chairman of the Punjab Public Service Commission (PPSC), Ravinder Pal Singh Sidhu, was expected—as a public servant—to appoint the best available candidates. Instead, he fixed pricetags on entry into the public services. Could such a thing happen without the full knowledge of the political class in Punjab?

Second, Punjab's neighbouring State, Haryana, witnessed a mockery of the law when some agitating groups "arrested" police functionaries. The High Court had to issue a Habeas Corpus for their release. Ghasi Ram Nain, the State President of the Haryana Bharatiya Kisan Union (BKU), could challenge law enforcement officers and Chief Minister Om Prakash Chautala by negotiating with the law breakers to seek the release of the detained men in uniform. How can rule of law prevail when a group of private citizens can be permitted to hold law-enforcing functionaries to ransom? Would the State government have shown the same concern if landless agricultural Dalit workers had broken the law, instead of the Haryana BKU?

Third, if the former PPSC Chairman destroyed the recruitment system to public services, the Uttar Pradesh Chief Minister (CM). Ms Mayawati, is in the news for recklessly 'transferring' government officials from one office to the other. Incidentally, the political class has used the instrument of 'transfer' both as a carrot and a stick. Every CM has appointed an obliging "Chief Secretary" to act as a "spy" over other ministers. Why did Ms Mayawati show an indecent haste in removing a Chief Secretary and bringing in her 'own man'?

Fourth, the DMK and AIADMK CMs in Tamil Nadu have always fought their political battles with the involvement of their loyal civil servants, particularly with regard to filing and prosecution of corruption charges.

Fifth, the Election Commission (EC) had to order state governments not to transfer officials on the eve of elections for the state assemblies. Can elections be 'fair' and 'free' if the machinery for their conduct is not impartial? Would democracy survive if people lost faith in the sanctity of the ballot? In the past, senior officials have been 'indicted' by the EC for indulging in electoral malpractices.

Next, communal blood-bath in Gujarat continued unchecked for about three months. Julius Ribeiro, a distinguished former police official, commented that the Gujarat police consists of "eunuchs". Mr. KPS Gill, security advisor to the Gujarat CM, maintained in an interview that "police forces act effectively if proper leadership is provided by the senior police officials". Justice Srikrishna in his report on the Mumbai riots of 1992-93 had specifically identified important police officials as "guilty" of dereliction of duty. How can the secular fabric be safeguarded if the common man is victimised by law enforcing agencies?

Finally, while every State Government is facing a "fiscal crisis", Andhra Pradesh CM Chandrababu Naidu demanded "powers for States to directly seek external funds" in his concluding address to his party's Mahanadu on May 29, 2002. This is a new development: Every State Government is trying to attract foreign capital for investment and every CM wants full freedom to negotiate with transnational investors in order to obtain capital.

An important implication of this development will be a division of our federal polity into 'economically developed regions' and 'relatively backward States'. Chandrababu Naidu has publicly alleged that "the performing States" are being denied assistance by the Central Government because of the so-called special needs of the "non-performing" backward States of Uttar Pradesh, Bihar, Orissa *et al.* Is this the meaning of autonomy, whereby every State looks after its own development needs without concern for a balanced development of every region? A democracy of regional imbalances will always be crisis-ridden and the so-called developed regions will always curse the backward States. This is an undesirable phenomenon, emerging out of the liberalisation process.

Incidentally, the so-called performing and non-performing states have not addressed themselves to the basic problem of de-institutionalisation of their State apparatus. Tamil Nadu or Gujarat lay claims to being "developed" and "performing" States. But their machinery of governance is in no way better than their neighbouring States.

It is the so-called developed State of Gujarat that experienced total administrative collapse during the recent riots. Mr. KPS Gill had to be inducted to improve the morale of the communalised Police force. Personal aggrandisement and breakdown of the State machinery is not only confined to Mr. Laloo Prasad Yadav's Bihar. It is an all-India phenomenon and hence is extremely worrying given that democracy and misgovernance cannot coexist.

The evil of misgovernance particularly in the so-called mainstream States cannot be ignored if democracy has to survive in this country. First, the social explanation for the growing privatisation of State Governments is to be found in the changing social composition of elected legislators. Land reforms in India ejected the traditional landholding high castes who were replaced when the backward caste middle peasantry emerged as new centres of power.

Consequently, the State Assemblies became an extension of the caste-based agrarian power structure controlled by middle peasants like the Jats, Yadavas, Koris, Kurmis and other land owning classes and castes. This mobilisation facilitated the formation of caste-based parties like Mr. Mulayam Singh Yadav's Samajwadi Party and Mr. Laloo Yadav's Rashtriya Janata Dal. Elections at the State Assembly level are contested as competition among castes and caste-based parties.

The implication is that the distinction between a party and its social base has been blurred and State Governments have become the handmaidens of the dominant caste groups. A Yadav CM or a Dalit CM has ceased to represent all sections of society. Mr. Ram Vilas Paswan, leader of the Lok Janashakti Party, admitted in a public interview that, as a minister, he is expected to look after the interests of his supporters—which in reality means his caste group. Similarly, the Sangh Parivar in Gujarat treats the Modi Government as its private property. How can

Bajrang Dal or VHP activists be arrested if they are protected by the State? Democracy at the State level has come to be equated with sectional interests, and winning an election has become a matter of caste *ijjat* or prestige.

In the final reckoning, India has entered a dangerous phase in its development, because the State apparatus has been 'privatised' and procedure-based democracy completely destroyed. Indian democracy is facing its worst crisis at the grassroots level because neither elected representatives nor permanent civil servants are insulated from 'localism' and parochialism. (*June 8, 2002, The Pioneer*)

When Government Betrays Trust

V.P. Singh, Chandra Shekhar, H.D. Deve Gowda, I.K. Gujral and A.B. Vajpayee have occupied the office of Prime Minister after delegitimising Rajiv Gandhi by actively campaigning that the late prime minister and his family had betrayed national interest by accepting bribe in the purchase of guns from Bofors Company of Sweden. The cycle has turned full circle and the five champions of clean public life have been caught — found thoroughly incompetent to fight against the cancer of corruption in public life. If Chandra Shekhar has been humiliated by the SC by ordering him to surrender 250 hectares of land grabbed by him, Vajpayee faced similar situation in Parliament so much so that he chose to resign and run away from the responsibility of explaining the role of PMO in the scam. These five Pandavs of Indian politics have strengthened the tradition that politicians have full control over public financial institutions and that the politicians are free to use, misuse and abuse public funds for private benefits. If Chandra Shekhar and Vajpayee have shown that they are masters of public resources, V.P. Singh drained away public resources by getting treatment for his personal ailment in England on the basis of millions of rupees sent by the Indian tax payers. Honest Indians pay taxes for dishonest politicians, bureaucrats and their friends, families and favourites. The Indian State has been privatised and watchmen of public funds are themselves involved in breaking the locks of public treasury in the midnight to transfer public resources to their private hidden accounts.

Politicians and bureaucrats are getting caught by the police and convicted by the judiciary for the misappropriation of public funds. Regional political commanders-in-chief along with their high-ranking civil servants had to be imprisoned because public funds were not safe in their hands. Narasimha Rao, Chandra Shekhar and Vajpayee have faced the worst public humiliation for their misconduct in dealing with public finances. Politicians have suddenly become rich. When Prime Ministers and Chief Ministers are busy in robbing the public money, politicians and bureaucrats from Panchayat to Parliament get fully encouraged to misuse and abuse public funds. During the last 53 years, India has reached a stage where distinction between criminals and politicians has blurred. Now, 20 million middle class share holders of Unit Trust of India's stocks have become victims because of the criminal activities of politicians and bureaucrats while dealing with public funds. It is not surprising that criminals are themselves entering Parliament, State Legislative Assemblies and other democratically-elected institutions. Elected Assemblies provide a sanctuary to the breakers of law because they are breaking only those laws which they have themselves enacted.

During Nehru's regime, the LIC had illegally helped an upstart industrialist Mundhra and Parliament was rocked. Judicial Commission under Justice Das indicted T.T. Krishnamachari, the Finance Minister. Nehru kicked out Krishnamachari. Yashwant Sinha cannot be kicked out because the game has allegedly begun from the PMO and under the protective umbrella of the Prime Minister. Every politician is safe to play with public money. Not only this industrialists who have manipulated the UTI cannot be punished because political and bureaucratic masters will have to be punished along with the beneficiaries of the loot. Everyone is safe because it is a wide network involving politicians, bureaucrats and industrialists. If one of them, *i.e.* the politicians, is punished, others cannot escape. A collective action of corruption leads to no punishment as is the case in the UTI scam. This encourages everyone to break the law and enjoy private wealth by devouring the public exchequer. Even the judiciary will take its own time for deciding the issues. The so-called Bofors bribery case which began in 1987 has not been concluded till now. The big sharks are protected and small fries are punished. The beneficiaries of public loot are the well-off and powerful sections of society and its victims are more than 500 million labouring classes. It has been revealed in every big scam and financial scandal that the 200 million prosperous Indian and poor workers, daily wagers and exploited women are helpless spectators to this drama of gross public misconduct by the politicians. Only Chandra Shekhar's ill-gotten property has been confiscated by the SC, while hundreds of others are going scot-free. Who can save India? The observation of honourable judges of the SC is noteworthy:

> "Corruption by public servants has now reached a monstrous dimension in India. Its tentacles have started gripping even the institutions created for the protection of the Republic."

Republic of India has become a banana republic because of politics of loot by the Indian elite. (*August 5, 2001, Deccan Chronile*)

Politics of Economics

It is surprising to hear our politicians admitting that economic development has been seriously affected by manipulative activities of various political groupings; and their making a fresh commitment to insulate and depoliticise the issues concerning economic development. But, if one compares some of their earlier statements, he will soon find that they are speaking in a language and using an idiom which are unheard of in any democracy. For instance, the Mandal messiah V.P. Singh had said that Indian voters are to be guided more by economic questions than caste considerations. L.K. Advani, the hero of Ayodhya politics, is on record claiming that India wants governance that is largely ideologically neutral, and believes that only de-ideologised governance can deliver the goods and take the country forward.

But how V.P. and Advani determined the political process of the 90s by practising sectarianism of caste vs. caste and religion vs. religion is an open secret. But, now both of them are united in their views about delinking of economics from politics. Not only this. During the 90s, every prime minister, (PM), regardless of his political affiliation, has sold new economic policy as a special feature of Indian political consensus despite the serious differences within the country. Successive PMs, Union ministers and industry leaders have been assuring foreign investors that the country is united on the new economic policy, despite an unstable politics at the Centre.

While the stability of the market is a legitimate concern of any investor, domestic or foreign, it is not given to the market leaders to determine the directions of political process. Politics of a country follows its own logic and many a time goals of various parties are opposed to each other, especially at the polls. The 90s had witnessed not only the launch of liberalisation, it also experienced serious and worst ever political instability; hence, every investor's demand from every PM is about the fate his money, and every PM has been publicly stating that liberalisation package has a national political consensus. Every world forum has been used by the successive governments to assure foreign investors about the stability of the economic regime. Even CMs have started speaking the language of national leaders on the imperatives of the liberalisation.

Even the three new states have been created on the plea that these regions suffered because they have been the 'victims of manipulative politics of powerful regional leaders in their respective mother states.' It is, however, true that politics of focusing on some regions at the cost of others has created regional imbalances in these states and, the answer lies in liberating the neglected regions from the discriminatory politics of regional leaders.

However, politicians' latest view that economic development should be insulated from conflicting political ideologies is highly debatable, for in a participatory democracy the direction of economic development has to be politically determined. Historically, only fascist and authoritarian regimes have imposed economic models of development after suppressing and banning political parties. Unlike dictatorial states, democracies discuss and debate every important economic issues. Moreover, it can be noted that in a democracy free and fair elections are held regularly either to endorse or reject the economic policies of contending political parties. Again, only in a functioning democracy any economic adventurism of the ruling party can be checked. Alternative models of economic development are decided only on political basis in democracy and, India is the best example of the view that economics divorced from politics can lead to disastrous social results, India has launched its liberalisation regime on the basis of a public political commitment of the ruling party and this model was scrutinised after every five years by the voters.

It could be recalled that the Parliament and the voter were called upon to politically approve/disapprove economic performance of the then governments; and in '67 the Indian voter did punish the Congress governments both at the Centre and the states for bad fiscal policies. During the 50s, 60 and 70s, the state assemblies were the centres of political contest on the land reforms issue. Land reform occupied the central stage in these decades, for politics was always a fundamental factor in determining the nature of the economy. Further, the public sector vs. private sector had its own political supporters and opponents. The Swatantra Party, Jana Sangh and the Forum for Free Enterprises were very active in their political opposition to the then economic policies under the licence-raj.

Since politics has been integrally linked with the formulation of our economic policies from independence, it is impossible to accept that suddenly from the 90s, politics and economics have entered into a divorce pact. On the contrary, liberalisation and globalisation has been hijacked by politicians by conspiring against the voter by not seeking his mandate on the economic issues, as also by pursuing a double standard on the issue, opposing it at the polls and endorsing it while in power. The Swadeshi Jagran Manch is now openly accusing its own fraternity, the BJP, for following an economic policy which the Parivar has opposed during the '96, '98 and '99 polls. The fact is that none of the political parties have taken an honest position for or against liberalisation in any of the hustings during the 90s. Is political dishonesty the real meaning of delinking of economic from politics?

To sum up, it is very dangerous for the democracy if economics is to be independent of politics. Politics in democracy sets social goals, including economics, for the society and this has been reiterated by the supporters of new global capitalism as well. US treasury secretary and a votary of free market Robert Rubin has recently warned every one, including India, that 'along with globalisation, we need a parallel set of policies that address to the effects of globalisation. You can't stop with technology, capital and trade'. While our leaders talk of 'keeping politics away from economics', Rubin advises us to keep politics nearest to economics. It is worth highlighting that politics of development transforms societies, and its absence has pushed UP and Bihar to backwardness. The central issue is that the Indian politicians lack any commitment to development, hence the backwardness. (*November 15, 2000, The Observer*)

The Politics of Economic Reforms

Prime Minister Atal Bihari Vajpayee, in his Musings II, *Call of the New Year: Clear Vision, Concerted Action*, astonishingly observed that "As is well known, these reforms have been pursued by all governments since 1991. Nearly all political parties in the country have been a part of these governments. Thus, a strong basis for a national consensus on the agenda of reforms already exists. We must further strengthen this agenda by depoliticising it".

Mr. Vajpayee's plea for depoliticisation of the economic policies pursued by his government deserves careful scrutiny because every crucial economic decision in a parliamentary democracy is based on weighty political considerations.

Mr. Vajpayee's assertion that economic policies of the 1990s are based on a political "consensus" is far from the truth. The Lok Sabha elections of 1991, 1996, 1998 and 1999 were not contested on the basis of the package of liberalisation, privatisation and globalisation. The new economic policy was instituted by the Rao government in 1991, post-elections, when India was bankrupt and we faced a fiscal crisis.

The Congress did not defend its new economic policy in the 1996 Lok Sabha election and the BJP, the socialists, the communists and the multiple Janata Dals attacked the Rao government's economic policies before the voters. The Sangh Parivar championed 'Economic Swadeshi' against the Congress policies of economic liberalisation. The prime ministers of 1996, 1998 and 1999 have opposed the Congress's new economic policies while contesting elections but followed the same economic path while in the government.

The new economic policy of the 1990s does not have the mandate of the voter. The founders of the Swadeshi Vichar Manch cannot claim that the policy is based on a national consensus. An important question is: What is the difference between the 1990s and the path of economic development followed by Nehru and Indira governments? The defenders of the new economic policies maintain that in the 1990s India witnessed a decisive break from the command economy established by Mr. Nehru and followed by the Congress. They are not telling the whole truth.

Every macroeconomic policy regime is based on the ideologies of human societies. The neoclassical economists are guided by the ideology of free enterprise and the individual's right of competition. The market fundamentalists have a political ideology based on the principles of individual freedoms. Their opponents on the other hand believe that the free operation of market forces deprives the poor from the benefits of economic growth.

Various models of economic development have always been accepted or rejected on the basis of democratic elections and every government in power is subjected to political pressure by multiple interest groups while taking so-called purely economic decisions. The Vajpayee government's coalition partners, from Mr. Naidu of Andhra Pradesh to Mr. Badal of Punjab, have openly campaigned for government intervention in paddy procurement in their states. Mr. Bhure Lal, an upright IAS officer, publicly maintained that the Food Corporation of India could not procure paddy in Punjab because it was mostly sub-standard. He was ridiculed politically as his views were politically dangerous.

The BJP is itself worried about the impact of World Trade Organisation agreements on the farming community. On April 1, 2001, quantitative restrictions (QRs) will have to be removed and its likely impact on the Indian agrarian sector has caused great concern to all parties including the BJP. The CPI(M) central committee, at its meeting on January 20, 2001 at Bhubaneswar, has come out with a resolution on the agrarian sector crisis resulting from the drastic fall in prices of agriculture commodities after the QRs on imports of 714 items were removed.

The CPI(M) has to be worried because coconut and areca nut growers in Kerala are in crisis and the forthcoming state assembly elections are on the horizon. Is minimum support price for wheat or paddy an economic decision? It is a political compulsion for Mr. Vajpayee to accommodate the Badals and the Chautalas. The same political reasoning compelled BJP leader Jana Krishnamurti to raise the issue of QRs in March 2000 and make a public demand that "the Congress must cooperate with the government. So must all other parties since a solution has to be found in unity. The issue is not political, but a fallout of the decision taken by the previous Congress regime". It is amusing that the BJP leadership is making pleas for political neutrality on purely economic issues.

Mr. Vajpayee's Musings are flawed because in a competitive democracy economic rationality and market imperatives have to be mediated by political considerations. It is the political class which gets brickbats or bouquets and rewards on its performance. Political parties mobilise social groups on "emotive" issues such as *Hindutva* and on the basis of the social and economic needs of the masses. The BJP is caught between purely economic issues and the Temple, an emotive issue.

Can Mr. Vajpayee "depoliticise" *rozi-roti* (jobs and food) and manage a coalition on the basis of an "emotive" issue? The answer is a big No because social mobilisation on the basis of the secular issues of *rozi-roti* is better politics for democracy than the politics of *Hindutva*.

Democracies have witnessed politics-led economics during the Great Depression when President Roosevelt responded with the interventionist policies of the New Deal. Democracies have also witnessed economics-led politics during the neo-classical economic regimes of President Reagan and Prime Minister Thatcher. Every democracy has been involved in a struggle to maintain an equilibrium in the politics of economics. Mr. Vajpayee's plea for "neutrality of politics" in economics is dangerous in a democracy. (*February 3, 2001, Financial Express*)

Power of Middle Class

Yashwant Sinha, the Finance Minister of India, has maintained that "Political Consensus" behind Phase II of Economic Reforms has weakened, and the critics have alleged that only the Indian middle class is the beneficiary of new economic policies and millions of the poor of India have not gained anything from the decade of "Economic Reforms". The Finance Minister himself observed that public finances are under great pressure because of the huge burden imposed by the implementation of the Fifth Pay Commission recommendations. The fountain source of existing fiscal deficit is the huge salary bill of the central and state government employees because of the generosity of the Fifth Pay Commission. P. Chidambaram, a self-confessed liberaliser in the governments of H.D. Deve Gowda and Inder Kumar Gujral, congratulated his governments for accepting the new salary structure of public employees as suggested by the Fifth Pay Commission and he did not pay any attention to its impact on fiscal resources of the Indian state. Incidentally, except the recommendation regarding high pay package for public services, none of the other recommendations of the Fifth Pay Commission, especially those concerning the "downsizing of the highly bloated bureaucracy" have been implemented. On the contrary Parliament was informed that the central government had 110 Secretary-level posts in April 1997, 116 in April 1998, 137 in April 1999 and 149 in April 2000. And such an increase has taken place at every level of the hierarchy in Indian bureaucracy. The story of increasing prosperity during the decade of economic reforms does not end only with bureaucracy. MPs, MLAs, Ministers, Chief Ministers and Prime Ministers of India are also looked after quite well by the public exchequer. It is quite frequent that salaries and multiple allowances of political class are revised and increased. On May 12, 2000 Parliamentary Affairs Minister, Pramod Mahajan, introduced a bill in the Lok Sabha "to allow the spouse of an MP to travel by rail in AC first-class or by air from the member's usual place of residence to Delhi eight times a year. Even after the dissolution of the Lok Sabha, this privilege will continue for MPs to avail of the "unutilised annual quota of free telephone calls, electricity and water from the date of dissolution up to the constitution of the new Lok Sabha". Thus politicians and bureaucrats who belong to the Indian middle class are very well looked after by the Indian state irrespective of its impact on the fiscal health of the country. Since politicians and bureaucrats belonging to the Indian middle class occupy real positions of power within the Indian state, they also protect and promote interests of their own class by following public policies which are relevant for the social needs of rural and urban upwardly mobile middle classes. It is not accidental that during the decade of economic reforms 250 million consumers of the Indian market have received special attention and reference by public policy makers during negotiations within foreign investors. Rahul Bajaj was asked by the Prime Minister Atal Bihari Vajpayee to submit a report on the actual functioning of the "economic reforms process" and Bajaj in his report on '*How can Indian Avoid the Pitfalls of Globalisation?*' has observed that: "the growth is being driven by the growing prosperity of the middle class, whose size is not more than 200 million". The Report further states "that India cannot claim the status of an economic super power by show casing its middle class".

The upshot of above description is that India is governed by the middle class and various groups of middle class occupy crucial position in the public life of India. A few facts may be mentioned to substantiate the argument that Indian middle class enjoys great power in the public affairs of democratic India. First, during the phase of economic planning, politicians and bureaucrats were the real decision makers and the process of planning facilitated the consolidation of the power of middle class political and bureaucratic groups. The commanding heights of public sector economy provided a great opportunity for the middle classes who were asked to manage about 240 central-government public enterprises and thousands of state government enterprises. The private sector industrial classes developed a good and workable relationship with the 'new owners and managers' of public sector enterprises, and politicians, bureaucrats and businessmen were closely integrated during the phase of economic planning. The real locus of power from 1947 to 1991 was in the collective hands of business class, politicians and bureaucrats.

Second, the upwardly mobile middle caste peasantry also followed the same route as was shown by the urban business classes and bureaucrats. The middle class peasantry used the levers of power for the promotion of their own interests. While the process of economic planning consolidated the power of urban/town middle classes, land reforms benefited the backward caste middle peasantry who successfully captured the levers of political power in the state legislatures and displaced the traditional high castes from their power: K. Kamraj, or Charan Singh or Pratap Singh Kairon emerged on the scene as a result of social and economic change in agrarian India. The rural middle class captured political power but it also found that the corridors of bureaucratic power were closed for them because their children could not compete against the children of highly educated middle classes. V.P. Singh, as Prime Minister of a shaky coalition in 1989-90, clearly understood the dilemma of the upwardly mobile and politically very powerful rural backward caste middle peasantry and he coopted them by accepting the Mandal Commission recommendations on reservations for the backward castes. Land reforms laid down the foundations of the power of the new rural middle class and implementation of Mandal Commission recommendations on reservations in public services completely consolidated the power of rural middle class. The Mandalisation and casteisation of the 1990s is nothing except the recognition of a fact that rural and urban middle class interests cannot be ignored by public policy makers. The caravan of caste reservations is becoming unstoppable because middle class political leaders like V.P. Singh, Mulayam Singh Yadav, Laloo Prasad Yadav, Ms. Mayawati have to promote and protect the interests of their own class and caste and it is not possible if backward caste middle peasantry is not represented in bureaucracy. Politics of reservations is the quintessential evidence of the fact that India is governed by rural and urban middle classes who are in full command of the levers of power.

Third, the decade of 1990s has witnessed the emergence of caste-based politics of rural middle caste peasantry and religion-based politics of the BJP which has a solid base in the middle classes. The RSS always attracted young, lower and middle class students, and it indoctrinated them in the ideology of 'one culture, one religion and one nation-state'. It is factually wrong to maintain that the RSS is a fringe of lunatic minority of Hindus. RSS is a backbone of the politics of *Hindutva* and it consists of highly educated middle class Hindus. Every leader of the RSS/BJP at every level of politics belongs to educated middle class Hindus. Atal Bihari Vajpayee, L.K. Advani, Murli Manohar Joshi and RSS chiefs beginning from Dr. Hedgewar to Sudarshan have been highly educated individuals. It is not only that the ideologies of *Hindutva* are from educated classes; they are present at every level of RSS/BJP organisation. Since the BJP is expanding its social base, it has appropriated the platform of reservations for the backward castes in public services.

Why has every political party accepted the doctrine of reservations in the public services? While economic liberalisation has opened a new job market for high caste Hindu children, the educated children of backward castes can be accommodated in public services. The controversy on Mandal recommendations died in the decade of liberalisation because Information Technology brought new opportunities to traditional educated middle classes and because of this new mobility of upper and middle class children, some space has been vacated for the entry of backward castes in public services. Mandalisation, casteisation, communalisation and liberalisation are all legitimised and vigorously supported by different segments of the middle classes. The party of *Hindutva* has not only abandoned its opposition to Mandal Commission, it has also buried its pet baby of *Swadeshi*. The Hindu middle class is attracted towards the ideology of *Hindutva* at cultural level, and the BJP's liberalisation is extremely satisfying to the consumerist Hindu Middle Class. Further, the forces of *Hindutva* have orchestrated successfully the idea of "Great India" and powerful middle class is a supporter of nuclearised, militarised Hindu India. Hence a natural relationship has emerged between the rising Hindu middle class and the politics of *Hindutva* because *Hindutva's* liberalisation takes care of rising economic aspirations of this class and the ideology of *Hindutva* or cultural nationalism of the BJP takes care of the identity problem of a Hindu.

If on the one hand *Hindutva* is one dimension of powerful middle class, caste-based politics is the other side of the coin. Mulayam Singh Yadav or Laloo Prasad Yadav or Ram Vilas Paswan or Sharad Yadav are all representatives of the emerging educated backward caste Dalit groups. Both the Yadavs of U.P. and Bihar claim that Yadav castes are our solid vote bank. If BJP uses the card of religion, the peasant caste leaders use the card of caste, and so the political mobilisation in the 1990s has been on the basis of either religion or caste. While caste versus caste and religion versus religion politics is dividing India, liberalisation is acceptable to every political group. V.P. Singh, P.V. Narasimha Rao, H.D. Deve Gowda, Inder Kumar Gujral and Atal Bihari Vajpayee are pushing forward the new economic policy of liberalisation and globalisation. Indian politics is witnessing a contradictory phenomenon of consensus on new economic policy and polarisation on the basis of caste or religion. This is the essence of Indian middle class politics. While Indian middle class is united on new economic policy because it has provided them new opportunities and prosperity, it is divided on its identity issue. Hindu identity or caste identity divides powerful political, bureaucratic and professional middle classes but they all get united on the opening of economy to foreign investors. This is the logic of globalisation. The Indian middle class in the age of new globalisation is trying to reconcile its high rising economic aspiration with the issue of cultural belongingness.

The upshot of above discussion is that the agenda of politics, economic and cultural identities has been formulated by different segments of the middle classes and unity among the powerful middle classes of India is revealed on national consensus on economic liberalisation and national conflict, and division among them exists on issue of cultural or caste identities. This is the essence of politics and economics of our governing middle classes who carry their contradictions in Indian politics. (*May 27, 2000, The Observer*)

6

Foreign Affairs

Foreign Policy without a Framework

Foreign, defence and international economic policies of every country, including India, have become completely integrated because the United States, the sole Superpower of the present epoch has decided to deal with every country in a holistic manner. Two telling examples of this new trend in international relations: first, George W. Bush declared, post 9/11, that countries which are not with the US in fight against global terrorism will not be accepted as friends; second, the message Indians got much earlier when President Bill Clinton imposed total sanctions against India as a punishment for the 'nuclear adventurism' of the BJP-led Government.

The Vajpayee Government has spent full two years mending its relationship with the US-led sanctions regime, with 9/11 giving this initiative unexpected impetus. It is worth mentioning that India has been very active during the last three months in improving its relationship with the US.

The so-called International Alliance against the Taliban led by the US attacked Afghanistan on October 7, 2001. George Bush, on the basis of the Government of India statements, declared on November 9, 2001 that "We (the US and India) will fight terrorism together" and the US has a new and "fundamentally different relationship with India". This statement should have pleased the Indian political and bureaucratic establishment but, Vajpayee, before meeting George Bush on November 9, 2001, publicly stated "our offered support has not brought about any concrete response from the American Government". The upshot of this description is that Indians were the first to proclaim their "full support" to the Americans on September 11, but the Americans did not ask for any material support from the Indians till November 9, 2001. India also suffered a big setback when the US stymied its efforts to squeeze into the 6+2 group around Afghanistan. The "six plus two" where Russia and US were the "two" and other six were neighbours of Afghanistan—China, Pakistan, Iran, Tajikistan, Uzbekistan and Turkmenistan—has no room for India. It is only on November 15, 2001, that a Group of 20 was established which included India, ostensibly "to bring Afghanistan's ethnic groups together in a transitional government". But again India found not even sideline space in Bonn in Germany where the talks have now concluded successfully. The Atal Bihari Vajpayee-George Bush Summit in Washington, had the PM say on November 13, 2001 that "In sum, my visit served to enlarge and deepen the areas of understanding and agreement with our friends and partners". In concrete terms, India and the US have established strong bilateralism in the fields of hi-tech commerce, hi-tech exports to India from the US, defence purchases by India from America and other economic related bilateral relations.

As a result of the Summit, military exchanges have increased between the two countries and Defence Minister Jaswant Singh and Prime Minister Vajpayee in their replies in the Rajya Sabha debates on November 26 and 27 reiterated that India's relationship with the US has been strengthened in every bilateral field. Many important questions about India's foreign policy as enunciated and practised by the Vajpayee Government must be raised to properly understand the totality of our relationships with the US-led Western Alliance against terrorism: Why could India not suggest that the war against the Taliban regime of Afghanistan should be endorsed by the Security Council? With all its limitations, the Security Council has much greater legitimacy than the American-led Alliance against terrorism. Not only this. The Western Countries in the name of fighting future "terrorism" can form an Alliance against any country and in the process destroy and destabilise any country in the world. A sovereign and democratic country like India should be very cautious and careful before aligning with the Americans and their Alliance against terrorism because the US has many friends and many enemies around the world and India has its difficulties only with Pakistan. President Bush, while speaking on terrorism at the UN on November 10, 2001, observed that "This threat cannot be ignored. Civilisation itself, the civilisation we share, is threatened. History will record our response and judge or justify every nation in this hall". Have we ever talked in such bombastic and arrogant language while dealing with Pakistan? The more worrisome situation for Indians is that Americans can unilaterally declare a state as "terrorist" or "rogue" and ask its friends like Vajpayee to support the adventurism of the Americans. George Bush observed on November 27, 2001, that "I can't make it any more clear to other nations around the world. If they develop weapons of mass destruction that will be used to terrorise nations, they will be held accountable".

Buying arms from the US is not the real issue. What is vis-à-vis our foreign policy is that the Government does not have any holistic framework in which bilateralism should operate. The telling example of such a missing "framework" in our foreign policy is that the Government of India failed to even suggest the alternative of the Security Council overseeing the war in Afghanistan. Since the Vajpayee government does not accept the Nehru-Indira framework of foreign policy, it deserves to be reminded that India had always promoted collective action by countries, whether from the platform of the Security Council, the General Assembly of the UN, the Non-Aligned countries or Afro-Asian organisations before interfering in the internal affairs of any country—civilised or rogue. Inspite of critics, Nehru preferred to refer our Jammu & Kashmir dispute with Pakistan to the Security Council. While Security Council during the Cold War phase showed some limitations, during the present unipolar, America dominated global scenario, the Security Council is the only hope for the defence of national sovereignty of Third World countries. Dose pax-Americana mean the irrelevance of many alternative global fora for the resolution of disputes among nations? The Vajpayee Government is not even sensitive to the new threats and dangers that are inherent in the American-led unipolar global system. George Santayana had alerted us that "those who cannot remember the past are condemned to repeat it", and this past of Indian foreign policy was based on an effective balance between "bilateralism" and "multilateralism".

Murasoli Maran, the Industry Minister, realised the importance of "solidarities among the developing countries" while dealing with the Western superpowers at Doha meeting of the World Trade Organisation. India got some concessions on pharmaceutical industries and some relaxation of TRIPS only with the backing of Brazil and 55 developing African countries. This real experience at Doha compelled Maran to observe on November 28, 2001 that "the developing countries ought to form a 'development alliance or a coalition' to carry forward their battle in the multilateral discussions". He wants a "rebellion of developing countries" because he himself experienced the might of Western countries at the WTO meeting. Are Vajpayee or Jaswant Singh or George Fernandes listening to their own colleague? Are they drawing any conclusions from the Doha meeting of the WTO. The Nehru-India foreign policy framework was based on the cognisance of creating "countervailing fora" in global affairs to checkmate the dictates and interferences by the big powers. Maran is talking precisely of Third World unity, which was believed, practised and strengthened by Nehru-Indira Gandhi during their regimes. The Vajpayee government is practising an adhoc "bilaterialism" with a real tilt towards America. It is unfortunate that Indian foreign policy makers have no large picture in this America-dominated unipolar world because the Indian corporate and business world is pushing the foreign policy makers towards the advanced western countries for capital, technology and trade.

The strategic thinkers of the BJP are completely focused on Pakistan and China; they have not addressed themselves to the conceptual framework of multipolarity versus unipolarity. Will India's national interests be better served in a multipolar global situation or in an American-led unipolar world? (*December 7, 2001, The Pioneer*)

Look Back, Mr. Bush

Every democratic country and every democratic movement, irrespective of its geographical and territorial location, has condemned the heinous crime committed by mindless terrorists who targetted innocent human beings working in the WTC and the Pentagon on September 11, 2001. Further, individual or group terrorists and even the state-sponsored terrorism of developing countries cannot achieve any political or military goal; the only satisfaction to the terrorists is that they are able to kill innocent human beings or a few soldiers. The essence of the 21st century is that political issues have to be resolved politically and political resolutions demand patient negotiations, mutual give-and-take and long struggles.

However, the most worrisome product of Black Tuesday is that public discourse has polarised between the American state and the leaders of the Taliban. The American state is talking the language of revenge by proclaiming "Bring Bin Laden, dead or alive", and "we will smoke out the terrorists". Not to be left behind, the Taliban leadership is also indulging in a loose discourse of "Islam in danger" and Sulaiman Abu Ghaith, the Al-Qaeda spokesman, has called on "Muslims across the world to wage a holy war against the US". He also praised the hijackers who carried out the September 11 attacks. In his riposte, US Secretary of State Collin Powell has said "...these are the kinds of words you expect to hear from an evil man".

This ghost of Islam versus Christianity should be buried because the real issue of Western hegemony over Arab/West Asian countries and anger of the people against it is not getting the attention that it deserves. Anti-America protests in some South Asian or South-East Asian countries by local Muslims have the same value as anti-war protests in America itself. The crux of the issue is why are the struggling and progressive forces of Arab/West Asian countries targetting the hegemonic Western power through methods which are not acceptable to the democratic forces in any country of the world?

A few well-known facts may be mentioned to substantiate the argument that the leaders of Western countries have to do a lot of self-introspection and explain to other people around the globe about their self-appointed role of "managing the world affairs" as sole policemen of the world. America or England or France or tiny Belgium have systematically destroyed democratic movements in Latin America, the Arab world, Asia and Africa. They have not stopped here. The above mentioned regimes have been involved in the physical liquidation of popular and tall leaders of the developing world.

In 1951, Dr. Mossadaq, the Prime Minister of Iran, was punished and liquidated because he exercised his national right to manage national resources like oil. Iran's history would have been different if Iranians had been allowed to manage their own domestic affairs in an independent manner. How could oil rich Iran be allowed national freedom by the oil consuming powerful Western nations? Western democracies have themselves to blame for the emergence of Iranian backward looking clergy against whom democratic struggles are going on in Iran.

The same story was repeated in Egypt, which was attacked by Western powers in 1956 because Nasser dared to assert his country's sovereignty over the Suez Canal. Then, Yasser Arafat, an unquestioned leader of the Palestinians, was described as the "most dangerous terrorist" because he wanted "a homeland for the Palestinians". The PLO was supported by all forward looking, modern, liberal and democratic sections of the Palestinian society. Where does the fault lie on the issue of freedom for Palestinians?

The above illustrations show that Islam is not the issue in the ongoing struggles in the Arab/West Asian countries. It is a struggle between freedom fighters and their oppressors and in the case of the Arabs, oppression is carried out by the puppet regimes supported by Western countries. The anger of the Arabs is against their own oppressive, feudal, monarchical, authoritarian and backward looking regimes which are surviving and thriving with the support of America. Is it an accident that a Saudi Arabian has emerged as the leader of the Taliban? The very existence of parasitical regimes in Saudi Arabia or Jordan or dictatorship in Egypt depends on full support by the American war machine. The Arab/West Asian countries have been witnessing serious ups and downs in their regimes and every challenge for regime change has been scuttled or manipulated by the Western countries.

The latest example is Afghanistan, where Tony Blair demands the need for a "broad-based government". UK Foreign Secretary Jack Straw has said: "We have an interest in a broad-based government and those within the Northern Alliance would play a part and there would also be a part of the people represented by the Taliban that is the Pashtu." Arrogant western countries have not learnt any lesson from the tragic events of Black September. The Belgians wanted to manage Congo and Patrice Lumumba was liquidated and replaced by a thug known as Mobutu. Americans have been managing the internal affairs of every country and their general style is revealed by the manner in which Allende of Chile was removed and a dictator Pinochet was installed. Americans want democracy only where it is protected by the Pacific and Atlantic Oceans but democracy is troublesome if it is a global phenomenon.

Samuel J. Huntington, through his faulty book, *The Clash of Civilizations*, has conditioned the Americans that in the 21st century faultlines are contest among civilisations like Christianity versus Islam. Huntington has noted: "There is little resource among Islamic countries for Western ideas of individualism, constitutionalism, human rights, equality, liberty, rule of law, democracy, free markets and the separation of Church and State." If the Professor is correct, he has not diagnosed properly the causes for the existence of such a situation in the so-called Islamic countries. Incidentally, Bangladesh, Malaysia, and Indonesia, are all involved in the struggle for practicing democracy and they happen to be Muslim majority countries.

Further, the US establishment should look at the role it played in destroying progressive movements by supporting military/dictatorial regimes in the Philippines, Indonesia and Pakistan. Army regimes have been favourites of American establishment in Pakistan and the troika that rules Pakistan is "Army, America and Allah (or Mullahs)". The Taliban leaders grew up in squalid campuses in Pakistan among the refugees fleeing Afghanistan during 1979-89. America has to own the parentage of the Taliban.

The upshot of the above description is that Arab/West Asian countries have been victims of western hegemony in the 20th century. Democratic and nationalist aspirations of Arab/West Asian societies and peoples have been crushed by puppet regimes supported by the Americans. Jean-Paul Sartre said: "I hate victims who respect their executioners." The methods employed by some Arab organisations in the struggle against domestic and foreign oppression have been sharply focussed post-September 11. But the causes underlying the anger and frustration of the struggling people of the Arab world have been brushed under the carpet. How long will the PLO and Mr. Arafat be expected to wait to achieve their legitimate democratic goals through purely democratic methods? If democracy is not practiced by Israel and its supporters in America while dealing with Palestinians, any expectation of civilised behaviour from the Palestinians would be unrealistic.

Francis Fukuyama in *The End of History* has celebrated the closing decade of the 20th century as the "Age of democracy". If this is true, the wretched of the Earth in Africa and the Arab world deserve to be left to their own resources to fight against their own oppressive rulers who are in reality the agents of America and other Western countries. This is the real lesson from the tragic events of September 11. (*October 25, 2001, The Pioneer*)

Handle US with Care

In the debate on foreign policy held in the Rajya Sabha in November 2000, Mr. Jaswant Singh conceptualised the BJP-led government's approach to international relations in the context of emergence of the United States as the "pre-eminent power". Mr. Singh observed that "the challenge in the post-cold war era is to meet the reality of 'unipolarity' and mould it to India's advantage".

Since Mr. Singh admitted that "This is a period of "transition" and "unipolarity" cannot be the basis of future international relations, the question is how to move in a multi-polar world and put it to India's advantage". Mr. Singh has very aptly problematised the methodology of a country operating its foreign policy in a New World Order. However, the manner in which the BJP-led government has charted its foreign policy during its three years in office has raised many doubts about its capacity to deal with the complexities of new unipolarity. A few facts may be mentioned to substantiate this argument. The BJP-led government has already accepted that it is the right of the United States to act as a new and unchallenged "global policeman". Can this assessment of the emerging India-US relations be accepted on face value? Has Mr. Singh forgotten that India continues to be under "economic sanctions" imposed by the United State in response to Pokharan II? Americans have given a clear message to India that either sign the CTBT or be ready for sanctions. In other words, it is the sole prerogative of the American government to reward a country like China or punish India, Pakistan and Iraq.

India defended its right to conduct nuclear tests in May 1998 by informing the American government that such an action was essential because "China and Pakistan are nuclear states." Obviously, the Americans have not accepted our "explanation." Otherwise, they would have removed the economic sanctions against us without linking them with signature on the CTBT. Not only this. America does not see India as a responsible nuclear regime because it has not agreed to sign the CTBT. The US is neither in support of nuclear programme of the Indian state nor is it in favour of India signing the CTBT. The above argument clearly reveals that Americans believe in following a policy of "carrot-and-stick" when dealing with India. The United States has economic and military capability to pursue its global and national interests and the Indian state has to show that it has an immense capacity to defend its national sovereignty. The relatively "autonomous" nation-state is the only buffer against American-led New International Order, and such an "autonomy" of the developing state cannot be protected without arriving at a national consensus on issues that concern Indians. The Rajya Sabha debate on foreign policy in November clearly revealed that the government and the major opposition party do not have any meeting ground with regard to India-US relations as projected by Mr. Jaswant Singh. If on the one hand, the BJP-led coalition government is handicapped by the absence of national consensus on its foreign policy goals, on the other, India-Pakistan and India-China problems continue to put brakes on our bargaining capacities with the western capitalist countries. It is prudent to maintain that relative autonomy of the Indian state while dealing with new global power system will be greatly enhanced with the improvement of India-Pakistan and India-China bilateral relations.

The geographical location of countries cannot be wished away and the quality of bilateral relations among neighbours is always a determining factor in a foreign policy. Thus, it is essential to warn Mr. Singh that his logic of territorially determined nation-state will make him sit in the company of "borderless globalisers" with complete subordination of the South by the countries of the North. The New American International Order is based on the ideology of the end of the nation-state. American scholars, who articulate ideas which are relevant to the promotion of the interests of the American state, are busy in pronouncing the death of nation-state project at a global scale. Not only this. The supra-governmental institutions of the North like the World Bank, IMF and WTO have emerged as unquestioned guides of neo-liberal economics which has to be followed by the developing countries if they want to be funded by the so-called multilateral global institutions. The market-led economic fundamentalism of the Americans and developed capitalist countries of the North have to be accepted by the Third World countries. Hence, foreign policy of India has to be integrated with world capitalist system. The most important implication of the present American-led global regime is that economic 'stick' will be used effectively for promoting Pax-Americana world-view and India has to find a space of its own in such a global order. This is a new challenge to India's foreign policy makers and India cannot realise its own potential if it is not able to develop a new framework for building bridges with Pakistan and China. While the Lahore visit of Mr. Vajpayee and unilateral declaration of ceasefire in Kashmir during the period of Ramazan are welcome steps in restoring India-Pakistan relations, they are not sufficient because India and Pakistan are in a deadlock at political levels. It is bad foreign policy to set conditions for starting negotiations with a quarrelsome neighbour. Further, the Vajpayee government has not shown any consistency of arguments when refusing to negotiate with Pakistan.

Earlier, India maintained that it would not negotiate with a military dictator who had destroyed democracy in Pakistan. It also hinted that negotiations cannot take place unless Pakistan stops infiltration of militants into the Kashmir valley. Incidentally, India welcomed a Burmese general for negotiations. However, General Pervez Musharraf remains untouchable for the Brahmins of India. A worrisome idea is being floated by a powerful establishment in the United States that India is a candidate to counter the growing strength of China. The American media is projecting that India as a friend of the US can checkmate China in Asia. Hence, it is essential for the BJP government to make its stand on India's relations with China clear. If India-China bilateral relations are perceived as conflictual as revealed by Mr. Vajpayee's letter to Clinton in May 1998, the Government of India will be pushed to the American way of looking at China. In such a scenario, the Americans will be happy to assist India to stand against China. If the Indian government is serious about multilateralism then China, Russia and India can together emerge as a counter centre to unipolar American-led world. India and the US cannot have mutual relationships on the basis of reciprocity as seen during Clinton presidency. The Clinton government imposed economic sanctions against India with no intentions of withdrawing them. Is this mutuality and reciprocity between two nation-states? The foreign policy of India under the Vajpayee government does not have any comprehensive framework for resolving India-Pakistan and India-China relations.

During its three years in office its responses and reactions have been of *ad hoc* character. It is in the national interests of India, Pakistan, China and Russia to come together and lay down the foundations of global multi-polarity by energising SAARC and involving India and Pakistan as partners in the ASEAN.

The upshot of the above argument is that unipolarity is a threat to territorially defined nation-state of India because the US believes and practices foreign policy of dictation. While state sovereignty is a dirty word for Americans, national self-respect is of great value for countries like India which have emerged after a powerful anti-colonial struggle.

The defence of state sovereignty in the age of unipolarity depends on countervailing multiple global centres of power. India should work on such a countervailing structure by following a foreign policy which stresses close friendship with Pakistan, China and Russia. (*December 28, 2000, The Pioneer*)

US Presidential Polls and India

The emperor has been caught without clothes. The Americans have become a target of jokes and ridicule and 'poetic justice' has been done to the arrogant Americans who were always sending 'observers' to inspect the actual conduct of 'free and fair' elections in developing democratic countries.

For the US, the new century has begun with a sad note as the ongoing drama about the Presidential Elections 2000 has not only revealed weaknesses but also serious defects in the whole electoral and political democratic edifice of the American political system. A few facts may be mentioned to substantiate the argument that arrogant American establishment has simply tumbled down and it would take time and effort to restore the image of the American ruling elite.

First, a governor of a state during elections died in an air crash, and ideally polls should have been countermanded as the candidate died during the campaign period. But, American democracy does not believe in this. His widow automatically became a governor of a state for two years on the basis of votes secured by her dead husband. Our Rabri Devi is much better as she is a duly elected MLA and Bihar CM.

Second, the pillar of any functioning and vigorous democracy is an active participatory citizenry. Only 50 per cent of the voters turnout was seen in the recent US polls. Such a low voter turnout is in spite of the media-led, market-led and money-led election in the US. It has been officially stated that $3 billion have been spent in the November elections. Not only this. Americans have always claimed some specialities about their great democracy and one of them is extensive public debate for about fourteen months. Even fund-raising dinners and social get together have been highlighted by the Americans as a great democratic exercise to involve large number of people in elections. Prestigious newspapers come out with special support for one or the other leading candidate in the contest. In spite of all these efforts with the help of powerful media, the voter participation is quite low as compared to the high turnover in our much maligned democracy.

Third, American system of conducting elections has been found quite defective and vulnerable in the face of unforeseen situations as witnessed in the recounting of votes in Florida and the results are hanging till the meagre absentee postal ballots do not arrive for the purposes of counting.

Further, American scholarship has always maintained that they have achieved all the 'pre-requisites' for the functioning of successful democracy; and in a very patronising manner American scholars would ask 'leading questions' in a sarcastic manner about the vote banks and patron-client based democracy of India especially during the 1950s and 1960s.

Fifth, the failure of technology may be ignored but the blunders committed by the high profile media cannot be brushed under the carpet because Americans have made elections a media-led commodity for influencing the public opinion. Not only this. It has gone into the head of American psychologists that they can conduct pre-poll and exit-poll exercises to find out the trends during and after the elections. All this is lying in a shambles because they have announced, rather misannounced the polls outcome.

American media, a very powerful element of the US establishment, has cut such a sorry figure during Bush-Gore elections that it stands exposed, humbled and humiliated.

Despite the above description about the US discomfiture, Indians cannot ignore the only super power in the real sense of the term and our government, industrial houses and important public and private policy makers would have to deal with the new occupant of the White House and likely Republican dominated Congress. President Bill Clinton declared India as a 'partner of the United States' but economic sanctions imposed on India in the wake of Pokharan-II in May 1998 were not lifted by the Clinton administration.

Similarly, the Clinton administration has refused to change its position on CTBT and even the supply of critical defence equipment is not easily available to India from the US. Hence, it is essential to examine the overall frame-work of American foreign policy which is always described as 'bipartisan' consensus-based approach towards countries around the world.

While the Democrats believe and practise the foreign policy of 'active interventions' and 'humanitarian interventions' in countries around the world, a statement by George Bush has been given an importance which it does not deserve. The democrats actively intervened in West Asia or Kosovo or the Yugoslavia, and George Bush observed that his foreign policy would be 'less interventionist' and his government would not go on fishing expeditions abroad.

This statement of the Republican Presidential candidate does not make him 'less hawkish' than the Democrats.

George Bush has clearly stated and many in the Clinton establishment have shown their concern on the emergence of New China in the twenty first century. It is probable that Americans may make India a candidate to counter China and some frantic anti-communist and anti-China groups and individuals in the BJP-led coalition government will welcome an American invitation to confront China. It is not accidental that the Vajpayee government in a confidential letter to President Clinton justified Pokharan-II by identifying 'Pakistan and China as our enemies." The imperatives of Indian foreign and defence policies lie in our geographical position where China and Pakistan cannot be wished away and hostility with both the neighbours would place a heavy defence burden on India and, if Indians play America's China card, India will become completely dependent on the US whims and fancies. Indians should review the 'unfolding' of American foreign policy after the Presidential elections.

We should also learn a lesson that Presidential system of governance as a recipe for India, propagated by the Hindu holy family, is so flawed that even elections cannot resolve the candidacy of the incumbent.

A parrot like initiation of the American Presidential system will prove disastrous for India because the quest of *Hindutva* forces for political stability will lead the country to many deadlocks as revealed by Bush-Gore elections. Moreover, after witnessing Hillary Clinton's victory and the powerful candidature of Bush Jr, the congenital critics of dynastic politics in India should simply keep quite.

It may be concluded by stating that the ongoing Presidential election process in America has completely exposed the myth that in a democracy American President has a mandate of the people because in spite of popular mandate in favour of one candidate, his opponent may win on the basis of 270 members of the Electoral College. How can an electoral college negate the popular mandate in favour of a candidate is possible only in the so-called great democracy of America? (*November 22, 2000, The Observer*)

US Jaunt—Reality and Rhetoric

Since Prime Minister A.B. Vajpayee has spent almost a fortnight in the US to promote Indo-US ties, the results of such an extended interaction between the policy-makers of the two nations deserve to be evaluated and analysed. The US being the sole superpower wields much more influence in the present world affairs, especially in the fast emerging new global capitalist scenario, where, on the one hand, the WTO, IMF and World Bank call all the shots and, on the other, every developing country, including India, has to deal with these supranational institutions that are highly influenced by Washington. New Delhi's foreign, economic and defence policy-makers have recognised this pre-eminence of the US; and the Clinton and Vajpayee visits were some of the concrete steps in this direction.

While analysing the actual contents of Indo-US ties as a consequence of the visit, a distinction must be made between the rhetoric associated with social occasions and the reality of actual results which have flowed or are likely to flow. It is mere rhetoric to maintain that India and the US have become 'natural allies' or a 'political partnership' has been established between the two after the Vajpayee visit. It has also to be noted that India's national security policy has always been different from that of the US' way of looking at global security and defence issues.

The Vajpayee government has taken great pride in proclaiming that India has emerged as a 'nuclear weapon state' after the Pokharan-II; and Vajpayee publicly told the US that India is a 'responsible nuclear weapon state'. However, it did not cut much ice with the Americans and, in spite of the US Congress' resolution to lift the nuclear sanctions, Clinton rejected the proposal. Further, Vajpayee was specifically asked to take concrete steps towards signing of the CTBT. And after leaving the US his first statement was in Frankfurt where he said, his 'government will try for a national consensus on CTBT'.

In his every address, whether made at the UN, or in the US Congress or in his deliberations with US policy-makers, Vajpayee focussed sharply on the deteriorating Indo-Pak relations due to the growing cross-border terrorism being sponsored by Pakistan in Kashmir. And every one knows what was the US response. 'India and Pakistan should negotiate the Kashmir tangle'. Does it show any 'tilt' in favour of India, and against Pakistan? Only Vajpayee's PMO or his MEA mandarins can say yes.

Indian policy-makers should make a clear distinction between the 'economic' and 'strategic' concerns and the interests of the US, as sometimes it can use its economic prowess to gain strategic advantages. It must also be noted that US foreign policy-makers have shown great deftness in using the carrot and stick policy for achieving their economic and strategic goals while dealing with foreign countries, and India cannot be an exception to this general rule of the US foreign policy.

At the most, the visit is a kind of 'first-step' towards 'a new bilateralism' between the two. Since India opened its doors to foreign investments, US investors with the support of their government have started exploiting the new economic opportunities in India. It is also a fact that the flow of American capital into India has been further facilitated with the visit. But there was no political consensus or understanding here. Matter of factly speaking, India wants US investments, and Washington is encouraging its capitalists to invest in India. But actually, India as a destination for the US capital has been the result of its new economic policy, and Vajpayee's visit is only a kind of 'footnote' in the process of ongoing bilateral economic relations.

The most important drawback of the visit is that India is back to square one on the nuclear issue, economic sanctions and on the CTBT. Again, Vajpayee repeatedly accused Pakistan for violating past pacts but it did not cut much ice with the Uncle Sam as Vajpayee was very clearly told to 'hold talks with Pakistan on the Kashmir issue'. Can Vajpayee assume that his updates on Kashmir would be music to the American ears? Isn't the US ambassador in India reporting to his HQ about the Indo-Pak deadlock over Kashmir?

Normally, the main purpose of a visit by a head of the government/state to another country is to create a conducive political climate so that visiting country's interests are taken care of by the host country. But Vajpayee, due to his ill-health and the inadequacy of linguistic felicity, completely failed to influence the powerful opinion-makers in the US. The contrast between Clinton and Vajpayee as communicators was quite visible. In a highly publicity-conscious society like the Americans, Vajpayee miserably failed to emerge as the chief public relations officer of his country. It is worth mentioning the editorial of *The New York Times* on September 21: 'On improving its friendship with India, the US needs to be particularly careful not to incite feelings of distrust in Pak and China. India should now move quickly to sign the CTBT — since failure to do so will not only provoke Pak but also raise anxiety in Beijing'.

This is the best commentary on the visit because in our euphoria of the so-called 'new chapter' in the Indo-US friendship, we are likely to forget that neighbours like China and Pakistan are a determining factor in our foreign and security policies. Actually, we don't need the NYT to tell us that growing friendship with the US cannot bring us peace without mending our fences with China and Pakistan. Not only this. While Vajpayee has been talking about 'multi-polar' world, he has been doing a lot of overtime work to evolve strategic relationship with the Americans. But such a relationship between Uncle Sam is not in our advantage as we are essentially an Asian nation and our strategic relationships depends mostly on our geographical location.

While letting the Indo-US ties grow further, it will be advisable for New Delhi not to put all eggs in the American basket without resolving our issues with Islamabad and Beijing. Hence, Clinton's observation that 'India and the US are not only natural allies but have common enemies' should alert New Delhi as the US as the sole superpower has global friends and global enemies, and India cannot be tied and linked with the list of such friends and enemies. (*September 27, 2000, The Observer*)

US Mediation is the Message

If September 11, 2001, was a defining moment for the Americans, India, on its part, was shocked on December 13, when terrorists succeeded in breaking the security cordon to attack the Parliament. The Government ordered full-scale military mobilisation. Its aim was to punish Pakistan militarily for indulging in cross-border terrorism. Not only this. Foreign and defence policymakers built a diplomatic front to convey a clear message to the US: The 'global coalition' against terrorism could not ignore the fact that Pakistan sponsored terrorist activities against India. India showed its determination by mobilising a one million-strong force to confront terrorists and their supporter, the Government of Pakistan.

India believed the military and diplomatic fronts against Pakistan-supported terrorism would activate its Western alliance partners, and that they would succeed in containing Pakistan. It believed the West had enough economic and military clout to do so. This premise concerning the West's capacities and intentions proved hollow. American soldiers were stationed in Pakistani territory and Pakistan was a frontline ally in the US's fight against Al Qaeda militants. Indian policymakers failed to realise that the Americans would play a wishy-washy role in the India-Pakistan dispute over Jammu & Kashmir (J&K).

Indian policymakers received another shock on May 14, 2002, when terrorists penetrated an army camp at Kaluchak near Jammu, and killed the family members of soldiers. The Government declared it would take the fight across the Line of Control (LoC), attacking terrorist camps in Pakistan-occupied Kashmir. Indian officials maintained it would be a "limited war" against terrorists based in Pakistani territory. Pakistan reacted strongly. One irresponsible Pakistani spokesman asserted that the war would be fought with nuclear weapons, since Pakistan did not have the capability to beat the Indian Army in "conventional weapons-based" war. The West became alert, worried as it was about the 'nuclearisation' of the India-Pakistan conflict. Both nations shouted from the rooftops: They would fight, even if it meant 'nuclear confrontation'.

War cries of the two 'nuclear power states' brought Western visitors to the subcontinent, who tried to stop them from waging a war that could end in 'nuclear disaster'. Not only this. The armies of India and Pakistan were standing eyeball to eyeball—any small accident could trigger a full-scale war. Events began moving fast as the US, Russia and China coordinated their activities. At the Conference on Interaction and

Confidence-Building Measures in Asia at Almaty, informal views were conveyed to India and Pakistan on the de-escalation of tensions at the borders. British and American policymakers launched an active campaign in the subcontinent. A breakthrough came after the visit, starting June 6, of US Deputy Secretary of State Richard Armitage. The Government permitted the resumption of civilian air flights to Pakistan. It withdrew Air Force warplanes and naval planes from forward areas. And it announced the appointment of a new High Commissioner to Pakistan.

These were concrete results of Mr. Armitage's mediation efforts. So "de-escalation" began even before the visit of US Defence Secretary Donald Rumsfeld on June 11. Mr. Armitage, in an interview to BBC in Washington on June 11, maintained that India and Pakistan had taken "de-escalatory measures". He added that "the international community would prefer as rapid a de-escalation as possible." He thus laid down the foundations for the Rumsfeld visit.

Conceding that Al Qaeda militants were present on the LoC, Mr. Rumsfeld proposed "monitoring" it. India, on its part, suggested 'the installation of sensors to detect infiltration'. The Defence Secretary appreciated India's de-escalation measures. As for border "surveillance", he said to the Press that he had "a whole series of proposals, any of which could lead to a step-by-step de-escalation of tension".

Bilateral de-escalation had been achieved, courtesy Western initiative. India had willingly invited Western 'mediation'. The West is now actively involved in India-Pakistan bilateral disputes. Addressing a gathering of the New York-based Asia Society on June 11, US Secretary of State Colin Powell talked of the Bush Administration's "interest in staying engaged in efforts to end hostilities" and in pulling the two countries "back from the brink of war".

A few aspects of Indian foreign, defence and diplomatic activities in June deserve attention because India seems to have, formally or informally, laid the foundations of 'Western mediation', 'arbitration' or 'engagement' in the dispute on Kashmir and cross-border terrorism. India and Pakistan have refused to enter into direct negotiations. The opportunity to break the ice in Almaty was not taken.

While India and Pakistan remained on the brink of war—with the nuclear *Democles*' sword hanging over them—the world's sole superpower was the first to exercise the option of asking its citizens to leave the countries on the ground that they were dangerous for Western tourists and investors. The message was: Let two 'nuclear weapons states' destroy one another. The West used a powerful weapon against India and

Pakistan by asking their citizens to pack up. Had this strategy continued for long, India would have still been bleeding, thanks to the impact on its economic interests.

Then, the superpower exercised its second option: If the Indians did not wish to be globally ostracised, they would allow Western mediation. There is no use pretending the de-escalation steps taken by India and Pakistan are not the result of American intervention supported by Britain and Russia. The Prime Minister should have backed Russia's President Vladimir Putin's proposal to arrange 'proxy talks' between India and Pakistan in Almaty. This step would have conveyed a message to the West: India has many options when it comes to dealing with Pakistan. A good foreign policy in a 'unipolar' world is to focus on multipolar centres of friendship. India, Russia and China could emerge as important centres of power, and Russia and China could play an important role in bringing India and Pakistan to the negotiating table.

Asian countries are seeking their own solutions to the problem of US hegemony. Just after the Almaty meeting on Asian security, the six-member Shanghai Cooperation Organisation (SCO) brought China, Russia, Kazakhstan, Tajikistan, Kyrgyzstan and Uzbekistan on a common platform. Has India made any attempt to develop multipolarity as a means to countering Pax Americana? The answer is a big 'No'. Consequently, Western countries have become active players in the India-Pakistan dispute. True, these powerful nations have succeeded in achieving a level of de-escalation between confrontationist neighbours in South Asia. But that only allows the world's sole superpower to monitor India's behaviour.

White House Press Secretary Ari Fleischer said on June 11: "This is a region ... that will require on-going monitoring." Does our foreign policy invite powerful Western countries to mediate in our disputes with neighbours? What about our tall claims to being a "nuclear weapons state"? Mr. Armitage came to India after talking to the Pakistani President. Mr. Rumsfeld visited India first, then Pakistan. The US message is clear. India and Pakistan were on the "brink of nuclear war"—and the Americans, as powerful mediators, would treat them as 'equals'. In the process, they would help us find a solution by monitoring the India-Pakistan border in J&K. This is what our current foreign policy means. (*June 29, 2002, The Pioneer*)

Growing Expansionism in Asia: India should be wary of American designs

Foreign and defence policy makers are throwing caution to the wind and unnecessarily becoming euphoric about the new levels of friendship between India and the USA. A few facts may be mentioned to substantiate the argument that the Vajpayee-led government should be highly concerned and worried about some of the policy decisions of the American policymakers because these decisions have an adverse impact on the security scenario of India.

First, the USA has decided to settle down with its military might in South Asia, South-West Asia and Central Asia. Mr. Robert D. Blackwell, the US Ambassador to India, was compelled to admit this fact. On January 24 at a "round table conference of journalists" he said that "there are no permanent plans yet, but there will be long-term engagement. The US has an interest in the vast oil reserves there".

Second, on the pretext of overseeing "operations in Afghanistan, the US-led coalition troops" have been provided a military base at Karachi airport. The US Commander of Afghan war, Gen. Tommy Franks, maintained that Americans "will stay put" in their allotted Pakistan bases.

Third, Russia, China and Iran are all worried because of the above mentioned developments in American foreign policy. Mr. Oleg Cherno of the Russian National Security Council expressed these fears on January 17 while stating that "the USA was establishing an airbase in the Central Asian republic of Kyrgyzstan, Uzbekistan etc."

Instead of showing concern on these developments in the region, the Indian leadership is enthusiastic in entering into collaboration with the Americans. Indian and US intelligence officials have decided to set up a "Joint working Group on Terrorism". The object of this bilateral relationship is that India and the USA will share "intelligence" on terrorism. Indians should be worried because "Intelligence on terrorism" is an extremely vague exercise and involvement of the CIA and the FBI with Indian agencies will lead to a complete "erosion of confidentiality" of intelligence meant for Indian national security. Indians will be creating great worries in China on this move for sharing of intelligence with the USA.

Mr. George Fernandes, Defence Minister, after his visit to the USA, declared on January 18 that "the revival of Indo-US defence relations is going to be strong and abiding". It deserves to be mentioned that defence deals between India and the USA are extremely profitable to the arms exporters and defence industry of the USA. Defence sales are a lucrative business for every arms exporter, including the powerful defence industry of the USA. After all, the Vajpayee-led government is moving with a shopping list for defence equipment and Americans cannot ignore the rising defence budget of the Indian government.

India has also sought US help on "vigil over our borders" and the US Coordinator for Counter Terrorism, Ambassador Francis Taylor maintained that "a key part of efforts is to enable nations to protect themselves" against terrorism and a "pilot project" has been launched in Jammu and Kashmir where Americans will "coordinate" with Indians on issues of cross-border terrorism". All these developments in the "new year" have naturally gladdened the Americans and Blackwell expressed these feeling by saying that "The Indo-US relationship, in most dimensions, is today unrecognisable from what it was a year back. But business relations are lagging behind. There is a lot of promise, but most of it is unrealised".

The growing dependence of India on the USA is a matter of great concern because America is the sole hyper-superpower of the present century, and so the Americans will get a new capacity to push their interests in India because the Indians are putting all their eggs in the American basket.

If Indian policymakers are not able to maintain an appropriate "distance" from the dominant American global interests, India will lose not only its "autonomy" of foreign policy, it may also complicate its relationship with Russia and China. A new tension between India and Russia has already developed because the Vajpayee government has welcomed George W. Bush Jr.'s Nuclear Defence Missile Programme and Russia feels threatened by this new development in American strategic thinking.

George W. Bush has not only talked about the abrogation of Anti-Ballistic Missile Treaty of 1972, he has made India a party to "his programme" of the "nuclearisation of the space". While Indians were in agreement with American Nuclear Missile Programme, the Russian Parliament (Duna) passed a resolution on January 16, 2002 that on ABM Treaty of 1972 the US move is not only "mistaken and destabilising", it could create "real conditions for a new round of arms race". India and Russia have very deep relationship and any strain between these two countries on account of Indian policy making lapses will be not only unfortunate, it will further push us into the American camp.

India, China and Russia are a "countervailing" force in the present unipolar world, and India will be ejected both by China and Russia if India accepts American Nuclear Defence Missile Programme. The Chinese Premier, Zhu Rongji, gave a clear message on January 15 that while China and Pakistan have an "all-weather friendship'; and as far as India is concerned, Zhu stated that "as the two largest developing countries in the world, China and India have on their shoulders the important responsibility for maintaining peace, stability and prosperity in Asia. We should strengthen our cooperation in international affairs and work together to promote the establishment of a just and equitable international, new political and economic order".

The goals of Chinese foreign policy as stated by Zhu Rongji, should be precisely our goals because the present global order has no checks and balances and everything depends on the Americans. A telling example of the pre-eminent status of American global agenda is provided by the Black Tuesday of September 11, 2001, when Americans declared a war against terrorism because they themselves were targeted. Not only this. It is becoming an unending war for the Americans and, under the pretext of fighting anti-terrorist global war, they have fully coopted the Indians and also put their armed forces permanently in our region. Will Americans stop here or put gentle pressures on coopted India for a "dialogue" on Kashmir?

What is the explanation for the Vajpayee government's fascination with the Americans? Atal Bihari Vajpayee and the Jan Sangh were always critical of Nehru-Indira Gandhi foreign policy framework of non-alignment because it was perceived by them as 'tilted' towards erstwhile Soviet Russia. Ideologically the Jan Sangh has been consistently anti-Communist and their anti-communism was logically extended to erstwhile Soviet Russia and China. Foreign policy of the Jan Sangh was based on anti-Russia and anti-China plank and Mr. Vajpayee as a Foreign Minister in the Morarji Desai's government of 1977-79 projected himself as a practitioner of "genuine non-alignment", which was without any "tilt" towards any superpower. In the present BJP-led government, Mr. George Fernandes as Defence Minister is ideologically against China and pro-Dalai Tibet, and thus Sangh Parivar and Fernandes are a stumbling block between the growth of healthy trilateral relationship among India, Russia and China. It also deserves to be mentioned that the Vajpayee-led government had informed President Clinton that Pokharan II test of May, 1998, was undertaken because India had hostile "China and Pakistan" as nuclear countries. Thus an ideological baggage of the 20th

Century is carried by Sangh Parivar and Mr. Fernandes while pursuing foreign and defence policies in a new global unipolar world.

Is Mr. Jaswant Singh, the Foreign Minister of India, able to reconcile actual policies of the government and his own rhetoric of global change? Mr. Jaswant Singh, while addressing an elite group on January 21, stated: "The world has moved from the glacial immobility of the cold war to the present. But the present has neither perseverance nor permanence. A constantly new frontier of diplomacy is the territory of change." Unfortunately, this sentiment is not translated into foreign and defence policy making because India has set its goal to reach only the frontiers set by Americans policies. If Americans are bringing Uzbekistan, Tajikistan, Turkmenistan and Karachi airport under their military presence, India will have no option but to stand as a mute spectator to America's presence in our region. But there is another option available to the Indian policy makers if they believe in the principle of "autonomy of national policy". While Putin's Russia has always been supportive of India, the Chinese Prime Minister has also been open to good relationship when he said that "we have border disputes, which are subject of discussion. But there is no conflict on the ground for over four years." Why not build on "correct and friendly relations" between India and China in the light of new American expansionism in South and Central Asia?

The foreign policy framework of the Vajpayee government is very restrictive because it has accepted the logic of existing America-led unipolar world. India's national interests cannot be served by accepting American hegemony. Indian policymakers have to explore every possibility and potentiality of opening new chapters of relationship with Russia and China. Russia and China are also wary of American presence in Asia and a convergence of interests should bring India-Russia-China around a trilateral cooperative agenda of dealing with the new global situation. The upshot of above description is that the first month of 2002 has brought great cheers to Indians who want very close relationship with the sole superpower but it has created anxieties in the minds of those who think that one power domination is a dangerous thing in world affairs. Hence there is a need for counter-strategies to limit the expanding military control by the Americans. (*February 16, 2002, The Tribune*)

Time to Back Down

President Musharraf's January 12, 2002 address made everyone sit around and ask: Does he really mean it? Can he really achieve it? Will he survive after making a powerful attack on "Military, Mosque and Militant" establishment of Pakistan which had become the centre of real state power. A few salient features of his scathing attack on the role of the clergy in determining Pakistan's state policy deserve to be highlighted. First, Musharraf unambiguously condemned *jihad* as a 'political weapon'. Second, he committed himself to "restore the writ of government" in Pakistan which had been eroded by mullahs, madarsas and mosques, and their patrons in the government. Third, he served a clear notice to the Pakistan's Intelligence Services that they will not be allowed to "use Islam to control the political process within the country and around the region". While denouncing the attempt of powerful religious fanatics, Musharraf observed that "Madarsas should not be used for spreading religious fundamentalism. It is humiliating for all Muslims that mosques are being used for *Jihad*". Fourth, Musharraf concertised his indictment of the *jihads* by banning five militant-terrorist Islamists like Laskshkar-e-Toiba, Jaish-e-Mohammad, and others. And finally, he declared his resolve not to allow terrorists to operate from Pakistan's territory.

India should trust the General because the Military-governing elite of Pakistan must have drawn a lesson that after 9/11, the world has decisively turned against religion-based terrorism. Not only this. The grand model of the Mosque-Military-Militant system of governance which was actually practised by the Taliban in Afghanistan collapsed like a house of cards before American military power. Since Pakistan Military-Intelligence-Mosque power group was deeply involved in Afghanistan, the collapse of Taliban regime also means the collapse of the model of Islamist terrorism for the simple reason that the defeat of Taliban in Afghanistan is also a crushing and humiliating defeat for the promoters and practitioners of religious fundamentalism/terrorism in Pakistan. President Musharraf could not have challenged the Mullahs and powerful military supporters otherwise. Pakistan and India are not able to start a meaningful political dialogue on the "Kashmir dispute" because our neighbour is not controlled by a political elite. Irrespective of the form of political regime, if Pakistan practices politics of diplomacy by displacing and replacing the terrorist *jihadis* and Mullahs, India, to use Jaswant Singh's observation of January 13, 2002, "...will not be found wanting. We are willing to take two steps for every one that Pakistan takes". If Pakistan state stops "export of terrorism" to India, bilateralism will definitely be in order in place of the present war-like situation.

Pervez Musharraf has made his commitment to the international community that religiously-inspired terrorism will be replaced by diplomatic and political negotiations between India and Pakistan to resolve the Kashmir dispute. The international community has also welcomed this new approach of Pakistan towards Kashmir dispute because secular policy issues of the state should not be made a hostage to religious fanatics. India should make every effort to bring Musharraf to the negotiating table because any other method of resolving the Kashmir dispute will be completely disastrous for these two nuclear-weapon sates. Military options are exercised only when diplomacy has failed. War is a recognition of a fact that diplomacy has not been successful in resolving inter-state disputes. Musharraf's rhetoric on Kashmir, or 'third party' intervention for the resolution of bilateral dispute is not to be taken seriously, because the US, Russia and China have rejected the option. This is the real message both to Pakistan and India by the international community that "war is neither necessary nor desirable" in the present situation and 'dialogue' between the two neighbours is the only option for resolving neighbourly disputes. The very idea of a war on the Kashmir issue in the context of nuclearisation of the two countries is irresponsible; it will amount to the worst kind of criminal adventurism by both countries. Further, Musharraf could not have made his agenda of 'redefining' Pakistan without sizable support from the powerful military machine of his country. The military general seems to have drawn correct lessons from the collapse of Pakistan supported model of Taliban regime and he has promised to cleanse Pakistan of 'Talibinisation of its own society'. It is essential for India to encourage 'secularisation' of Pakistani politics because it will bring great political dividends. If Kashmir dispute is "delinked" from the *jihadi* terrorists, normal diplomatic channels will start operating between the two neighbouring countries. In summation, it may be mentioned that it is in India's own enlightened national interest to change the war-like atmosphere which is prevailing in this country because January 12 marks a beginning of a new thinking in Pakistan's powerful military establishment. Political democracy of India is based on the principles of 'negotiation, bargaining and accommodation' and these are precisely the principles which should be practiced in diplomacy especially between the two neighbouring countries. (*January 20, 2002, The Sunday Pioneer*)

Putin Visit: An Assessment

Russian President Viadmir Putin's recent visit to India has great political and strategic significance for our foreign and defence policies.

The old Communist system has collapsed and Russia is facing the obstacles of transition from the old to the new system. Even amidst these domestic troubles, Putin has a world view which is in harmony with Indian interests.

What kind of a global framework is beneficial for India? The collapse of the Socialist system in Eastern Europe and the USSR was celebrated by ex-US president George Bush as the end of the Cold War and emergence of a new world order, and the end result was the emergence of a unipolar world under US policing.

It's worth recalling a former national security adviser to the US President, Zbigniew Brzezninski's observation at a recent ICSSR seminar held in New Delhi: "The US should strive to prolong its dominance, not only because it is good for the US but also because there is no substitute for it". Brzezinski represents the prevailing consensus among the Americans that the US is the most powerful country in the new world order. Will it serve New Delhi's national interests to operate its national security and defence policies under the US supervision? The answer is a big no. It's worth quoting Prime Minister A.B. Vajpayee's statement at the India-EU summit in Lisbon on June 28, 2000: "In an increasingly interdependent world, a plural security order alone can deal with the challenges of the new era... It is part of India's resolve to build a multipolar world where she has strategic space and autonomy in decision-making."

The announcement of new strategic partnership by Putin and Vajpayee is a confirmation of the desire of these two countries to strive to create a democratic multipolar global order. All the 17 agreements signed between the two leaders, including the strategic partnership document, inter-governmental commission on military technical cooperation and the pact on peaceful uses of nuclear energy and space, are very significant as this powerful bilateralism between New Delhi and Moscow is an important step in creating a stronger foundation for a multipolar world order.

Even on specific national concerns of India on terrorism, Afghanistan, and security threats from Pakistan supported religious terrorism both the leaders emphasised the importance of joint efforts to establish a solid global legal basis for cooperation in combating world terrorism. Putin unambiguously stated that he was prepared to show hard evidence of a common pattern of religious terrorism from Kosovo to Kashmir and Chechenia to other Central Asian republics. And Putin even went to the extent declaring unambiguously that the LoC in Kashmir was sacred.

Moscow along with New Delhi will have to make more concrete efforts to lay down a solid foundation for a multipolar world, based on the sovereign equality of all states: and for achieving this goal, Russia is working for a triangular axis between Moscow, New Delhi and Beijing. If it works out, then other Asian countries can also follow suit. The upshot of this discussion is that Putin has conveyed a very well-thought out strategy of safeguarding the sovereignty of all states in the present unipolar world. Moreover, this proposed multipolar world order is not against any other country and, specifically not anti-Western. Also such a multipolar world order, having many centres of power is a guarantee for the security of every state. Russia, India and China can emerge as one centre of power in Asia because all of them have enough economic and strategic strengths to safeguard their collective national interests as also promote the national interests of other friendly Asian states. Is this idea not worth pursuing by New Delhi?

It will be extremely unfortunate if the BJP-led coalition government failed to promote the proposed Asian triangle idea, because while exploding nuclear devices in May 1998 the Vajpayee government identified China and Pakistan as our major enemies. The Sangh Parivar has been consistently anti-China and pro-Tibet as it is ideologically opposed to Communism. It can be recalled that Nehru organised the Asian Relations Conference in New Delhi with a view to promote cooperation among the victims of colonialism, and in spite of the derailment of Sino-Indo relations in 1962, Rajiv Gandhi had re-launched the idea of Sino-Indo friendship.

Putin's visit is extremely important as relationships between India and Russia in every field have been comprehensively discussed and mutual pacts have been signed. His visit to the BARC was even historical as he endorsed India's peaceful use of nuclear energy and offered to strengthen nuclear cooperation.

It is an irony that despite all the strategic importance, the Putin visit was underplayed and accorded a very routine affair by the Vajpayee regime which is euphoric about the growing Indo-US friendship. But the visit has given a new message to India that Moscow and New Delhi do not have any conflict of interests, a message which Clinton could not give during his visit.

Even the die-hard pro-American and anti-Russian groups here have been put on the defensive because concrete agreements in the field of defence, nuclear energy, trade and the commonality of approach towards religious terrorism clearly gave a message that Putin meant and valued serious friendship with India. It is difficult to find any gap between Putin's speeches to the Parliament or to the corporates. The declaration on strategic partnership, covered trade and economy, defence, science and technology, culture and other fields. The political dimension of this declaration was quite significant that both countries asserted their desire to work in close cooperation in the bilateral as well as in the world arena: and if any assurance was needed, the document clearly stated that it was based on mutual respect and benefit.

Finally, it needs to be mentioned that the Vajpayee regime is quite enthusiastic when it comes to Indo-US relations, but it has some mental and ideological reservations and hesitations while dealing with the Russians or the Chinese. Since New Delhi is committed to establish a multipolar world order, every effort should be made to expand and extend the Indo-Russian friendship and cooperation. New Delhi has a choice. Either a hegemonic unipolar world or a multipolar democratic world order.

South Asian State Systems

The collapse of East European Socialist State Systems and the end of cold war in the beginning of 1990s created euphoria of victory in the Western capitalist countries because the demise of planned socialist economies was attributed to the absence of democracies in the erstwhile socialist countries. On the basis of flawed logic, the failure of socialism was immediately equated with the success of Western capitalist system and their values of governance. A few salient features of the post-1990 ideological pronouncements of the arrogant leaders of the Western capitalist countries may be highlighted to understand the reality of new global milieu in which South Asian state systems will have to function during the first decade of the twenty first century. George Bush, the former President of United States, proclaimed that the end of cold war has led to the creation of a New World Order which in reality means American-led global system. America is the sole super-power and every country will have to grapple with Pax Americana. The foundational principle of Pax Americana is neo-liberal economic theory which is a glorification of a market-led democracy. The collapse of Soviet socialist system was not only proclaimed as a victory for capitalism, it was also declared that the whole world has achieved the goals of liberty, equality and fraternity for which the journey began in 1789 with French Revolution. In a self-congratulatory mood, the Western political leaders are projecting the victory for their values of democracy, human rights, rule of law, market-led democracy and retreat of the state and it is now a global project for the Westerners, and every country is expected to conform with the ideology, values and philosophy of governance of Western democracies. It is not only a rhetoric for the New Age for Democracy, the Western countries propose to reward or punish countries which either conform to the Western agenda of democracy or fail to protect human rights and rule of law. This is the new global setting in which South Asian state systems will have to conform to the standards of governance laid down by the Western capitalist countries.

Feudal-monarchical Bhutan and Nepal, feudal-bureaucratic-army rule in Pakistan are deviant cases in the Western proclaimed Age of Democracy. South Asian state systems are authoritarian or democratic, and in the latter category are included India, Sri Lanka and Bangladesh and even Maldives. If on the one hand South Asian countries have differences among themselves on the basis of systems of governance, on the other, all of them are dependent and integrated with world capitalist system. Not only this. While South Asian countries have some serious conflicts among themselves or within their own countries, as far as New Global capitalism is concerned, all of them have unanimously accepted the hegemony and dominance of the capital surplus and capital exporting countries. South Asian state systems are "subordinate" sub-systems of the Western capitalist hegemonic countries because all fractions of the ruling classes in South Asia whether military generals, or monarchy/kings or capitalists or feudal/landlords have accepted that that they cannot manage their economy, society and polity in a relative autonomous manner while dealing with the Western capitalist countries and their institutions like the World Bank, IMF and WTO. The "subordinate status" of South Asian state systems was dramatised when India and Pakistan decided, very foolishly, to declare themselves as Nuclear Weapon states in May/June 1998. The so called Nuclear Weapon states of India and Pakistan were punished by the G-7 countries and economic sanctions were imposed against them. Not only this. The G-7 countries imposed a condition on India and Pakistan to sign nuclear Non-Proliferation Treaty if they wanted the withdrawal of economic sanctions imposed against them. The upshot of this discussion is that our democracies or monarchies or feudal-military regimes, inspite of their proclamations, have compromised their "sovereign rights" to govern over their own countries.

If growing dependence and subordination of the South Asian state systems is one side of the social dialectics of these societies, the other side is represented by powerful democratic movements and struggles which are taking place in these societies to establish egalitarian social structures internally and to confront dictations imposed by powerful capitalist countries and their institutions. This contradictory social dialectics explains the realities of all South Asian countries which are facing serious internal oppositions to the established social order. It is better to substantiate the above formulation from the Indian experience of democracy. Democracy is not a gift of the British colonial rulers. The struggle for democracy was integrally linked with India's very powerful anti-colonial national movement and it is during our national movement that the Indians learnt their lessons in democracy. All the pre-requisites of democracy as defined by Western social scientists like Lipset or Barrington Moore or Larry Diamond were conspicuous by their absence in India. Not only this. The Indian feudal and landlord classes alongwith a section of intelligentsia maintained that Indian social soil was not hospitable for the launching of the experiment of universal adult franchise. During the last fifty years, democratic elections held on the basis of universal adult franchise have played a "*revolutionary*" role in bringing a qualitative change in social relations among Indians. Indian democracy was launched from "above" and as the journey continued democracy has penetrated the remote villages of India. An important fact to be noted about Indian democracy is that it has become a part of political culture of the masses and it is not confined to the narrow social elite. The voter's turnout during the Lok Sabha, or State Assembly or Panchayati Raj Institutions has been gradually increasing and many a time it has crossed 65 to 70 per cent of actual voting during the elections at various levels of democracy. Indians have not witnessed any fatigue or passivity or cynicism of the voter during the elections is demonstrated by the fact that voters come out and stand in the queues for elections inspite of the terror exercised by musclemen and criminals who want to capture the election booths. The established caste-based rigid hierarchical social order has been completely shaken because the poor, the Dalits and women consider that right to vote is their instrument of power. While the decade of 1990s has witnessed the erosion of state sovereignty and subordination of the ruling classes, during the same decade, political and social assertions of Dalits, depressed and oppressed castes have been witnessed in India. The language of vote as a right is spoken by the Dalits and they practice it during the elections. Further, the Indian voter has learnt to punish his elected representatives and voters are electing and rejecting their representatives. This new capacity of the voter to punish his representative has compelled the political classes either to respond positively to the people's demands or face humiliating electoral defeats. India is witnessing a 'grand democratic transition' from the stage of feudal-landlord high caste-class established rules of a social order towards a stage of challenge to all the premises and assumptions of inherited feudal-landlord hierarchical caste based and caste determined social order. It is a long and difficult journey of ups and downs and the direction of future social developments cannot be predicted during this stage of transition but one thing is quite clear that the Indians are on the road to the weakening of the authoritarian social order by using their democratic right to vote.

Since social dialectics is based on a contest between the positive and the negative, it is essential to highlight some significant negative features of Indian democracy. A process of social fragmentation of India is at work and political mobilisation is undertaken on the basis of manipulation of sectarian identities of the voter. The decade of 1990s has witnessed the emergence of identity politics of caste versus caste, sub-caste versus sub-caste, region versus region, tribe versus tribe; and political parties in the traditional sense of the term have simply collapsed and have become just an extension of identity or sub-identity groups. Democracies operate on the basis of well-organised competing political parties which become *relatively autonomous* from their supporters and voters while governing democratic countries. Party is not a mere extension of caste or sub-caste, or religion or sect, or language because parties are required to mobilise their social constituencies to promote alternative agendas for governance of the country. If on the one hand, all parties or groups in coalition governments led by H.D. Deve Gowda or Inder Kumar Gujral or Atal Bihari Vajpayee have followed the economic policy of globalisation, privatisation, liberalisation, free market economy, open invitation to foreign capital etc. on the other, all partners in the coalition government are promoting their sectarian agendas of *Hindutva* or caste or region or personal benefits. Coalition governments at the centre do not have any social cohesion because they are a conglomerate of sectarian groups and factions which have specific social constituency and specific agendas of their own. The Vajpayee government is working successfully as a promoter of *Hindutva* because other groups of the coalition have been allowed to promote the interests of their limited social constituencies. A question is always raised. How can a socialist like George Fernandes or

Sharad Yadav or Ram Vilas Paswan or Nitish Kumar or an atheistic party of M. Karunanidhi sit with the party of *Hindutva* in a coalition? The answer to this question is not difficult to find. While the BJP is party of the Hindus, for the Hindus and by the Hindus, all other groups in the coalition are personal shops of chieftains of various castes and regions and the Prime Minister is happy to permit them to pursue their local-caste specific agendas so that they do not ask any inconvenient question about the anti-Muslim and anti-Christian activities of the BJP-led coalition at the centre or BJP-led state governments in Uttar Pradesh or Gujarat or Himachal Pradesh. The claims of managers of coalition governments like V.P. Singh that he was competent to deal with contradictions of supporters or Atal Bihari Vajpayee that he is a practitioner of the *Dharma* of coalition culture is an empty rhetoric because in reality all coalition governments at the centre are conglomerates of sectarian social groups. It is not without reason that leaders publicly identify their social support and social constituency with some sectarian/sectional group in society.

A few important challenges to Indian democratic state may be highlighted to substantiate the argument that the deepening of democratic process in the society and the emergence of new social assertions are threatening the various fractions of the ruling classes; and class leaders and class parties are responding to new social situation by fragmenting the society so that large social solidarities of the exploited masses do not emerge on the political scene. It is not a conspiracy theory to suggest that in the garb of identity politics the ruling classes are destroying large social solidarities of the working classes whether in urban or agrarian India. India is witnessing a riot of identities and sub-identities and more than 45 parties and political groups have emerged on the scene to promote and protect fractured identity groups. India at least had an agenda of development for the poor and socialism during the much maligned period of Nehru-Indira Gandhi planned economic development. During the decade of 1990s if, on the one hand, identity-group demands have been raised in a very vocal manner, on the other, socialism, equality, concerns for the poor and demands for a just social order have ceased to be even talking points in the 1990s. In a poor country like India, democracy has to especially care for the poor and downtrodden but during the 1990s, democratic governments are promoting the interests of various factions of the exploiting classes and masses are being offered the *opiate* of identities and sub-identities. It is wrong to examine the causes of decay of the Congress Party. The legitimate social science question is: Why has the Congress social agglomerate been replaced by a social-political conglomerate? A related question is: why have the fractionalised and fragmented identities of caste or religion emerged on the social scene in the decade of globalisation of the Indian economy? The shift from Congress led social agglomerate to a shapeless social-political conglomerate has taken place because the ideology of nation-building has been replaced by the logic of identity of power and power for the sake of an identity group. Democratic development for the whole of India has been abandoned because globalisation means social disparities within the country and among the countries of North and South. The globalisation of Indian economy is beneficial only to the well-off sections of society and democratic state of India in the age of globalisation has been captured on the well-off strata of society.

Since elections are regularly held, voters are mobilised on the basis of emotive issues of defence of Hinduism or self-respect for the Dalits or protection of the so-called regional or sub-regional demands. A rupture has emerged between mobilisation during elections and the actual governance in a democracy. The telling example of this phenomenon of vote on identity basis and governance for the better-off social strata is provided by the New Economic Policy of India. During the decade of 1990s, Lok Sabha elections were held in 1991, 1996, 1998 and 1999 and during none of these elections, any party or group campaigned on the basis of support for the policies of liberalisation, privatisation, deregulation and open invitation to foreign capital and multinational corporations. Not only this. During the elections, the New Economic Policy of India was a whipping boy of all opposition parties and just after the elections these policies became the darling of every ruling coalition. The Swadeshi Jagran Manch became a Videshi Manch and the party of *Hindutva* became an aggressive champion of globalisation. This sums up the real challenge to Indian democracy where voter's verdict has lost its meaning and it is manipulated by small time *identity wallah* politicians.

To sum up, while South Asian countries are struggling to defend even "formal democracy" from feudals, monarchies and military rulers, Indians are facing a challenge of a very different kind. The real agenda of the masses in India is to deepen democratic forces and establish a just social order but this agenda has been hijacked by globalisers and fragmented identity-based political groups. How to bring back the united masses to confront the present unequal social order and unjust global order? The choice for democratic forces in India is to create a social agglomerate or formless and shapeless social conglomerate which will operate Indian democracy in "*subordination*" and accept dictations of the Western capitalist countries. (*Vol. 21, Nos. 10-11-12, Oct.-Nov.-Dec., 2000, World Focus*)

Kashmir on the Negotiation Agenda

The entire nation is focused on the ongoing developments in Kashmir where leaders of the National Conference and those of the Hurriyat Conference and Hizbul Mujahideen, the two most important militant groups based in the Valley, have been involved in talks with the Centre. It is noticeable that instead of its earlier cavalier approach to the autonomy resolution, wisdom has dawned on the Vajpayee government this time as it has adopted a constructive view towards talks with ultra groups. However, these talks are going to be quite difficult and one may see light at the end of the tunnel or more collisions and deadlocks between the two sides. The problem gets further confounded with the conflicting demands of various militant groups. While the NC is demanding maximum autonomy under the Constitution, the Hurriyat and Hizbul are talking of their 'maximalist' agenda of independence along with an adamant demand to involve Pakistan in talks, thus making it more of a non-negotiable situation.

It could be recalled that the Centre had dealt with such situations in the North-East where various Naga groups, Laldenga of Mizoram or even the All-Assam Students Union and Assom Gana Parishad came to the negotiation table with a kind of 'ultimatum' to the Centre but the agreement was the outcome of many compromises between the parties. Not only this. The Centre has its won extremist groups who always oppose any talk with any group which does not believe in their philosophy. The Sangh Parivar has always rejected any effort to talk with Kashmiri militants. So is the BJP, which still wants to scrap Article 370.

But the logic of power and a proper understanding of the ground reality made Vajpayee, on August 3, to publicly call and urge all the militant groups which believe in peace to join the Centre's efforts for a peaceful resolution of the Kashmir issue.

This statement and the first meeting between the Union Home Ministry officials and Hizbul on August 3, was the first meeting of its kind between the militants and the Centre during the past 11 years of militancy. When the Hizbul commanders in Kashmir called for a three-month unilateral cease-fire on July 24, all the Pak-based terrorists condemned the Hizbul on the decision and some described it as ill-timed and ill manoeuvred. If in spite of this the Hizbul decided to negotiate with the Centre, the government must make serious efforts to enter into a meaningful dialogue with militants as well as parliamentary groups of Kashmir. It is important that the Centre gives equal importance to the views and demands of those groups which have been participating in the electoral process of J & K and groups like Hurriyat and Hizbul which were boycotting it, so as to make an impression that the government is impartial.

While every political proposal for the solution of the problem may be discussed, some of the proposals which are already floating around may be summarily rejected. A proposal has been made that J&K should be divided into the Hindu majority Jammu, Buddhist majority Ladakh and the Muslim majority Kashmir Valley as this is a dangerous route towards finding a solution to the 11-year-old ills of the Valley.

J&K as a composite cultural entity deserves peace with unity and not through partition of communities. Pakistan looks towards J&K as an 'unfinished agenda' of the Two-Nation theory and the Pakistani leadership makes claims on the Valley because it is a Muslim-dominated area. While Pakistan as a theocratic state can approach any issue on the basis of religion, a secular India has to find a solution on the basis of the secular Kashmiriyat identity irrespective of the religion.

Another important approach for negotiations could be involving a 'third party' so as to facilitate talks between Indian, Pakistan and various Kashmiri groups on both sides of the border. But the Hizbul call to involve Pak was spurned by the Centre which led to breakdown of the talks and resumption of conflict. The Centre has shifted its position many a time in the past on the 'third party' involvement as the 'third party' in this specific context means the US. But the Americans' track record in finding a solution to a dispute between any two countries has always been dubious, and it has never been a neutral party to any dispute anywhere in the world.

Moreover, during the initial stages it is always prudent to keep the talks confined to Kashmiri groups on the Indian side alone. Further, the BJP-led coalition should evolve a national consensus on the content of the negotiated peace. If on the one hand, Kashmiri groups are divided among themselves on the form and substance of demands, on the other, Indian public opinion and political parties also make conflicting views on the problem. The historical burden of more that 50 years has conditioned our national psyche over the issue.

Meanwhile, the Vajpayee regine's policy of total disengagement with Gen. Musharraf is quite unhelpful in resolving Indo-Pak row. It is hardly an argument that Musharraf is a pretender to power or that the ISI is responsible for the cross-border terrorism in Kashmir.

The logic of neighbourhood is a compelling factor that India should always be prepared to negotiate with anyone, under any circumstances, including Pakistan. The Nehru, Shastri, Indira and Rajiv governments never hesitated to negotiate with Pak dictators and even after fighting three wars in '47, '65 and '71, they never missed an opportunity to talk to Pakistan.

A sea change has taken place in the global arena and the mindset of the Sangh Parivar is not valid for the 21st century because the new century is the age of globalisation and of regional groupings like the EU, Association for South-East Asia Nations, the Organisation of Asia-Pacific Rim countries and also the SAARC. In the age of globalisation. South Asia will swim or sink together or the choice before South Asian countries is simple surrender before the powerful capitalist countries.

The Kashmir problem should be resolved by keeping in mind the fast changing global power equations which is definitely weighed against the Third World. The Indian chauvinists should see the reality around and they will find that South Asia, including India, cannot afford the luxury of wars because the problems of development are demanding greater priorities.

The Kashmir problem can be resolved through talks which will be long drawn but necessary to achieve the large national goal of peace and prosperity. After all, the Hizbul must have some weighty reasons to declare casefire for three months and opt for the path of negotiations instead of confrontation. It is an important opportunity for New Delhi and for all major political parties to make every effort at finding a solution to the Kashmir problem without the involvement of the United States. (*August 19, 2000, The Observer*)

7

Opposition and BJP

Congress at Crossroads

The Congress leadership is involved in an in-house post-mortem for identifying the causes for its poorest ever performance in a Lok Sabha election. The party leadership should be extremely worried because even when the voters of India decisively punished the Congress for imposing the 'Emergency', the party could secure 54 seats and maintain its presence in the southern states. The Congress showed an excellent electoral performance in 1998 by winning decisively the state assembly elections of Rajasthan, Delhi and Madhya Pradesh but just after ten months, the voters of these states have punished it.

Mrs. Sonia Gandhi, while owning her responsibility for the party's poor performance, observed that "the results call for introspection, frank assessment and determined action." A few important leaders of the party like Kamal Nath, Rajesh Pilot, Siddhartha Shankar Ray and Digvijay Singh have focussed their attention on the growing organisational weaknesses. The Congress has also appointed a committee under the chairmanship of A.K. Antony to suggest remedial action and Ram Niwas Mirdha has announced an election programme for the office-bearers of the party.

It may be mentioned here that party organisation is a necessary but not sufficient condition for the survival and rejuvenation of a party which has secured just 112 Lok Sabha seats. If organisational capabilities were a major factor in electoral victories, the cadre-based parties of the communists and the BJP would have won great electoral battles in the highly competitive political system of India. It is worth mentioning that the BJP could win 182 seats in 1999, *i.e.* one more than the Lok Sabha elections of 1998 while the party's national share of votes went down from 25.59 per cent to 23.07 per cent. While the CPI-M is able to maintain its limited political influence, the decline of the CPI is continuing with every election and it has secured only 1.45 per cent share of the national vote in the 1999 Lok Sabha elections.

In spite of its organisational fragility, the Congress has an all-India presence in the real sense of the term. While the BJP is able to spread its influence in the eastern, north-eastern and southern states with the support of regional political formations like the Telugu Desam Party, or the AIADMK-DMK, or the Biju Janata Dal or the Janata Dal (United) or Trinamool Congress and others, the Congress has a presence of its own from Arunachal Pradesh to Punjab and from Kashmir to Kanyakumari. In the 1998 Lok Sabha polls, the party contested 477 seats and obtained 25.82 per cent of the votes polled. In 1999 elections, the party fielded candidates only in 453 constituencies, but still increased its share of national votes to 28.42 per cent, *i.e.* five per cent more than the BJP.

The Congress has either contested or won elections in every northern, eastern, north-eastern and southern state and it has formed governments in Karnataka, Arunachal Pradesh and Maharashtra along with the Nationalist Congress Party. The BJP which is the main competitor of the Congress cannot form governments in the north-east or eastern or southern states, while the Congress has been winning or losing elections on the basis of its own strength in all these states.

The above description helps us in establishing the fact that the Congress leadership is searching for only organisational solutions for the recovery of its lost political space while its competitors are challenging it on an 'ideological level'. The Rajiv and post-Rajiv Gandhi Congress is suffering from ideological bankruptcy and this is the reason why it is not able to respond to the new social challenges of a fast changing India. The senior leadership of the Congress represented by Arjun Singh or Narain Dutt Tiwari or K. Karunakaran are intellectually bankrupt and petty factional fights have completely exhausted them. The 'new leadership' of the Congress inducted by Rajiv and Sonia Gandhi is de-ideologised because their perspective of the future India is limited to a techno-economic transformation of the country.

If these new faces of the Congress were not ideologically neutral, Arun Nehru and Arun Singh would not have walked out of the Congress to the BJP and P. Chidambaram would not have been comfortable with every political group. The tragedy of the Congress is that its 'old leadership' is completely tired and its 'new leadership' which includes Sonia Gandhi have not learnt the best lessons of the history of their own party. A few facts may be mentioned to substantiate the argument that the completely de-ideologised and de-historicised 'new leadership' of the Congress can learn a lot from their party's history which will help in the revival of the "grand old party" of India.

To begin with, Nehru made Congress a vehicle of democratic change in India by linking the destiny of the country with changing global power relations. The Congress fought ideological battles within the party for resolving basic issues of domestic and foreign policies. An ideological pillar of the Nehru-Indira Congress was the "relative autonomy" of the Indian state in world affairs. The new Congress leadership deserves to be reminded that Nehru on his first visit to the United States in 1949 made it clear that he had come to the US to promote mutual understanding, not to make "any deals" but to become acquainted with the American scene.

Is relative autonomy of the Indian state in global affairs valid for the 1990s? The Congress could have made full use of the powerful heritage of the Nehru-India foreign policy by standing firm against the completely unequal new international economic, information technology and defence order by projecting the non-negotiable national concerns before the patrons of the New World Order. If the Congress had followed in the footsteps of its own very tall leaders, it would not have surrendered its right as a defender of the sovereignty of the Indian state during the 1990s. The BJP-led government in 1999 could successfully sell to the whole country that the western countries were supportive of our posture on Kargil. If the Congress had been perceived by the people of India as a defender of our sovereignty, it could have effectively challenged the BJP by a counter-argument that Indians do not need "testimonials of good conduct" from the partisan western countries.

Nehru and Indira stood against illegitimate external pressures and the people of India supported their leadership on foreign policy. The most important Nehruvian tradition was that the Congress was always involved in intensive ideological debates and ideological contest which provided an opportunity for ideological clarity for the rank and file. Nehru's contest against Purshottam Das Tandon was ideological because while Nehru stood for "progress", Tandon represented the "conservative" forces within the Congress. Not only this. The socio-economic programme of the Congress was discussed in all the forums of the party and the leaders reflected sharply different ideological views on issues like the Hindu Code Bill or cooperative farming or democratic socialism or the socialistic pattern of society. Nehru and Rajendra Prasad clashed on the Hindu Code Bill; the lobby of the Kulak farmers represented by

Charan Singh fought against Nehru's ideas on cooperative farming, and Rajaji walked out of the Congress because of the ideological differences of opinion on Nehru's model of economic statism and Rajaji's belief in the private sector's role for a solution of India's poverty and backwardness.

For a while, this tradition of joining ideological battles within the Congress continued with Indira Gandhi when the split of 1969 was projected as a contest between the forces of progress represented by her and the forces of conservatism represented by the leadership of party organisation. However the 1999 polls did not witness any powerful contest on ideology where the Congress could sharply differentiate itself from the BJP. Nehru and the Indira Congress faced ideological opposition and fundamental challenges from within the party and outside. The Rajiv and post-Rajiv Gandhi phase in the Congress has failed to mobilise either the party workers or the people by focussing on any distinct social philosophy of its own. This is a break with the history of Congress as represented by Nehru and Indira. (*October 30, 1999, The Hindustan Times*)

The Congress under Siege

The Congress, which laid the foundations of the ongoing process of capitalist modernisation and political liberalism in India, is under siege not only from its political opponents but also from 'insiders'. They are working overtime to destroy the grand old party. The latest assault on the Congress has come in the shape of the judgement against Mr. P.V. Narasimha Rao and Mr. Buta Singh who have been found guilty in a case of corruption. Irrespective of what happens to the case on appeal, the party has been put on the defensive. It will have to make Herculean efforts to restore its political credibility as an upholder of public morality. Incidentally, even an unproven allegation against Rajiv Gandhi in the Bofors bribery case assumed political significance and the Congress was punished by the voters in the Lok Sabha election of 1989. Mr. V.P. Singh got political dividends by projecting himself as a campaigner against 'corruption'.

In the case of Mr. Narasimha Rao and Mr. Buta Singh the Congress is caught on the horns of a dilemma because allegations on corruption against party stalwarts now have a legal sanction. The faction-ridden Congress will find it difficult to completely rally around Mr. Rao and Mr. Singh because a powerful anti-Rao faction within the Congress will use this opportunity to make the party "disown" these political liabilities. If

Mr. Arjun Singh and others succeed in achieving their goal of making the party "disown" them, then the people of India will have a right to conclude that the party leadership is totally "opportunist". This is because Mr. Rao and Mr. Buta Singh have been caught because they were defending the party's interests in 1993.

There is already a long list of serious problems and difficulties which are currently confronting the Congress. A political party survives and thrives on the basis of its organisational strength and ideological positions on public issues. Unfortunately, the Congress faces serious challenges both at the level of its own party organisation and also on the acceptability of its ideological position on public affairs. The Congress is involved in an internal Hobbesian war of all against all on the issue of forthcoming organisational elections to be: held, if at all, on November 1, 2000. The Congress's internal organisational elections are like mini-Indian elections in which every possible manipulative activity is undertaken to capture the party organisation. Mr. Ram Niwas Mirdha, the head of the Central Election Authority, is performing the same role which is performed by the Chief Election Commissioner of India for ensuring "free and fair" poll in the country. The first step in the Congress's internal election involves 2.5 crore voters. It is precisely at this stage that every effort is made by the various competing factions of the party to rig the elections. Mr. Mirdha faces the challenging job of appointing District Returning Officers and Block Returning Officers who are expected to conduct the "free and fair" elections. Mr. Mirdha, had to cancel the list of District Returning Officers for Uttar Pradesh because factional leaders in the party levelled charges and counter-charges against them. While the election programme of the party is in motion, Mr. Salman Khurshid, the UPPCC President, has been removed by the party president and another person has been appointed PCC president. This story of 'infighting' among Congress factions is repeating itself with a vengeance in every State. A free-for-all struggle is on to capture the organisation of the party. The Congress model of internal democracy as seen now clearly reveals that it is not only a divided house but has a place for political manipulators of the worst kind. It should not come as a surprise that Congress leaders are always involved in getting some of their own party nominees defeated during the Lok Sabha and State Assembly elections. This is because their faction is more important to them than the interests of the party. The divisions and factions within Congress have a weakening, even crippling, effect on the capacity of the party organisation to reach the voter and effectively convey the message of the party. The BJP, which is the real opponent of the Congress, has the monolithic Rashtriya Swayamsevak Sangh at its beck and call, while the Congress always faces a challenge from its own party factions. The organisational strength of the BJP is its great asset during elections, while the disunited Congress factions are always busy competing against their own factional opponents.

The Congress also faces serious difficulties on its ideological positions on public issues. The new economic policies of liberalisation, privatisation and globalisation was fathered by the Congress. The BJP has enthusiastically appropriated these Congress policies. The Congress is totally confused by this turn of events. In a system of parliamentary democracy, the Congress, as the main opposition party, has to project itself as an ideological alternative to the ruling alliance. However, the party can neither disown its own economic policy nor it can be allowed to be seen as a B-team of the BJP. Ms. Sonia Gandhi, as the Congress president, has appointed a 'committee' to resolve the basic dilemma faced by the party on the issue of economic policies which are being projected by the BJP as Congress policies. It may be suggested that here too the factional leaders are fighting their factional battles. The opponents of these policies try to attribute every failure of the party to their factional opponents. A completely divided house cannot unite on the policies and programmes of the party.

The Congress has always had factions within itself. In the face of serious opposition to the party, Congress factions either united or some faction walked out of the party. The current problems of factionalism within the party are different from those that the party experienced under the leadership of Jawaharlal Nehru, Indira Gandhi and Rajiv Gandhi. These Congress leaders had an unassailable pre-eminent position within the party and they could deal with its factional challenges and conflicts. Ms. Sonia Gandhi does not have the same standing and she did not succeeded in winning the elections for the party.

Hence, Ms. Sonia Gandhi's own leadership and capacities are problematic for many Congress factional leaders. She is not perceived as the leader of the party who can effectively resolve internal factional feuds. Mr. Sharad Pawar walked out of the party because the party president herself felt insecure and threatened by Mr. Pawar's presence in the party. As a result of this struggle between Ms. Gandhi and Mr. Pawar, the Congress emerged decisively a loser in the Lok Sabha elections. Further, while a Nehru or an Indira or a Rajiv had depended on important party leaders it was difficult to pinpoint any one or a few party leaders as their "coterie". Ms. Sonia Gandhi has important Congress Working Committee members who cannot win even municipal council elections. In spite of this, they seem to have great clout within the party because of their proximity to the party president. Thus, Ms. Gandhi is perceived as a "factionalist" herself.

How can a Congress President who is seen as a factionalist command authority within the whole party? Congress is under siege because it has serious weaknesses within itself while its political opponents are very well organised. Ms. Sonia Gandhi is a necessity for the Congress because she is its only all-India face. But she has not shown any political acumen while dealing with her so-called "loyalists". Indira Gandhi and Rajiv Gandhi knew quite well that Congress factional-leaders were turncoats. A completely de-ideologised opportunistic group of leaders cannot be loyal to the party.

It is an unfortunate development that a "socially inclusive" party is not able to set its own house in order to confront "exclusivist" formations based on religion, caste or region. Even now, at the all-India level, about 30 per cent of the voters look towards the Congress for leadership of the country. In spite of this the party has failed to revitalise itself. (*October 5, 2000, The Pioneer*)

Congress Democracy?

The old death wish of the Congress party has come back in the form of the nomination of 24 CWC members by the so-called elected President. Does it mean that the drama of election of the president of the party was in a sense enacted in an absent-minded manner? Any healthy democratic development within the Congress deserves to be welcomed. A sound democratic opposition is an important countervailing force in a parliamentary system because it can check the ruling party. The contest for the office of Congress president did rejuvenate the party rank and file and Mr. Jitendra Prasada has willy-nilly emerged the spokesman of grass-root workers who want democratic participation in the decision making bodies of the Congress — from the President to District Congress Committee and *taluka* levels. It is post-Jitendra Prasada phenomenon that the PCCs authorising the party President to nominate the PCC presidents have attracted opposition within the Congress party.

Congress Election Commissioner Ram Niwas Mirdha was forced to admit that the presidential elections were far from being above board. By making this statement, Mr. Mirdha encouraged provincial Congress committees to push for democratic functioning of the party at provincial, district and taluka levels. Ms. Sonia Gandhi versus Mr. Jitendra Prasada contest made Congress workers and grass-root leaders take a serious look at the party. It deserves to be mentioned that Mr. Sharad Pawar or late Rajesh Pilot's challenge to the leaders of the party had no impact. By writing letters, Mr. Jitendra Prasada generated a debate within the Congress. Further, Mr. Prasada challenged Ms. Sonia Gandhi and questioned her leadership and capacity to act as an independent and impartial head of the party. By raising the issue of a coterie exercising real control over the party from behind the scenes, Mr. Prasada compelled Ms. Sonia Gandhi to acknowledge that a coterie has been functioning and that he himself was part of coterie politics during Rajiv Gandhi's and P.V. Narasimha Rao's tenure.

In the post-independence Congress history, Rajiv Gandhi was the first to talk of "power-brokers" within the Congress. He expressed these views at the party's centenary session in Bombay in 1985. Mr. Prasada has reiterated that Ms. Sonia Gandhi is a "captive of a coterie of power-brokers." It is a healthy democratic development for any party, and especially the Congress, to raise questions and engage in a debate on the internal functioning of the party because if a party does not practice "inner democracy", it is likely to scuttle democracy when in power. Many serious scholars have warned us that intellectuals and media should take serious note of the inner functioning of parties.

Robert Michaels gave an "Iron law of Oligarchy" in which he stated that real power within the parties gets concentrated in the hands of a few leaders. This should be vigilantly exposed for the safety of democracy. Robert Merton, an important American sociologist, has warned against party bosses who control the real levers of party. According to Merton elected presidents are creations of "party bosses" who exercise control over elected presidents of the country. This has led the critics to say that the US democracy is controlled by a "ruling elite."

Trotskyites had talked about a "law of substitution" in the Russian Communist Party, that is, the proletariat had been substituted by the Communist party, the party by the politburo which in turn had been substituted by Stalin. The so-called democratic centralism of the Communists had given birth to the politics of personality cult. At least, the Communists publicly maintain that their party constitution is based on the principle of "democratic centralism" and the secretary-general of the party is the key elected leader. Parties which proclaim their faith in "inner democracy" and in actual practice scuttle it to create a leader-oriented organisation face a worrisome situation.

In India, every party, national or regional, suffers from the malaise of authoritarianism. Samajwadi Party's Mulayam Singh Yadav, Rashtriya Janata Dal's Laloo Prasad Yadav, DMK's M. Karunanidhi, AIADMK's J. Jayalalitha, TDP's Chandrababu Naidu, Trinamool's Mamata Banerjee, BSP's Kanshi Ram and Mayawati are all running their "shops" as personal property. The BJP, as an extension of the RSS, practices politics of elitism. The Sarsanghchalak of the RSS is nominated by the incumbent and Mr. Atal Bihari Vajpayee and Mr. L.K. Advani as unquestioned leaders of the BJP have nominated Mr. Bangaru Laxman as party president. The practice of nominating a Sarsanghchalak of the RSS was started with its founder K.B. Hedgewar, who nominated his successor, M.S. Golwalkar. The BJP continues to follow this highly undemocratic practice while managing its inner party affairs. Moreover, the emergence of a high command within the Congress has a history of its own, but the emergence of high command within the BJP is not even three years old. The BJP high command of Mr. Vajpayee and Mr. Advani nominated BJP chief ministers in Uttar Pradesh, Uttaranchal and Jharkhand. Like the Congress, the BJP high command issues a writ to silence its dissidents. Recently this happened in Uttaranchal and Jharkhand where a near revolt occurred against Vajpayee-Advani choice of chief ministers.

The upshot of the above description is that every political party throttles and kills inner democracy. The specifics of Sonia-Prasada contest go much beyond the Congress presidential elections. An imperfect democratic election within the Congress is better than fiefdoms of the regionalists. The focus of Mr. Prasada or coterie surrounding Ms. Sonia Gandhi may be dismissed as trivial because Messrs Arjun Singh, Natwar Singh, Ghulam Nabi Azad, M.L. Fotedar, *et al*, want personal benefits from the family. Mr. Arjun Singh's son is a minister in Madhya Pradesh, Mr. S.C. Shukla and Mr. Moti Lal Vora's sons are ministers in Chhatisgarh, Mr. Karan Singh's son is a minister in Jammu & Kashmir. Mr. Natwar Singh's son could not be elected else he too would have been accommodated by Mr. Ashok Gehlot in Rajasthan.

The issue of coterie surrounding the leaders has serious implications which deserves to be examined. Mr. Bansi Lal of Haryana used a proverb that if a calf is in your hands, the mother cow will be your captive. He caught hold of Sanjay Gandhi and exercised influence over the Indira Government. L.N. Mishra, the Railway Minister in the Indira Government, was a pillar of inner coterie and he had developed a practice to convey to Indira Gandhi concocted news about important Congress leaders or chief ministers through Congress workers whom he would select to visit her.

It is well known that political leaders at the top are insecure because in politics there are neither permanent friends nor foes. The coterie around Mrs. Indira Gandhi could be tackled by her because she practiced manipulative politics; she could tame the manipulators around her. On the other hand, Ms. Sonia Gandhi's capabilities to deal with her coterie are highly suspect. Only real inner democracy of the party will be able to prevent her from falling into the trap laid down by the coterie. Democracy within the Congress is a healthy check over the elected president and her group of advisers. It is expected of the PCCs to continue with the practice of democratic elections as shown by the Prasada-Sonia contest. If the Congress leadership allows real democratic elections at every level within the party, it will not only lead to its rejuvenation, but will also bring leaders with alternative viewpoints and experiences from the grass-roots. (*January 5, 2001, The Pioneer*)

From TINA to Tiny: The Congress Journey

The seeds of the Babri Masjid dispute were laid down by Gobind Ballabh Pant in 1948 and fruits of Masjid-Mandir controversy were harvested by the forces of *Hindutva*. Mr. K.C. Pant, who is the inheritor of his father's legacy, has not found shifting from politics of soft *Hindutva* of the Congress to the pure brand of *Hindutva* of the BJP. The other heroes after the erstwhile Congress leadership like Mr. Ajit Singh, the son of Chaudhary Charan Singh, or Sunil Shastri, the son of Lal Bahadur Shastri, find great comfort in *Hindutva*. The BJP in UP could form its Government because a sizeable group of the tiny Congress in the State Assembly walked over to the BJP and helped it in coming to power. The hero of this activity was a *Bania*, Mr. Naresh Agarwal, whose family grew up in the Congress party.

Dr. Sampurnanand was a practitioner of Hindu rituals and Nehru had to publicly snub him in 1961-62 by saying that he was an obscurantist who believed in the evil consequences of *Ashta Graha* or "conjunction of planets". Kamlapati Tripathi continued to be a practicing Hindu priest, a Chief Minister and a Congress leader. And, finally, N.D. Tiwari wrote Rajiv Gandhi's political obituary in 1989 elections by taking him to Ayodhya with the slogan of "*Ram Rajya*". The UP Congress firmly established the political culture of social conservatism and soft *Hindutva* and these two tendencies have finally matured — the State is today a citadel of social conservatism and full fledged communalism and casteism. In the emerging milieu, the Congress naturally finds no place.

Since ideologies do not hang in the air, the material foundations of UP's ideological backwardness are linked with its economic backwardness, where traditional industries like jute, textiles, etc., were allowed to die without any replacement; and social productive relations in agrarian society of UP suffered a serious setback because UP Congress implemented the most regressive programme of land reforms. The social consequences of recommendations of UP Zamindari Abolition Committee and UP Zamindari Abolition Act was that rural economic and political power was transferred from traditional high caste land owners to backward caste middle peasantry. The theory and praxis of land reforms in Uttar Pradesh tells an interesting story of replacement of high castes by the middle castes without bringing any change in social attitudes.

If the Congress practiced politics of caste alliance, its successors too are playing the caste card in a big away, not only for winning an election but also for making caste a factor in the governance of the State. It is not without reason that casteisation and communalisation of UP State apparatus has become unstoppable. Ms. Mayawati, Mr. Mulayam Singh Yadav, and Mr. Rajnath Singh have privatised State Government apparatus for the welfare of their own social constituency.

Further, politics of the decades of 1990s has impacted comprehensively not only UP but also the Centre. Mr. V.P. Singh, who learnt his lessons in the classroom of the Congress, played the caste card to keep himself in power by proclaiming the acceptance of Mandal Commission Report on reservations for the backward castes in public services and public institutions. Caste fractures in UP society got institutionalised because caste identity became a route to political and State power. Mr. V.P. Singh's politics of caste sharpened the social contradictions in UP and society was horizontally and vertically polarised around caste and sub-caste labels.

If on the one hand, caste versus caste confrontations took place between the "forward" and the "backward castes", on the other, many new caste identities emerged among the subaltern castes like the Dalits and the Most Important Backward Castes, etc. Mr. V.P. Singh administered a deadly injection to UP's casteised society and caste war has become the order of the day because struggle for the ballot is being fought through caste confrontations and violence. Not to be left behind, the forces of *Hindutva* burnt the UP society by injecting the deadly needle of communalism. Hence riots, killings, atrocities and cooption of the State apparatus by criminals and thugs has become the order of the day.

And now the BJP is trying to combine communalism with new casteism. The greatest victim of the ongoing drama of casteisation, communalisation, and criminalisation in UP is "civil society", where every institution has been infected by socially regressive forces. Can Messrs Murli Manohar Joshi, K.C. Pant or N.D. Tiwari feel proud of the state of affairs in the Allahabad University? UP has decisively entered the dark ages because power for the sake of power is being practiced by various caste and communal groups.

It is intellectual laziness to describe the present social milieu of UP as a testimony to great social churning which is taking place in a highly traditional society. Social churning is also taking place in Rajasthan and MP, and these historically backward societies are gradually moving forward. It is one kind of politics which makes a State and society enter the "dark ages", and it is another kind of an alternative politics which lays down the foundations of progressive development of a society. UP is suffering because of its backward looking casteist and communalist political formations and leadership. Governance and economic development of the State will suffer greatly by competitive casteist politics of Mr. Mulayam Singh Yadav, Ms. Mayawati and Mr. Raj Nath Singh — the three main players in the forthcoming elections. (*October 4, 2001, The Pioneer*)

Where is the Congress? Down in the Dumps

The explanations for the rapid decline of the Congress lie within the Congress party. Enemies of Congress are sitting within the party and with such a CWC and leadership, the party does not need any outsider to write its political obituary. It is worthwhile recalling the history of fifty years of factionalism and splits of the Congress party to properly understand and appreciate the present weaknesses of the party. After independence, Congress party fought its internal ideological battles around the issues of forward looking progressive modern and secular groups represented by Jawaharlal Nehru and the Conservative Right Wing Hindus represented by Sardar Patel, Rajendra Prasad, Purshottam Das Tandon and others like them. This battle between the two ideologically opposite groups was fought by Nehru against right wingers on the issue of presidency of Purshottam Das Tandon in 1951. The right wingers wanted to capture the Congress parliamentary party after the elections of 1952 by nominating their candidates under the umbrella of Congress President Tandon. Nehru saw through the game and fought out against Tandon and his other Hindi—Hindu supporters in the Congress. Tandon resigned and Nehru established the supremacy of forward looking progressive social philosophy in the Congress. Another battle was fought between Indira Congress and the party forces represented by K. Kamraj, Atulya Ghosh, S.K. Patil, Nijalingappa and others and Congress was split in 1969. This first grand split of the Congress took place around the rhetoric of progressivism versus conservatism. In reality, it was a struggle for power between Indira Gandhi and party bosses who controlled the party 'Machine'. The Lok Sabha elections of 1970-71 established full control of Indira Gandhi over the Congress party and party bosses licked the dust before Indira's slogan of "*Garibi Hatao*" versus her opponents' slogan of *Indira Hatao*. Indira Gandhi's phase of Congress leadership brought party to power and also started the processes of its decline and degeneration. From 1971 to 1975, Indira Congress became synonymous with personality and authority of the only Leader and all other levels of leadership and Congress organisation were trampled under the feet of the Leader. As if this was not enough to weaken the 'grand old party of India', during the emergency of 1975-77, the Congress party and the Constitution of India were completely destroyed.

Sanjay Gandhi with his clique of Bansi Lal, Jagmohan, Maneka Gandhi, Arjun Das, Rukhsana Sultana practiced a culture of illegality and immorality and Congress leaders were helpless spectators of 'lumpenism' of India's politics under the leadership of Sanjay Gandhi and his cronies. Congress was again split in 1978 and Indira Gandhi won the Lok Sabha elections of 1979.

No lesson was learnt from the humiliating defeat of 1977. Indira and her lumpen son started the same practice of destroying the institutions of governance and of the Congress party. After Indira Gandhi's assassination in 1984, Rajiv Gandhi won the elections and declared in Bombay that "power-brokers should be shown the door" because everyone within the Congress became completely "deideologised". Rajiv inherited a Congress which had been completely destroyed and corrupted by his mother and a wayward brother. New struggles began within the Congress. Nehru's Congress was dead and the Congress of Rajiv, V.P. Singh, P.V. Narasimha Rao, Sita Ram Kesari and others stood for pure quest for 'power, privileges and perks'.

Everyone who walked out of the Congress in the late 1980s or in the 1990 wanted a 'lion's share' in public resources. Congress party was gripped by the vicious logic of power for the sake of patronage. How can such a party deal with the challenges of the 21st century? Sonia Gandhi has leaders like Arjun Singh, K. Karunakaran, Natwar Singh and others who want their children to become MPs, Ministers and MLAs. Further every leader and Chief Minister of the Congress is only effective, if at all, in his/her own state. An all-India party like the Congress needs all-India leaders and late Rajesh Pilot and Madhav Rao Scindia were two all-India leaders of the Congress. The Congress is completely bereft of all-India leaders and the so-called leaders are either unable to win their own election or busy in promoting their useless family members. Poor Sonia Gandhi has to shoulder the burden of carrying the coffin of tired Congress leaders over-her shoulders. A telling example is from Uttar Pradesh where the Congress does not have a single leader who can take on Mulayam Singh or Mayawati or party machine of the BJP.

Today Congress has a caricature of party organisation. India needs the party and the voters keep on coming back to the Congress. The situation is like England. The King is dead, Long Live the Crown. The Congress leaders have destroyed their own great party which is dead but the voters of India say Long Live the Congress. (*October 7, 2001, The Sunday Pioneer*)

Congress and Left must Co-operate

The CPI(M) held a three-day special conference on October 19-21 at Thiruvananthapuram to update the party programme because earthshaking changes had occurred in the 1990s both internally and externally. In the light of these new developments, the party discussed and deliberated on its theory and praxis of socialism.

The forces of caste, communalisation, and globalisation, liberalisation and deregulation made a major impact in the 1990s. That decade can thus be appropriately characterised as the era of Mandal, mandir and economic Darwinism in which a decisive break was made with forty years of post-Independence politics. Not only this. The collapse of the east European Communist state systems of Soviet Russia, Yugoslavia, Romania, Albania, Hungary, Poland and East Germany was a kind of earthquake for the European and Asian communist parties because the capitalist West celebrated the end of socialist ideology as a vindication of the theory and practice of the capitalist path of development. While Mr.

George Bush, the former US President, declared that the decade of 1990s had given birth to the new international security, economic, technological and information order, communists everywhere were on the retreat. Only Mr. Fidel Castro of Cuba, stood firm. Even communist China changed its ideology by proclaiming the doctrine of market socialism as a new path for development.

These global and domestic political developments were compelling reasons for the communists to look afresh at their ideological and theoretical formulations. The CPI(M) had not grown beyond three states of Kerala, West Bengal and Tripura and it had also got a shock when, on mere technical grounds, the Election Commission derecognised it as a national party. Why has the CPI(M) not grown according to the expectations of stalwarts like A.K. Gopalan, E.M.S. Namboodripad, B.T. Randive and others who split the Communist Party of India in 1964 with the majority of party members? What has happened to the promise of achieving the goal of people's democracy?

It is important to note that one of the elements in the ideological divide between the CPI and CPI(M) was their differing evaluations of the split between Russia and China on the basis of the dispute between Khruschev and Mao, which does not have any relevance now. Mr. Harkishan Singh Surjeet while inaugurating the special conference observed that the current situation demanded the strengthening of Left and democratic forces to take on communal forces and imperialist-driven globalisation. In the same tone, Mr. Jyoti Basu maintained that it is necessary to mobilise the forces that are willing to fight against communalism and the attacks on the people's economic interests. Communalism and new economic policy packages have been identified as the primary enemy of the people. A party which believes in the establishment of people's democracy will have to make every effort to create a Third Front which maintains equidistance from the Congress and the BJP.

An important modification made at the Thiruvananthapuram conference was that it abandoned its previous ideology of not participating in a coalition government where it was not in a position to decisively make its presence and power felt by other members of the coalition. The party also decided to be in the opposition and organise people's struggles against socially reactionary policies of the present government. This policy of not participating in a coalition government was followed in 1989 when the party supported the V.P. Singh government from outside and also in 1996 when H.D. Deve Gowda and Inder Kumar Gujral formed coalition governments at the Centre.

In 1996, the non-Congress, non-BJP formation asked Mr. Jyoti Basu to lead the coalition government at the Centre. The CPI(M)'s refusal was later described as a historical blunder. This was not the first time in the history of communist movements that blunders have been made because of ideological rigidity. But the communists have shown the ability to learn from mistakes, which was demonstrated at Thiruvananthapuram. An important issue regarding the experiment of coalition government at the Centre during 1977-79, and 1989 should also have been discussed and examined because an anti-Congress, anti-BJP Third Front with the active support and participation of the CPI(M) has been proved to be unviable. The crux of the issue is that BJP and the Congress are all-India parties and every other political group or leader, except the communists, are regional forces. Indian politics has decisively shifted away from one-party dominance to the total fragmentation of society and politics. In this situation the Congress and the BJP cannot create a bipolar polity, nor can regional groups provide cohesion at the central level because their political horizons are limited. That is why regional groups are forming shifting coalitions at the Centre on the basis of local political situations.

If Ms. Jayalalitha is in opposition in Tamil Nadu, her target is Mr. M. Karunanidhi's DMK. Only one of them can support a coalition at the Centre and if one supporter withdraws from the coalition, the other joins it. The Left and democratic allies of the Third Front like the AIADMK and the DMK have supported the communal BJP. The convener of the United Front of 1996, Mr. Chandrababu Naidu, is actively supporting the BJP-led coalition at the Centre because his party is fighting the Congress rather than the BJP in Andhra Pradesh.

Only Mulayam Singh Yadav, the practitioner of casteist politics, can be a trusted member of a CPI(M)-led anti-BJP and anti-Congress front. Everyone else, Mr. Laloo Yadav or the Janata socialists like Mr. Sharad Yadav, Mr. George Fernandes and Mr. Ram Vilas Paswan are clear that in this unstable political situation, ideological purity is a road to political suicide. Mr. Laloo Yadav has openly said that a future coalition at the Centre should include the Congress, but this assertion is only for the present moment. He can join some other Front later. Mr. H.D. Deve Gowda has also said that he can work with the Congress.

The CPI(M) has the correct theoretical position that the new economic policy package is a breeding ground for religiosity and the growth of BJP because the poverty-stricken masses are easily swayed by tradition, which is represented by the believers of religion-based politics. Moreover, the BJP has created a powerful social constituency among capitalists, entrepreneurs, professionals, capitalist farmers, upwardly mobile agrarian and urban middle classes because these classes are the real beneficiaries of the new economic regime as well as votaries of *Hindutva* because all these affluent social groups have global linkages where an assertive Hindu identity is advantageous.

This is also a social limitation of the BJP because in a poor country like India, a party or a government cannot attain democratic legitimacy without a programme of "*garibi hatao*".

The 1990s have seen an intensification of social conflicts. Minorities are also under threat. Socially affluent groups, small property holders and millions of shopkeepers want political stability, and either the party of *Hindutva* or a credible political alternative will be able to secure political support by promising stable government.

The CPI(M)'s Third Front without the Congress is not a viable or stable option. The CPI(M) has to resolve this riddle before it launches a democratic and secular alliance to confront the BJP and its economic policies. If the CPI(M) follows its own interpretation of the existing political reality of India, it has to have a serious dialogue with the Congress. Otherwise the Congress and the communist parties cannot come to power. (*November 10, 2000, The Pioneer*)

The Real Face of Third Front Warriors

Mr. Harkishan Singh Surjeet of the CPI(M) and Mr. A.B. Bardhan of the CPI have proclaimed that a revival of the Third Front is once again on the agenda. According to them, many secular regional parties are ready to walk out of the BJP-led National Democratic Front and the Congress has shown no capacity to re-energise itself and emerge as an effective alternative to the BJP.

A few developments have compelled the Communist leadership to once again float a front of parties which would claim to practice a politics of equi-distance from the BJP and Congress. One, the Bengal Pradesh Congress Committee leadership is ready to float a grand alliance with Ms. Mamata Banerjee to contest the forthcoming State Assembly elections in Bengal. This political development in Bengal has alerted the Communists. If an anti-Communist alliance emerges, it will pose a very powerful challenge during the Assembly polls. Two, the Bengal developments have further convinced the Marxist parties that the

Congress is a sinking ship because the Bengal PCC leaders have acted on their own initiative without consulting the high command. If such an alliance is formed in Bengal, the so-called secular credentials of the party will become a big political joke. Three, the Left parties have felt encouraged to revive the idea of an alternative to the BJP and the Congress because its former warhorses, Messrs V.P. Singh, Chandra Shekhar, H.D. Deve Gowda and Inder Kumar Gujral, have proclaimed their availability for a Third Front regrouping. The four former prime ministers have begun making public noises on public issues to project themselves as leaders-in-waiting to grab power should the NDA disintegrate in the near future.

A few facts may be mentioned to substantiate the argument that there never was a so-called Third Front Government at the Centre during the 1990s. First, the V.P. Singh Government in 1989 was formed with the outside support of the Communists and the BJP and the combined strength of outside supporters was more than the MPs of Mr. Singh's Janata Party. Mr. Singh accepted the diktat of the BJP leadership on Jammu & Kashmir; he appointed Mr. Jagmohan as Governor. Two, the Chandra Shekhar Government had only 56 MPs and it was sustained in power by the largest opposition party, the Congress. It was the same story during the 1996-98 phase of Indian politics. The outside supporters of the Deve Gowda and Gujral governments were numerically more than the MPs of the Janata Party. Three, every Third Front Government of 1989 or 1990, or 1996-1998 was supported either by the BJP or the Congress. What kind of equi-distance was maintained by the Third Front from the BJP or the Congress? Hence, it is a myth to maintain that Third Front governments have been an alternative to the BJP or the Congress. On the contrary, all the four Prime Ministers of Third Front coalition governments at the Centre were political beneficiaries of those parties from which they were maintaining equi-distance during the elections. Whenever the Congress decided to withdraw the support, these temporary governments fell like a house of cards.

This story does not end here. Messrs Surjeet and Bardhan have maintained that the Third Front partners are secular political groups and that they are partners in their common fight against the politics of *Hindutva* on the one hand, and the soft *Hindutva* of the Congress variety on the other. This tall claim is not based on facts. The V.P. Singh Government was supported both by the BJP and the Communists. The secular regionalists like Telugu Desam, DMK, and Socialists like Mr. Ram Vilas Paswan and Mr. George Fernandes have embraced the BJP by opting out of earlier Third Front governments. How can these birds of transition be characterised as secular political groups? Mr. Chandrababu Naidu, Mr. K. Karunanidhi, Mr. Parkash Singh Badal, Mr. Farooq Abdullah and Mr. Chautala are neither secularists nor forward looking socially alive leaders. They have changed their clothes frequently depending on calculations of political losses and gains. A group of completely de-ideologised regionalists cannot be torch bearers of secular politics.

If the claim of secular regionalists is phoney, equally wrong is the other claim of the Marxists—that they want a Third Front alternative which should follow economic policies that are different from those of the BJP and Congress. Marxist parties argue that the Congress has failed to perform the function of a genuine opposition party because its own economic policies are being pursued by the BJP-led coalition Government. They describe the Congress as the B-team of the BJP Government and they assert that a new opposition front must be established to oppose the politics of *Hindutva* and the policies of economic liberalisation. The claim of the Marxists that Third Front political groups have a package of alternative economic policies is not based on facts.

Mr. V.P. Singh pursued policies of economic liberalisation by stealth and Messrs Deve Gowda and Inder Gujral's Finance Minister, Mr. P. Chidambaram, was a great liberaliser. Economic liberalisation has been the main policy plank of Third Front partners like Mr. Chandrababu Naidu and Mr. Karunanidhi. The economic agenda of the Third Front allies has been either "economic backwardness" or very fast track liberalisation. Mr. Laloo Prasad Yadav and Mr. Mulayam Singh Yadav have been messiahs of "economic backwardness" and under-development of Bihar and UP respectively and other regionalists believe in fast track liberalisation of the Naidu variety.

The Third Front political alternative in India has been a coalition of power seekers and opportunists who have aligned together to enjoy the fruit of power. It has been neither anti-Congress nor anti-BJP. It has been essentially pro-itself.

The Central Government has been decisively weakened because heterogeneous political groups have shared power to pursue their sectional and personal political agenda. Third Front coalitional governments had no coherent social and national agenda while they were in power. Mr. V.P. Singh announced the acceptance of the Mandal Commission Report on reservations in public services for the backward castes in 1990 because he was fighting a grim factional battle within his own party. Mr. H.D. Deve Gowda felt hamstrung on the Cauvery river water dispute between Karnataka and Tamil Nadu because while he himself belonged to Karnataka, Tamil Nadu's DMK was also part of the Government he led at the Centre. All coalition governments at the Centre have been weak, shaky and vulnerable to domestic and foreign pressures.

A collection of disparate individuals and political groups does not become a political alternative. The politics of alternatives is always based on alternate ideologies and basic programmes of governance. The politics of secularism is the real politics of alternative world views and ideologies. Third Front allies did not show any commitment to the ideology of secularism. Every leader and group of the Front made fundamental compromises with the believers of religion-based politics.

Communist parties of India have been genuine champions of anti-Congress and anti-BJP politics and they have paid a heavy price for floating an opportunistic and ideologically bankrupt politics of alliances in the 1990s.

Even if the Third Front is revived in the near future, it will be a short-lived experiment like in the past. The Third Front warriors will keep fighting for the loaves and fishes of power. Front partners have traditionally failed to evolve a common public agenda for the governance of the country. This is the reality of our Third Front warriors. (*April 20, 2000, The Pioneer*)

Crisis of Coalitions

Messrs V.P. Singh, Chandra Shekhar, H.D. Deve Gowda, I.K. Gujral and Atal Bihari Vajpayee have been the only beneficiaries of unstable, faceless, shapeless and directionless coalition governments at the Centre, and all these five Pandavas of Indian politics have been betrayed, publicly abused and kicked around by their own coalitional partners; the latest victim of this humiliation is Prime Minister Vajpayee who felt the need to suggest quitting office after a virulent attack by Mr. Sanjay Nirupam of the Shiv Sena, a part of the NDA. The Hindu fascist Shiv Sena leadership added insult to injury by again publicly stating that Mr. Bal Thackeray had asked Mr. Nirupam to apologise to the Prime Minister not because the norms of coalitional government had been violated but because the BJP wanted such an apology.

A dominant public discourse in India is that the decade of the '90s has witnessed the end of the Congress's dominance over national politics; there is no all-India umbrella party today. It has been maintained that India has decisively entered coalitional era of governance at the Centre and on the basis of trial and error, Indian political class will develop coalitional culture, or *Dharma* of governance. It must be stated that coalition governments will be unstable and it is wishful thinking to suggest that India will develop a coalitional culture of governance in the foreseeable future.

A few facts may be mentioned to substantiate the argument that Central governments in the coalitional era have become weak, unstable and more corrupt. Mr. V.P. Singh received support from Communists and the BJP to become the Prime Minister in 1989 by proclaiming from house top that he was extremely competent to manage political equations of the Lok Sabha of 1989. Mr. Singh's 11-month prime ministership proved disastrous for the nation because he handed a disturbed Kashmir over to his successors. He committed three blunders as prime minister which laid the foundation of blood-soaked Kashmir. Kashmir has always been an extremely sensitive problem for the Indian state, and the appointment of a Kashmiri as the Union Home Minister was based on a total misunderstanding of the dynamics of the Kashmir issue.

The V.P. Singh government handed over public initiative to terrorists in Kashmir because they now had a most important family as a soft target, and they successfully used this opportunity provided by the Central Government to abduct the Home Minister's daughter. The next step of the Central Government sealed the fate of peaceful democratic process in Kashmir, when it surrendered before a group of terrorists and arranged for the freedom of Mufti Mohammed Sayeed's daughter. The terrorists have never looked back ever since. Then Mr. Singh gave the charge of Kashmir to Mr. George Fernandes, a loose canon of Indian politics; under him the situation worsened.

Many such illustrations can be given to substantiate the argument that all the five prime ministers of coalition governments have contributed to the weakening of the Central authority. The Union Government has become directionless because partners in coalition governments have nothing in common with one another and every minister or a group representative in the Council of Ministers is engaged in the pursuit of individual political agenda. A minimum cohesiveness amongst coalition partners is a prerequisite to any meaningful governance, but sadly coalitions under all the five Pandavas of Indian politics have been completely divided.

Mr. Singh announced abruptly the acceptance of the Mandal Commission recommendations on the reservation of backward castes in public institutions to fight his internal political battles with Chaudhary Devi Lal and Mr. Chandra Shekhar. The so-called National Commission on Review of Constitution has been appointed to suggest measures to deal with political instability of the coalitional era of the 1990s. How can any commission suggest any method to deal with the problem of walking-in and walking-out by coalition partners? How can any constitutional commission suggest remedies for open opposition among the allies of coalitional government? Can any retired chief justice of India lay down any law for a fascist Shiv Sena to behave correctly till the party is a partner in government?

If on the one hand coalition governments lack minimum cohesion, on the other the experiment has institutionalised political immorality, corruption and opportunism. Mr. Narasimha Rao showed his talent by purchasing elected MPs to continue in power. He pales into insignificance compared with what Mr. Thackeray says, that the Shiv Sena was not given "lucrative ministries" in the Vajpayee ministry. Mr. Rao and Mr. Thackeray are honest people. Politics in India is a means to personal prosperity. The Samata Party was caught by the famous Tehelka episode for collecting funds for its own party because every leader or group in the coalition needs funds for himself or his own group. In the process corruption has multiplied in our public life. Coalition governments have institutionalised politics of opportunism and corruption. Every partner in a coalition is busy blackmailing the other. The thirteenth Lok Sabha has 40 parties; tiny groups and so-called Independent members — out of 545 members of the Lok Sabha, the BJP has only 192 members. Messrs Vajpayee, Gujral, Deve Gowda, Chandra Shekhar and Singh constructed and manipulated majority support for forming their governments and every partner manipulated the prime minister and extracted personal concessions and benefits.

In a coalition, everyone is manipulating everyone else so that they can continue in power. How can Indians expect clean government from so many shareholders of the coalition enterprise? Small parties are sitting on the back of crippled and lame elephant, because only such a disabled beast can carry the load of politics as desired by the warring partners. Small in Indian politics has become beautiful and any shop with even two members like the Shiromani Akali Dal can tame public policies in favour of the capitalist farmers of Punjab.

The explanation for the emergence of immoral, corrupt, directionless and incoherent coalitional government lies in the logic of opportunistic politics which has become the hallmark of Indian political class. If caste war brings votes, parties and leaders championing caste and sub-caste causes and interests come on the scene. If on the one hand champions of caste versus caste politics are active, on the other, votaries of *Hindutva* or regional identity or sub-regional identity are busy manipulating voters for a few seats in the Lok Sabha.

The Congress was the first and last party to champion the cause of development of the whole of India. Since the party stood for large social solidarities, it could be displaced only by those who could play the politics of not large but sectional and sectarian fragmentary social identities. The large social class agglomerate platform created by the Congress has been replaced by faceless, shapeless, and fragmented social conglomerate and the result is that one dominant party has been replaced by a motley crowd of groups based on limited social constituencies. This is the social essence of transition witnessed by Indians in the politics of the decade of 1990s, and its concrete expression is felt through weak and vulnerable coalition governments.

Coalition governments are a result of collusion among opportunist political groups and since opportunism cannot be a permanent bond of friendship, coalition partners confront one another. The result is coalition governments are always involved in crisis management and partners of a coalition are always engaged in looking after the interests of their own sectarian constituencies. The Government for the whole of India is only in name; coalition partners are actually ruling either for Hindus or for Dalits or for Yadavs or for Jats or for their regions. There is no saving grace in the experiment of coalitional governance in India, which consists of practitioners of politics of immoralism. (*August 29, 2001, The Pioneer*)

Socialism has met with an Inglorious End

The collapse of the erstwhile systems of the Union of Soviet Socialist Republics and Eastern Europe in the early 1990s has had a devastating impact upon traditional socialist parties in India and Europe. The leading lights of Indian socialism like Mulayam Singh Yadav, Laloo Prasad Yadav, Sharad Yadav, Nitish Kumar and Ram Vilas Paswan have completely abandoned socialist ideology and enthusiastically adopted the worst kind of casteist politics. Socialism has thus been replaced by the completely regressive ideology of casteism.

The key element of socialist ideology is a belief that rigorous development of modern socio-economic productive forces in society will lead to the establishment of a new egalitarian social order. But, the tall leaders of socialist movements in Uttar Pradesh and Bihar have vigorously contributed to the total underdevelopment of these two states, by equating backward caste based politics with economic backwardness and underdevelopment.

The 1990s have seen the great traditions of the Congress socialist party of the 1930s—as represented by Acharya Narendra Dev or Mr. S.M. Joshi — being completely perverted by their successors. Some Indian socialists have even abandoned secularism and joined hands with the forces of *Hindutva*. George Fernandes, a great trade union leader, today sits with Hindu communalists and believes he can influence public policies for a progressive social agenda by joining backward-looking forces.

In Europe, new socialist parties in many countries have — since the dawn of the 1990s — started talking the language of market fundamentalists — language which has in the past been associated with conservative parties of private property owners. Prime Minister Tony Blair of England and Chancellor Gerhard Schroeder of Germany have given a new social content to their Labour Party and Social Democratic Party respectively. This 'Third Way', which is described as "social market economy", is based on public-private partnership. The New Labour completely rejects the previous socialist model which is alleged to have given rise to a "dirigiste state" and inefficient state owned economic industries. During the June 2001 election campaign Mr. Blair campaigned on the basis of the slogan "We accept market economy, we do not accept market society". Chancellor Schroeder of Germany, like his British counterpart, believes that public sector undertakings should go to the market and social public services like health, education and transport ought to remain in the purview of the state.

Why has the socialist alternative to market based capitalism come to an inglorious end in Europe? European socialists maintain that their societies have entered a post-industrial stage, one in which the 21st century will experience technology-knowledge based development; one where the 'new economy' will dominate over the 'old manufacturing economy'. As a result of this changeover, the old anti-capitalist trade unionism of skilled and semi-skilled workers has become a thing of the past. Further, globalisation has "de-territorialised" economic operations, therefore country and industry specific trade unions no longer remain a determining factor.

Interestingly, while European socialists have explained their acceptance of 'market forces' as an attempt to adapt to a very different kind of capitalism Indian socialists have not offered any explanation for their abandonment of socialist ideology. Let me attempt to do so. Indian socialists are in total disarray for at least two reasons. First, in the 1990s Indian socialists bid farewell to their ideology and embraced the ideology of political opportunism. The practitioners of socialist ideology became men of clay and power hungry self-seekers. This happened when the traditional communist parties foolishly supported the casteist politics of Mr. V.P. Singh.

Since the communists tied up with the protagonists of Mandalised politics, they could neither oppose casteist politics nor could they practice it as casteist politics is a natural opposite of socially progressive communist ideology. As a result, communist parties got completely marginalised in UP and Bihar. CEM Joad, a British writer had perhaps met the Chandra Shekhars, George Fernandes, Mulayam Singh Yadavs and Laloos when he wrote "socialism is like a hat which has lost its shape because everybody wears it".

A second explanation for the total confusion among Indian socialists is their failure to renew ideology, to ask new questions about the fast-changing Indian and global reality. At least the European socialists are engaging themselves in an intellectual exercise of adaptation, but Indian socialists are busy making or breaking ministries. The latter have failed to reckon with a new social reality — that the powerful Indian middle class has turned against the state-led economic model of planning.

A very important plank of Indian Marxists has been that if the Indian market is deep-ended, the need for foreign capital will get marginalised. Indian Marxists argue that by creating purchasing power in Indian villages, the crisis in the Indian economy can be overcome. One of the corollaries of this logic is that the unfinished programme of land reforms should be completed so that the rural masses benefit from a rejuvenated rural economy. Is Mulayam Singh Yadav or Laloo Prasad Yadav or any other ally of the communists committed to radical land reforms in UP and Bihar? The answer is in the negative because now it is the backward-caste middle peasantry which is a roadblock to any restructuring of land relations. How can the communists ally with the messiahs of new vested landed interests?

Indian communists are suffering from a mismatch between their ideology and the politics of their allies who do not accept the communists' ideological planks. Socialism has been let down by the socialists themselves — they have no one else to blame. Socialist ideology does provide a framework for future progressive and egalitarian social order but its practitioners in India are living for the present political games of power. (*August 11, 2001, Financial Express*)

Index